ITALIAN *CUCINA*

"We hope our book will be a tool in your kitchen and will introduce you to some basic techniques involved, as well as show you how easy the preparation of Italian food can be.

"We have concentrated on dishes that are not only classic but that also answer the needs of today's family.

"The most enjoyable sort of field research has convinced us that the old basic recipe is usually the best. These original recipes are the foundations of this book.

"THESE EVERYDAY DISHES GO UNDER THE NAME OF *PIATTI ALLA BUONA* . . . QUICK AND EASY, MAKE-DO, SIMPLE, AND FAMILY STYLE, TO—QUITE SIMPLY—DELICIOUS."

—Margaret and Franco Romagnoli

Margaret and G. Franco Romagnoli

THE ROMAGNOLIS' TABLE

Italian Family Recipes

Photographs by G. Franco Romagnoli

BANTAM BOOKS
TORONTO • NEW YORK • LONDON

*This low-priced Bantam Book
has been completely reset in a type face
designed for easy reading, and was printed
from new plates. It contains the complete
text of the original hard-cover edition.*
NOT ONE WORD HAS BEEN OMITTED.

THE ROMAGNOLIS' TABLE

*A Bantam Book / published by arrangement with Little, Brown
and Company in association with The Atlantic Monthly Press*

PRINTING HISTORY

Little, Brown edition published April 1975
2nd printing .... August 1975   4th printing .. December 1975
3rd printing .. September 1975   5th printing .... February 1976
6th printing .... April 1976
Cook Book Guild edition published June 1975

*Portions of this book have appeared in
McCall's Magazine May 1975*

Bantam edition / January 1977
2nd printing .... January 1977
3rd printing .... February 1978
4th printing .... January 1981

*Bantam Books are published by Bantam Books, Inc. Its trade-
mark, consisting of the words "Bantam Books" and the por-
trayal of a bantam, is Registered in U.S. Patent and Trademark
Office and in other countries. Marca Registrada. Bantam
Books, Inc., 666 Fifth Avenue, New York, New York 10103.*

PRINTED IN THE UNITED STATES OF AMERICA

13 12 11 10 9 8 7 6 5 4

*To all of you
who have shared
your tables with us*

Contents

Introduction

On our return to America from a work-oriented stay in Italy a few years ago, we gathered our friends around our table again. As usual, they asked us for the secret of our latest sauce and demanded to know what we were doing about our collection of recipes. We are at last turning it into a cookbook, we said firmly and optimistically. But another project soon claimed our attention: we started cooking on television. We were delighted to find a host of new friends whose interest in "The Romagnolis' Table" eventually brought us back to our original plan, the compilation of our traditional Italian recipes in book form.

We realize a lot of books have been written on the subject of Italian cooking, and surely many more will be. Some have been written with the sole purpose of recording the "real, true, original" recipe, and some for the veiled purpose of rebutting the former. We found most of them beautifully accomplished, elegant tomes. (Some, very few fortunately, were by foreign writers whose instant love for the Italian *cucina* was greater than their knowledge of the Italian language and dialects and led them to misinterpretations.) We hope our book will be a tool in your kitchen and will introduce you to some basic techniques involved, as well as show you how easy the preparation of Italian food can be.

Deciding on the recipes to use was not easy. We have concentrated on dishes that are not only classic but that also answer the needs of today's family (with its limitations of time and budget), as well as use ingredients available on the American market. It has been a matter of selecting among thousands of time-honored recipes, an almost infinite variety with, nonetheless, a common simplicity.

A brief look at Italy's history and geography will explain, we hope, both the simplicity and the variety. The country until quite recently was a conglomerate of independent states that were, for geographical or political reasons, sealed off from each other. Give or take a few exceptions, they were agrarian states. The Italian farmer has never been rich; everybody in his large family has had to work, dawn to dusk, in the fields. There was not much time to spend in the kitchen, and only enough money to pay for essentials. Very little, if anything, that was not grown on the spot ever reached his table. Food then, apart from being a necessity, was also one of the few sources of enjoyment, distraction, and gratification. It had to be tasty, economical, reasonably quick or easy to prepare, and had generally to go around for a crowd. (If, by and large, these are national characteristics of Italian cooking, we do not want to say that all Italian cookery is peasant style. After all, where money and power flourished, so did a more sumptuous table whose dishes, when exported, became *haute cuisine*.)

As for variety, Italy is a long, thin peninsula stretching from north to south in the form of a boot. Trimmed at the top by the arc of the Alps, it is ribbed down its length by the Apennines, with the triangular island of Sicily a stone's throw from the toe. To the west of the mainland is Sardinia, the next largest of the Mediterranean islands. With the generous sprinkle of smaller islands, Italy ends up with an area just about that of California, but with all the geographical variations of the North American continent.

Many people simply divide Italy into North and South, but that is too elementary a distinction. The country has nineteen major regions, each in turn subdivided into provinces, and then into counties, most of which differ not only in topography, climate, and economy, but also in dialect, history, folklore, and ways of cooking. Moreover, through the ages foreigners (from Albanians to Zouaves) have come and stayed in one region or another of the Garden of the Mediterranean, thus leaving their cultural and culinary imprint. Accept all these factors, and you can begin to understand Italy's quantity and diversity of regional dishes.

Today, in spite of fast produce delivery, more money, and more widespread availability of everything throughout the country, there are still many dishes that are best when made and eaten in a particular region. Modern ingenuity and social changes in Italy, plus a recent tendency to gloss over humble origins, have created many embellished variations of the same dish. The most enjoyable sort of field research has convinced us that the old basic recipe is usually the best. These original recipes are the foundations of this book.

Some Italian dishes have crisscrossed the oceans and become rich and flamboyant. Even if the origins of these exported dishes remain the same, the local habits, economic conditions, and many of the ingredients are different. An American pizza pie, for example, is to a pizza in Naples what an apple pie is to a *torta di mele:* a wild mutation of the original. This is not our kind of cooking.

Traditional Italian cookery emphasizes not only flavor and texture but also color and contour. To regard as important the hue and form of a food may sound frivolous, but having watched a thousand tables set we feel that they are important considerations. The sense of color and shape that expresses itself throughout Italian life dominates the way a display in a store window is set up, the arranging of the glorious fresh produce at the open market, the planning of a vegetable garden, the way a meal is presented.

Italians very rarely consider a dish all by itself, but set in the context of the meal as a whole. For them a meal has a certain definite pattern: there is a distinct first, second, and third course, with each dish congenial and complementary to the others in taste, texture, color (where possible), and of course in substance.

Most of our recipes are for what we call everyday dishes, which have the characteristics that the Italian peasant meal once had. Today in Italy these everyday dishes go under the name of *piatti alla buona,* which loosely translated means everything from quick and easy, make-do, simple, and family style, to—quite simply—delicious. All of our recipes, unless otherwise specified, are for six people.

We have also included some *piatti domenicali,* or Sunday dishes. They are food for a *festa* or for the day when you have some time on your hands to dedicate to the preparation of a meal. These *piatti domenicali,* like Sunday best clothes, are something special, elegant, and out of the ordinary. Usually our recipes for Sunday fare are those that millions of Italian families have used for centuries for celebrations and holidays.

Many of our recipes are specific souvenirs of our working trips to well-known cities or remote villages of the peninsula. They have been tested by our friends on both sides of the ocean. For our Italian *amici,* a description of the dish, where it came from, and an approximation of the ingredients was enough, but it didn't work that way in the United States. For American cooks, Margaret has translated the pinch and handful and veil into teaspoons and cups and sprinklings. We also recognize that some American ingredients don't taste exactly as their Italian counterparts, so we have adjusted quantity and handling, when possible, to strive for the traditional result. All of the recipes have been used constantly by us, working parents who are well acquainted with the American kitchen, the vicissitudes of the world economy, and the increasing lack of time to prepare and enjoy a good meal.

We have listed the dishes in the same order as they would appear on a family table or on the menu of a *trattoria,* Italy's small, informal family restaurant:

> *Antipasti*—before the meal, appetizers
> *Primi piatti*—first courses, which include pasta, soup, rice *polenta,* and other traditional offerings
> *Secondi piatti*—meat, poultry, fish, eggs
> *Contorni*—vegetables and salads
> *Dolci*—sweets, both fruit and pastry (usually the Sunday variety)
> *Svogliature*—snacks, pizza

Needless to say, we've found that two cooks in the kitchen do not spoil the broth. A cooking partnership, in addition to being more entertaining for the participants, saves a lot of time. How do we divide the labor? There is no formula, really. When there are familiar recipes in a menu, we each tend to make our own old favorites. When learning any new dish, each of us naturally does the part he or she likes and does best. Everyone has a certain attraction to particular kinds of cooking techniques. After anyone has made a few dishes, it's usually obvious which details he performs most skillfully. Some cooks thrive on chopping, others on basting or frying. In our case, anyway, our two distinct self-assignments in kitchen duty seem to balance out and complement each other. We also might say, "Choose your battle station, and stick with it." In short, neither partner should encroach on the other's work unless asked. Divide the labor, and double the rewards.

It would be unnatural if two cooks always agreed completely about methods. Margaret is inclined to rely on her measuring spoons and cup; Franco depends more on his instincts and experience. Finally, our advice is: follow the weights and measures, but remember that everything can be bent a little—to your taste.

ALL RECIPES, UNLESS OTHERWISE INDICATED,
SERVE SIX PERSONS.

With special thanks to our children, Gian Giacomo, Marco, Paolo, and Anna, who over the years helped to chop and mince, taste-test, make notes, run errands, and joined us around our various tables to share with our Italian and American friends in little and big celebrations of living.

And with gratitude to Sylvia Davis, Michael Rice, Margaret MacLeod, and all those members of WGBH-TV who aided and abetted in putting the first of the Romagnoli recipes on the air.

ANTIPASTI
Appetizers

Antipasto is literally translated as "before the meal": an appetizer. It is designed to stay hunger pains, whet the appetite, and fill the pause while the pasta water or broth is coming to a boil. Frankly, it seldom shows up on the everyday Italian family table, but is mostly reserved for Sundays and feast days to decorate and enrich the meal.

While the fancier Italian (the so-called international) restaurants list all kinds of *antipasti*, the family cook makes good use of only a few. These few seem to have been born of the season's best offering: in summer, the fresh sweet figs or cantaloupe coupled with lightly salted *prosciutto*; perfect slices of *salame* the right number of months after butchering; fresh green olives in late September; or a handful of delicate fruits of the sea when the fishing is good.

The most common *antipasto* is a mixed platter of *prosciutto* and several varieties of *salami* accompanied by hearts of artichokes in olive oil, olives, butter curls, and decorated with bits of vegetables (peppers, cauliflowers, pearl onions, eggplant, pickled in wine vinegar).

Some *antipasti* wear two hats, and appear also as side dishes or part of a cold meal. Like sauces, they are the cook's choice, and anything goes: think of something delightful, light, and cheerful, a springboard for your palate.

ANTIPASTO DI MARE
Seafood Cocktail

This seafood medley includes tiny baby clams, and the smallest squid, shrimp, and mussels simmered with seasonings. Serve with olive oil, lemon, chopped fresh parsley, and chopped capers.

½ pound tiny squid
1 pound small shrimp
½ pound baby cherrystone clams
1 pound mussels
1 carrot
1 celery stalk
1 onion
1 bay leaf
1 teaspoon salt (approximate)
5 peppercorns
½ garlic clove
1½ tablespoons chopped fresh parsley
1 tablespoon chopped capers
6 tablespoons olive oil
   juice of 1 lemon

Clean the squid. Cut it into small strips or rings, leaving the tentacles whole. Shell the shrimp. Scrub the clams and mussels with a stiff brush, and rinse well under running water.

Put the squid in a pot big enough to hold all the other shellfish. Add the carrot, celery, onion, and bay leaf, about a teaspoon of salt, and the peppercorns. Add enough water to cover the squid by about 2 inches. Bring to a gentle boil, reduce the heat, cover, and simmer for 15 minutes. Add the clams and mussels, and cook for 5 minutes more. Add the shelled shrimp, stir carefully, and cook another 5 minutes, or until the shrimp are tender and the shellfish have opened. Strain, reserving the liquid. Scoop the clams and mussels out of their shells.

Rub the inside of a medium-sized serving bowl with the garlic. Put in the shrimp, clams, mussels, and squid. Sprinkle with the chopped parsley and capers. Dress with the olive oil, lemon juice, and a tablespoon of the reserved fish stock, and toss gently. Chill and marinate for half an hour before serving.

CARCIOFINI ALL'OLIO
Artichoke Hearts in Olive Oil

This favorite antipasto is also a popular way of cooking, serving, and preserving the young artichokes that appear at the beginning of the season. They're cooked in wine, spiced with bay leaf and cloves and lemon. To preserve them, substitute more white wine for water and add lots more oil.

> 2 dozen small artichokes
> 1 cup lemon juice
> 5 cloves
> 14 peppercorns
> 8 bay leaves
> 5 thin slices lemon
> 1½ cups dry white wine
> 2 tablespoons vinegar
> 1 cup olive oil (approximate)

Prepare the artichokes (pages 225 to 226), and continue paring until all the green leaves have been removed. This process is like paring an apple, and it leaves the artichokes looking like tightly closed flower buds (about the size of a big peony bud). Although Italian artichokes have no chokes, the American kind, even when small, tend to have spiny centers: cut yours in half and scoop out any spines with a sharp knife. Dip the halves in lemon juice and put them in a medium-sized saucepan.

When all the artichokes are ready, add to the pan all 5 cloves, 10 of the peppercorns, 4 of the bay leaves, the lemon slices, white wine, vinegar, and enough water so that the artichokes float. Bring to a boil, cover, reduce the heat, and boil gently for about 10 minutes, or until the artichokes' bottoms are tender when stuck with a fork.

Drain thoroughly, discard the cooked spices, and put the artichokes in a jar with the remaining 4 bay leaves and 4 peppercorns. Pour in enough olive oil to cover. Let stand a few days before serving.

FINOCCHIO ALL'OLIO
Fennel with Olive Oil

A crisp, different, anise-flavored salad makes an ideal *antipasto* for hearty first courses. Many a cook will use it as a *contorno* with a solid second course.

- 3 big fennel bulbs, chilled
- 3 tablespoons olive oil
- 1 teaspoon salt, or to taste
  freshly ground black pepper
- 1 teaspoon wine vinegar (optional)

The secret of this salad is the choice of fennel: a good fennel is bulbous and firm. The outer layers of the bulb should be almost smooth, with the ribs just barely showing. The dill-like plumes on the stalks should be fragrant and not wilted. The more oval-shaped fennel (or a tired fennel) has to be peeled considerably to reach the tender, crisp, edible part.

Cut off the stalks of the fennel, and peel away the stringy, pulpy outside layers of the bulb. Then cut it in quarters and cut out almost all of the core. Slice it into thin wedges. Wash in cold water, drain, and shake out in a towel as much water as possible. Spread out on a deep platter or in a salad bowl. Add the olive oil, salt, and pepper. Toss gently, or tip the platter and baste until all the fennel is dressed with oil. (Optional: add the vinegar and toss again.) Serve with extra salt and pepper on the side.

FUNGHI ALL'OLIO E LIMONE
Mushrooms with Oil and Lemon

Mushroom caps and stems, cooked in garlic-flavored olive oil and seasoned with lemon juice, are served cold as an *antipasto*. A similar treatment but a different cut is used in Mushrooms, "Truffle Style" (pages 235 to 236), which is served as a side dish.

> 1 pound small white mushrooms
> ½ cup olive oil
> 1 medium garlic clove
> ½ teaspoon salt, or to taste
> ¼ lemon
> 1 tablespoon chopped fresh parsley

Peel and clean the mushrooms, and cut caps from stems. Slice off the very bottom of the stems where they are slightly dried out.

Put the oil in a medium-sized frying pan, add the garlic. Sauté over medium heat until golden and then discard. Add the mushrooms, raise the heat, and cook quickly. Keep stirring them so they don't burn. When the mushrooms start to give up their juices, add the salt. When they are tender but still firm (about 4 to 5 minutes), squirt them with the lemon, stir well, add the parsley, stir again, and take them off the heat.

Serve cold in their own flavored oil.

POMODORI AL RISO
Tomatoes Stuffed with Rice

Big, ripe tomatoes are filled with rice, seasoned with basil, parsley, and garlic. They can be made in large quantities and served either hot or cold.

6 **really big tomatoes**
4 **tablespoons chopped fresh parsley**
6 **fresh basil leaves**
½ **garlic clove**
½ **cup long-grain rice**
½ **cup olive oil**
½ **teaspoon salt**

Preheat the oven to 375°.

Wash the tomatoes and cut off the tops about a quarter of the way down, so that you can get at the insides. Save the tops. Scoop out the seeds, and the inner pulp with its juices, and strain through a sieve into a small bowl. Chop the parsley, basil, and garlic very fine and add them with the rice to the tomato juice. Add ¼ cup of the olive oil and the salt. Mix well.

Put this mixture into the tomato shells, filling them no more than half full. Place them in a shallow baking dish just large enough to hold them. Sprinkle with the remaining ¼ cup of the olive oil, and cover each tomato with its own top.

Bake (at 375°) for half an hour. Then reduce the heat to 350°, and baste the tomatoes with the juice from the baking dish, using a bulb baster to get the liquid into the rice without disturbing the tops too much. Bake another half an hour or so, until the rice is really tender.

PEPERONI ARROSTO
Roast Peppers

Roasting the peppers gives them an incredibly different taste. After roasting, they're sliced in strips and bathed in lemon and olive oil. Roast peppers are frequently served as a vegetable course as well as an *antipasto*.

6 to 8 large peppers (red, green, yellow, sweet and meaty)
2 lemons
8 tablespoons olive oil
salt to taste

To use a gas stove: turn the grates of the top burners upside down to cradle the peppers and set the flame at medium high. Put the peppers on the grates and keep an eye on them as they roast. As soon as one side of a pepper is blackened, turn it a bit to the next uncharred portion. Keep turning until all the outer skin is blackened and blistered.

To use an electric stove: put the peppers in the broiler, as close to the heating element as possible, and keep turning them as they blacken. We have to admit that this broiling process doesn't cook the peppers as well as the gas burners: it tends to overcook them. If, however, you use really fresh, plump peppers, the results are good. Roast until the outer skin of the peppers is completely charred.

Put the charred peppers under a cold stream of water and peel off the black with your fingers. This makes a great mess in the sink, but the taste of the peppers will repay you for the cleanup.

Cut off the top stems, take out the inner seeds, and slice the peppers lengthwise into ¼- to ½-inch-wide strips. Drain briefly and put in a serving dish. Squeeze the lemons and pour their juice over the peppers. Add the olive oil, and salt to taste. Baste well.

The roast peppers can be served right away, but they improve if they marinate for half an hour or so.

PROSCIUTTO E MELONE
Prosciutto and Melon

This is probably the best known and easily the simplest of all the *antipasti:* chilled cantaloupe and the cured, unsmoked Italian ham known as *prosciutto*.

1 large cantaloupe
12 thin slices *prosciutto*

Chill the melon thoroughly before opening it. Cut it in half, scoop out the seeds, and then cut each half into 6 wedges. Finally, cut the melon meat away from the rind, place the rindless wedges around a platter, alternating them with loosely rolled slices of *prosciutto,* and serve.

PROSCIUTTO E FICHI
Prosciutto and Fresh Figs

Fresh, ripe figs, chilled and peeled, when combined with *prosciutto* make a very, very simple *antipasto* with a splendid taste.

12 ripe figs, either the purple or the green variety
12 slices *prosciutto*

Chill, then peel the figs before serving. To peel, cut off the very tip of the pointed end of the fruit. Make 4 shallow incisions in the skin as if you were going to cut the figs into quarters. Slide the knife underneath the incisions at what would be the top of a quarter and peel back the skin, cutting it away from the fig at the very bottom. Place figs and *prosciutto* alternately around a serving platter, and that's all there is to it.

PRIMI PIATTI
First Courses

No proper Italian meal can begin without a *primo piatto* (a first course) of either *minestra* (soup, with or without pasta) or *pasta asciutta* (pasta without soup, cooked in water, drained, and married to a sauce) or a variation of the two. This last category includes rice dishes, *timballi* (casseroles) such as the famous *lasagne, gnocchi* (dumplings), or *polenta* (northern Italy's corn-meal concoction) with a sauce.

The *primo piatto* has a definite purpose as a course: it soothes the appetite with something important, for on the traditional Italian table it is still the main part of the meal. It also sets the pace for the dishes that follow.

First courses reflect regional variations in climate, economy, and the availability of products. Colder and more prosperous than the South, the North of Italy tends to serve rich soups, dishes made with rice, and sturdy *polenta*—all in all, a rather serious, no-nonsense cookery. In the sunnier South, the *primo piatto* is zippier and, because fewer rich ingredients are available, frequently more inventive.

In choosing a first course, depend on what's in your larder or the local market, and remember to make it complementary to the rest of the meal in color, texture, taste, and consistency. A spicy second course should be preceded by a bland first, a delicate meat by a hearty *minestra,* and so on. Never forget the weather, and above all, the mood of the moment.

13

PASTA
Pasta in General

For simplicity's sake we divide pasta into two major categories: commercial and homemade.

A glance at a shelf in a store will show you how many, many commercially produced shapes and sizes there are. We've never stopped to count the number. Moreover, as a pasta shape is adopted by one region or another, it may even change its name. What's *tagliatelle* in Bologna could be *fettuccine* in Roma. Every once in a while a pasta-maker further compounds the confusion by coming up with his own original creation. To update the list would be both an impossible task and a rather useless exercise.

No matter whether pasta is homemade or mass-produced, its shape dictates how it will end up: either in *minestra* or as *pasta asciutta*.

The smaller shapes are generally used in soups: *quadrucci, stellette, pastina, capellini* to name a few. They will make their appearance in the *minestre* (soups) section.

The longer and bigger shapes are generally used for *pasta asciutta*. The overall title of *pasta asciutta* (literally, dried-off pasta) means that it is drained of the liquid it's cooked in and then is served with a sauce. Spaghetti, *rigatoni, ziti, perciatelli, vermicelli, linguine, fettuccine*, all these are only a few names on the *pasta asciutta* roster.

Most commercially packaged pasta is made with flour and water, and it is the flour you have to watch out for. If the box is labeled "Made from Semolina" or "Made with Durum Wheat," you can be sure it contains pasta that will keep its character during the cooking process as no other kind will.

Pasta fatta in casa (homemade pasta), whether for soup or for use with sauce, is made with all-purpose unbleached flour, eggs, and a pinch of salt. (All-purpose flour contains a higher percentage of hard wheat flour, a requisite for good pasta, than does pastry flour.) Also called *pasta all'uovo* (egg pasta), it is the most delicate of all, the Queen of Pasta (the gender of *pasta* is feminine in Italian).

In Italy, there are many shops that make *pasta all'uovo* daily, and you can simply buy the amount and shape you wish, just as you might buy fresh bread at a bakery. In America, few towns offer such a luxury, but don't despair. The knack of making pasta is not difficult to master, and you'll find it a positive pleasure to be your own supplier, especially when you consider the enormous culinary rewards you'll receive.

PASTA ALL'UOVO, FATTA IN CASA
Homemade Egg Pasta

The only utensils you really need are a clean, flat surface no smaller than 24" × 24", a fork, and a rolling pin, ideally no shorter than 24 inches.

As for ingredients, the Italian rule of thumb is 1 (American medium) egg and a scant ¾ cup of flour per person, but remember that the average Italian portion of pasta could be considered over-abundant for the American serving. Also, as the number of servings grows, a process of de-escalation takes place, i.e., a 6-egg batch for 8 servings, a 7-egg batch for 10, a 9-egg batch for 12, and so on. These, then, are the ingredients you'll need to make a batch that will serve 6 American portions:

> 3½ cups all-purpose unbleached flour (approximate)
> 5 medium eggs at room temperature
> ¼ teaspoon salt

Incidentally, for beginners we advise starting with a small batch of pasta: let's say 2 eggs, approximately 1½ cups of flour, and a pinch of salt, for 2 to 3 people. This will give you not only expertise in the making of pasta but also a good idea of how many eggs and cups of flour you will eventually need for the exact number and size of portions you wish to serve.

Roll up your sleeves, remove your watches, rings, and bracelets, and make a mound of the flour in the center of your working area, which may be a pastry board or kitchen counter or table. Stirring with your fingers, make a hole in the top of the mound, and keep on stirring until you touch your working surface and have turned the mound into a crater with walls high and thick enough to contain the eggs, which you now break into the middle. Add the salt.

Start beating the eggs with a fork held in one hand. As the beaten eggs try to flood through the walls, your other hand should embrace the crater and keep building up the outside all around, bottom to top, simultaneously managing to spill some flour inside. The two motions combined will make the eggs inside absorb more and more flour, and will turn the two elements into one thick paste.

When it becomes too difficult to continue with the fork, flour your hands and work the paste with your fingers, admittedly a sticky business at first. Adding more flour slowly will turn the paste into a real dough. Keep on flouring your hands and the work surface until the dough can't absorb any more flour.

(By the way, if your ball of dough is too hard, flaky, and in general doesn't want to amalgamate smoothly, it means that more flour has been used than the eggs can absorb. To reestablish the balance, mix in a little water, a few drops at a time. Do it when nobody is watching because this procedure is scorned by the professionals. Nobody else will know the difference.)

At this point, you'll have some flour left over (the quantity depending on the size of the eggs, quality of flour, moisture of room, and other variables), but it won't be wasted. Push it aside, and scrape the surface of the working area clean of loose or caked dough. This is the moment also to clean your hands if they're still sticky. As you get more proficient, you'll reach this point with almost clean hands.

Once you've tidied everything up, flour your hands and working surface and begin to knead the ball of dough. Everyone develops his own technique for kneading, but the standard one is to push the ball of dough down with the open palms of your hands and roll it away from you. At the end of the roll, press hard with the heels of your hands spreading the dough out into an oblong shape. Fold it over so that it becomes even more oblong. Then lift it and, while bringing it back toward you, double it over on itself and slap it onto the working surface. The dough is almost a ball again, and is ready for another kneading cycle.

Keep repeating the process over and over again for about 10 minutes, sprinkling flour on the working surface from time to time, or until you have a ball of dough that is smooth, golden, and elastic. By this time, the working surface should be almost spotless (clean it up if it isn't), and you are ready to roll.

Break off a piece of dough the size of a tennis ball and pound it flat with your hands. Flour your rolling pin, and roll it over the dough so that the spreading action is from the center toward the edges. When the dough is visibly thinner, turn it by 90° and roll again. Since this process tends to squeeze the moisture out of the dough, keep dusting the working surface, rolling pin, and dough with flour. Keep rolling this way until you reach the desired thickness, which we can best describe as about that of a dime.

A faster way of rolling thinly and uniformly requires a long rolling pin. To follow this method, once you have rolled down the ball of dough to ¼-inch thickness, dust it generously with flour. Position the rolling pin on the edge of the dough closest to you. Roll the pin away from you and, as you roll, let the pasta wrap itself around the pin. This gives you more leverage on the dough itself.

Start with both hands together at the center of the

pin and, as you roll, gradually let your hands work their way from the center to the outside edges of the sheet of pasta, while still maintaining pressure on both dough and pin. It's a neat trick but possible, like patting your head and rubbing your stomach at the same time. Unroll the sheet, turn it partway around, and repeat the process.

When you have reached the thickness desired, by either method of rolling, put the sheet to rest on a clean, dry towel, and get to work on the remaining dough. If you don't have enough space for rolling pasta, or you are mechanically inclined, you can use a pasta-making machine, which will also do some of the kneading for you. If you are using one, when the dough has absorbed as much flour as it can, and is relatively unsticky, break off a piece just smaller than the palm of your hand. Flour the piece, and send it through the adjustable rollers, which are set at their widest distance apart. Keep on putting the dough through at this setting, folding the piece in half each time and flouring it a bit until it loses its wrinkles and is smooth and elastic. Then bring the rollers closer together, flour the dough, and send it through again. Keep on reducing the space between the rollers and sending the pasta dough through until it has reached the desired thickness.

When you have rolled the pasta, only your imagination limits what you can do with it. Some of our friends, at their first success, just stood and looked at it in awe. Others quickly started cutting it for *fettuccine, lasagne, tonnarelli, cannelloni, cappelletti,* and *tortellini,* just to mention a few options. You'll want to check individual recipes for variations in drying time before and after cutting.

Generally speaking, if using *pasta all'uovo* for *fettuccine* or *tonnarelli,* let it dry 15 minutes before cutting, cut, and spread it out on dish towels to dry further, up to 3 or 4 hours.

If using it for *cannelloni, lasagne,* or *manicotti,* let your pasta dry 15 minutes before cutting, then cut and spread it out on dish towels for no more than half an hour before cooking. This larger cut becomes too brittle if dried too long, so that it breaks easily and spoils the layering or filling.

If using it for *agnolotti* or *cappelletti,* let your pasta dry only as long as it takes you to finish rolling out the whole batch. Fill and fold immediately, as the pasta must still be pliable in order to be folded and sealed tightly around the filling.

PASTA VERDE
Green Pasta

Green pasta is used in *lasagne* and for making green *fettuccine,* and is just like *pasta all'uovo* but with fresh or frozen minced spinach substituted for 1 or more eggs, depending on how many servings are made. This recipe is enough for 6 servings of *fettuccine verdi* or 12 servings of *lasagne verdi.*

   3½ cups all-purpose flour
    3 medium eggs at room temperature
   10 ounces fresh or frozen spinach
    1 teaspoon salt

To use fresh spinach: wash and remove the stems. Cook the leaves briefly in as little water as possible with 1 teaspoon salt. Drain thoroughly, pressing the spinach against the sides of a sieve. (If you've got cheesecloth handy, wrap the cooked spinach in it and squeeze dry.) Mince the spinach thoroughly with a sharp knife on a cutting board until it is practically a paste.

To use frozen chopped spinach: cook in boiling salted water, drain and squeeze dry as above, and mince finely.

Now proceed as with *Pasta all'uovo* (pages 15 to 19), putting the flour in a mound on the work surface, turning it into a crater, and breaking 3 eggs into the center of the crater. Then add the cooked, minced spinach to the eggs. (Ten ounces boils and minces down to about 4 heaping tablespoons of spinach—approximately the volume of 2 eggs.)

Here are a few advance warnings on the idiosyncrasies of *pasta verde*. You'll find that because of the spinach this dough takes a bit longer to get to the hand-working stage and also to its final rolling. If you use a pasta machine, the dough tends to shred a bit on its first trip through the rollers, because of moisture in the spinach. Pay no attention to looks, flour the dough, and undaunted keep on sending it through.

The first time you knead or roll out *pasta verde*, you'll notice that the green is by no means uniform throughout, but as you keep on kneading or rolling, the color becomes the same throughout, and the pasta gets as smooth as heavy silk. Let it dry on a dish towel according to cut and use desired.

HOW TO COOK PASTA ASCIUTTA

The proof of the pasta is in the eating, which means that, packaged or homemade, it has to be cooked correctly. An old Italian saying is, "The death of the pasta is by boiling it: it can go to hell or to paradise in the process." For a saintly pasta, the rules are few and simple, and so are the tools. Essential are a pot big enough to contain at least 1 quart of water per serving of pasta (if you are cooking only 1 or two portions, however, you should start with at least 3 quarts of water), a long wooden fork or spoon, and a capacious colander for draining. Advisable are a couple of potholders, to say nothing of the strength to lift the pot if you are serving a crowd.

The water: The water should be brought to a rolling boil, then salted with 1 teaspoon of salt per quart of water. Salting at this time makes the water boil more than ever. Only then is it ready to receive the pasta, which should not be dumped in all at once but in portions, to minimize the cooling of the water, and should be stirred gently to avoid sticking. The water should then be brought back to a full boil as quickly as possible. Covering the pot helps immensely at this time. Once the water is back to the full boil, uncover, and stir the pasta. Purists insist this should be done with a wooden implement, as a metal one lowers the temperature and the susceptible pasta suffers, but then purists wouldn't cook pasta at a high elevation either; at mountain altitudes water boils at a lower temperature, and pasta doesn't like that.

The cooking time: Cooking time varies with different varieties of pasta. It ranges from 7 to 8 minutes for thin spaghetti to 12 to 15 minutes for the sturdiest *rigatoni*. Generally, the time is a few minutes less than that recommended by commercial manufacturers. Homemade pasta is much more sensitive, and cooks in about 4 to 5 minutes. It also floats to the top of the water when almost done.

The main goal is to cook it *al dente*. Some sort of literary prize should be given to the poet who can describe *pasta al dente*. The term means that it is bitable but not raw, can be felt under the teeth but is neither crunchy nor rubbery; it means that each piece of pasta retains its individuality and texture, yet is just tender enough to please. Overcooked pasta is a mushy affair and a terrible offense to the ingenuity of generations of pasta-makers: all their creations in sizes and shapes are turned to an indifferent blob. *Al dente,* then, is what you must achieve in cooking, and the only way to find out when this occurs is by testing.

In Naples, homeland of *vermicelli,* the cook would extract one piece of pasta out of the boiling pot and fling it at the tiled wall: the pasta, when *al dente,* would stick to the tile for the count of three, then plop to the floor. If it didn't stick, it wasn't done yet. If it stuck longer, it was overcooked, and the cook would commit suicide. This kind of testing is not recommended.

A much simpler method is to fish out periodically,

using the wooden implement, one piece of pasta, blow gently on it, and bite it. The *al dente* stage will make itself known.

The draining: When this critical moment has arrived, the pasta has to be drained. So, have a good-sized colander ready in the kitchen sink. Pour the pasta water into it, slowly at first, and when most of the water has been poured away, dump the rest with the pasta into the colander. Then put the colander over the empty pot to finish draining. This lets the last of the hot water drip into the pot, and its steam keeps the pasta warm a minute or two. For some sauces, you may need a tablespoon of that water at serving time. Anybody who rinses hot pasta with cold water should be punished and condemned to eat cold pasta all of his life. (There is one exception to the above: *lasagne* or *manicotti* pasta cuts may be put under cold water for a brief minute to aid in quick handling.)

Mixing with the sauce: With the pasta cooked and *al dente,* there is little time to waste. The pasta should be married immediately to the waiting sauce, served, and consumed.

PASTA ASCIUTTA: IL SUGO
Sauces for Pasta Asciutta

Even properly cooked, *pasta asciutta* is nothing without a sauce. Italians call the sauce *il sugo.* The Italian-English dictionary translates *sugo* as "juice, gravy," and also as "essence, substance, pith (essential parts, strength, vigor)." We like to think Italian *sugo* is juice, gravy, strength, vigor all combined. *Pasta asciutta* has to be married to a *sugo,* even the simplest, to become a full-bodied, satisfying entity. With the hope of being as clear as possible, we'll refer to any *sugo* as a sauce, which is the most common term used in English, and get on with the game.

Some Italian sauces take hours to prepare, but

many of them take only minutes. They are devised to be ready by the time the pasta is cooked. Many of them have lovely romantic names, frequently geographical, but you don't have to be a map reader or live in Italy to make the most of them. Their ingredients are generally readily available in the United States. Several standard rules apply to practically all sauces.

Use fresh herbs whenever possible, because they are always more flavorful. Probably the most frequently used herbs are basil, which combines magnificently with tomatoes, and parsley, the flat-leafed Italian variety (it has more taste than the curly type), together with its cousins celery and carrot. All herbs and other seasonings in the Italian kitchen should be used sparingly, so that no one overpowers the other. Garlic is a case in point.

As for the spices, the two most commonly used are pepper and nutmeg. Freshly ground pepper, whether white or black, is so much better than the packaged preground variety that we recommend the use of pepper mills. If you can't find white peppercorns, use black but a smaller quantity. As for nutmeg, packaged grated nutmeg can't hold a candle to freshly grated, and we strongly urge you to use a nutmeg grater. If you can't get one, however, use packaged nutmeg but about half the amount specified in our recipes.

Use the red pepper pod stripped of its seeds to give a hot taste that can be controlled depending upon how long the pod sits in the sauce it is flavoring. Ground red pepper tends to burn easily and get bitter, and is impossible to remove once it's done its job.

Use unsalted butter if possible, because it has a lighter, sweeter taste. If you're using salted butter, use less salt than indicated in the recipe.

Many sauces begin with the mincing of a mixture of *odori* (literally, aromas): fragrant seasonings, celery and onion and carrot, combine with one or more herbs and a slice of salt pork. The *odori* and herbs are piled on top of the salt pork, and are sliced through into tiny pieces. Then the combination is chopped again and again, with the knife going back and forth over the pile until it is reduced to a paste. The end product is called a *battuto* (the word is the past participle of the verb *battere,* to beat, to pound). If *odori* are not treated in this way, they neither blend well nor flavor quickly. A good sharp knife and a wide cutting board are fine tools for making a *battuto.* So are the half-moon chopper (*lunetta*) or the hand-operated spring choppers that you push up and down, turning as you chop.

Salt pork, which is called *pancetta* or *guanciale* in Italy, is unsmoked, cured bacon. We've found American-made *pancetta* in Italian food stores here, but nine times out of ten it is too strongly flavored with pepper, and the curing process leaves a different taste from the one we want. So use American lean, cured salt pork (cut in ⅛-inch slices), which is very close to Italian *pancetta* in both taste and texture. It is generally soft to the touch, lightly salted, as streaked with lean as a good piece of bacon. Sometimes you'll get a piece that is heavily salted, in which case, blanch it before use. An alternative to salt pork is rindless slab bacon. Regular thick-sliced bacon can be used, but it adds a smoky flavor that is not characteristic of the original sauce.

When they are in season, use really ripe fresh plum tomatoes. Their flavor, without a doubt, makes a superlative sauce. If fresh ones aren't available, use peeled whole canned plum tomatoes. They are produced in both California and Italy. Some, however, are canned in a very thin watery liquid (instead of thick tomato juice), in which case drain and use the tomatoes only. As for tomato paste, handle it warily. It is a real concentrate, and can completely overpower all other flavorings.

Olive oil is another important ingredient of many sauces. It is somewhat expensive, but its flavor justifies the cost, and most sauces don't use an awful lot. Olive oil varies, however, in grade and brand. Look for pure virgin olive oil, which is delicate in flavor and light gold in color. Its taste should be unmistakably that of olives, and should linger on the tongue briefly and then disappear. Buy small amounts of various kinds until you find the one you like. Tasted on a morsel of Italian bread, olive oil delights the palate.

Use Italian bread for tasting sauces as they simmer. It has more body and is less sweet (it should be made with wheat flour, yeast, salt, and water, with no sugar or other additives) than the average American bread. A morsel dipped in a cooking sauce will show the way that sauce will taste with pasta and is a much more accurate test for the ultimate combination than a sampling of straight sauce.

In all sauces, consistency is very important. When a sauce has simmered the proper length of time, it begins to coat the spoon used to stir it. Some sauces take longer than others to get to this point, but you can tell when they're getting there when the juices have boiled away a bit, the color has generally deepened, and the flavors have blended and mellowed subtly.

When we suggest cooking times for sauces, we realize that stoves differ greatly. Some burners go too hard and fast, others too slow. So, after you've made a sauce or two that has clung to the pasta properly, make a note of your timing and stick to it. When making quick-cooking sauces, it's fairly simple to judge when you should start cooking the pasta in order to have both pasta and sauce ready at approximately the same time: to simmer a sauce for 20 minutes takes about the same amount of time required to bring cold water to a boil and cook macaroni. But, if you're using homemade *fettuccine,* which cooks in 5 minutes, your sauce should be about ¾ of the way through its 20 minutes of simmering before you put the pasta in the boiling water.

Finally, while cooking a sauce, remember a bit of Italian advice, "A simmering sauce should not scream but murmur," which means it should bubble along gently and slowly. It should never be simply abandoned to its fate. A sauce is a living thing, and so requires attention as it murmurs on the back burner: stirring, tasting, covering, uncovering, as the case requires.

When served, many of the sauces are topped with grated cheese: *parmigiano* or *pecorino*. *Parmigiano* (Parmesan cheese) comes grated and ungrated to the American market. A properly aged, imported, ungrated Parmesan cheese is recommended if available. Its delicate flavor compensates for the slightly higher cost and the extra time you spend in grating it as needed. Packaged American grated Parmesan, however, is quite acceptable. *Pecorino,* a sheep's milk cheese, is harder to find, and therefore we usually resort to its American counterpart marketed under the name Romano. It is a sharper cheese than Parmesan, and some find it too sharp, in which case it can be blended with Parmesan.

We found that selecting the following sauces and pasta was like trying to catalog old friends: it was impossible to choose which should come first in either popularity or importance. So we decided to group them in families—taste, the use of a particular ingredient, and mood being the common denominators.

Sauces for Pasta: First Group

The first group uses butter and cheese as the principal ingredients, is marked by the absence of tomatoes, and has a mellow, soothing taste. Geographically these recipes have their roots in northern and central Italy.

PASTA, BURRO E PARMIGIANO
Pasta with Butter and Parmesan Cheese

Here we have pasta served with the simplest of all sauces: unsalted butter and Parmesan cheese. If made with homemade *fettuccine,* this dish becomes a work of art, most delicate and pleasing to the palate. *Fettuccine* means ribbons, which are what you cut your homemade pasta into.

SAUCE
   8 tablespoons unsalted butter
   6 tablespoons grated Parmesan cheese

PASTA
   6 quarts water
   6 teaspoons salt
   1 5-egg batch *Pasta all'uovo* **(pages 15 to 19) cut into** *fettuccine,* **or 1¼ pounds egg noodles or spaghetti**

If using homemade pasta: roll it out in big sheets, flour lightly, and let dry for at least 15 minutes. Then fold it up gently in flat rolls about 4 inches wide. With a good, sharp knife slice the rolls in ribbons about ¼ inch wide. Every 10 or 15 slices, stop cutting and pick up the *fettuccine,* shake them out so that they unfold, and put them on a dry, clean dish towel. They may be used at once, or they may continue to dry for up to 3 hours.

Heat the serving dish. You may set it as a cover on the pasta pot until you're ready to cook the pasta, or you may place it in a warm (200°) oven. In either case, let the butter melt on the dish as it warms.

When the water boils, add the salt and put in the pasta. Transfer the warm platter to a warm oven, if it isn't already there. Let the pasta cook at a good boil, stirring frequently until it is *al dente.*

Then drain the pasta thoroughly, and pour it on the warm serving dish. Using a serving fork and spoon, turn the pasta over and over until it is all buttery, adding the grated Parmesan cheese as you do so until everything is nicely coated. Serve immediately on hot plates.

FETTUCCINE ALLA PANNA
Fettuccine with Cream Sauce

This embellished modern version of the old *burro e parmigiano* is sometimes known as *fettuccine all' Alfredo*. The butter is melted with the cheese on a serving platter, and then turned into a smooth, creamy sauce without benefit of saucepan.

SAUCE
- **8 tablespoons unsalted butter**
- **½ cup all-purpose cream**
- **8 tablespoons grated Parmesan cheese**

PASTA
- **6 quarts water**
- **6 teaspoons salt**
- **1 5-egg batch** Pasta all'uovo (pages 15 to 19), cut into fettuccine (as in the preceding recipe)

Put the butter and cream in a wide, shallow serving bowl or deep platter in a warm (200°) oven or, even better, on top of the pot containing the heating pasta water. When the butter has melted, stir in about ⅔ of the cheese. Keep this cream sauce warm while the *fettuccine* cook.

When the pasta water comes to a good boil, salt it, and put in the *fettuccine* by the handful. When *al dente*, drain it thoroughly, and put it on the platter with the cream-butter-cheese sauce. Turn it over and over until the sauce is well distributed. Serve immediately, and sprinkle with the remaining cheese.

RIGATONI, BURRO E SALSICCE
Rigatoni with Butter-and-Sausage Sauce

This is another quick sauce that practically makes itself in the serving dish while the pasta is cooking. Made with butter, sausage, cream, and cheese, it is also excellent with *fettuccine*, big shells, or any large pasta of your choosing.

SAUCE
  8 tablespoons unsalted butter
  2 Italian sweet sausages
  ½ cup medium cream
  8 tablespoons grated Parmesan cheese
    salt to taste

PASTA
  6 quarts water
  6 teaspoons salt
  1¼ pound *rigatoni* or *fettuccine* made from 1 5-egg
    batch *Pasta all'uovo* (pages 15 to 19)

Put half the butter in a serving bowl or platter,
which you then either put in the warming oven or use
as a cover for the pasta pot as the water comes to a
boil, and let the butter melt.

Meanwhile, skin the sausages (they should be the
kind made without fennel and other spices) and mash
them up in a small frying pan with the rest of the butter. Sauté over medium heat until cooked but not crisp.

Add the sausages and their butter to that in the
serving dish, stir in the cream and half of the Parmesan
cheese. Once well mixed, salt to taste, and put the dish
in the warming oven while the pasta cooks.

Cook and drain the pasta (page 20) and put it on
top of the cream sauce in the serving dish. Turn the
pasta gently over and over until coated with sauce and
sausage bits. Serve immediately and sprinkle with remaining cheese.

TONNARELLI ALLA BURINA
Thin Noodles, Peasant Style

Tonnarelli are also called *pasta alla chitarra* because of
the ancient contraption strung like a *chitarra* (guitar)
that was once used to cut the thin, thin noodles that
look like square spaghetti. Here, *tonnarelli* are served
in a sauce made of mushrooms, peas, salt pork, cheese,
and cream.

SAUCE

- ½ cup all-purpose cream
- 6 tablespoons grated Parmesan cheese
- 8 tablespoons unsalted butter
- 2 slices lean salt pork, or 4 slices *prosciutto*
- 1 cup fresh mushrooms
- 1 cup fresh or frozen peas

PASTA

- 6 quarts water
- 6 teaspoons salt
- 1 5-egg batch of homemade pasta (pages 15 to 19) or 1¼ pounds folded egg noodles.

Put the pasta water on to boil, and place your serving dish on the pot as a cover. Pour the cream onto the dish, add 4 tablespoons of the cheese and half the butter. (If you like a really rich, thick sauce, use heavy cream.) Stir gently with a fork to get the cheese spread around, and let the dish sit over the warming water until the butter has melted and blended with the cheese to form a creamy sauce.

Put the other half of the butter into a big frying pan and melt it over medium heat. Dice the salt pork and add it to the butter, cooking it until it has become translucent. The pork should add just the right amount of saltiness to the dish. (If you want to be really fancy, substitute *prosciutto* for the salt pork.)

Chop the mushrooms into pea-sized bits. If you use fresh peas, add them to the frying pan, and cook 5 minutes. Then add the mushrooms, and cook another 5 to 10 minutes, or until both are tender. If you use frozen peas, add both mushrooms and peas together and cook 5 to 10 minutes, or until both are tender.

If you make your own pasta (pages 15 to 19), dry it for 15 minutes, and then cut it as you would *fettuccine* (page 27) but much narrower: each noodle should be no wider than it is thick. Once cut, the pasta can sit on a dishcloth for a couple of hours before cooking, but it should not dry as long as *fettuccine,* or it will be so brittle it breaks on being put in the pot.

Cook and drain the pasta (page 20), and pour it over the cream sauce in the serving dish. With a fork and spoon, turn the pasta over and over, well distributing the cream sauce. Then add the mixture of salt pork, peas, and mushrooms, turn some more, and finally add the remaining 2 tablespoons of Parmesan cheese. If you wish, add even more cheese.

FETTUCCINE AI FUNGHI
Fettuccine with Mushrooms

An elegant way of serving pasta, this sauce uses fresh, sliced mushrooms and crisp, chopped parsley, whose flavors are blended with butter and heightened with grated Parmesan cheese.

SAUCE
- ¾ **pound fresh mushrooms**
- 8 **tablespoons unsalted butter**
- ¼ **to ½ teaspoon salt, or to taste**
  dash of freshly ground pepper
- 3 **tablespoons chopped fresh parsley**
- 3 **to 4 tablespoons grated Parmesan cheese**

PASTA
- 6 **quarts water**
- 6 **teaspoons salt**
- 1 **5-egg batch** Pasta all'uovo **(pages 15 to 19) cut for** fettuccine **(page 27), or 1¼ pound egg noodles**

Slice the mushrooms, stems and all, into thin wedges, and sauté them in half the butter over medium heat. After about 5 minutes, or when the mushrooms start to give up their own juice, add the salt and pepper. Sprinkle with the chopped parsley and cook another 2 or 3 minutes, or until the mushrooms are tender. Remove the pan from the heat, but keep it warm.

Cook and drain the pasta thoroughly (page 20), and put it on a serving platter. Dot with the rest of the butter. Toss lightly. Pour the mushrooms with their sauce over the pasta. Toss again, and serve with Parmesan cheese.

Sauces for Pasta: Second Group

The recipes for this second group of sauces are country cousins of the first. Again, they include no tomatoes, but the sauces are zippier. Butter has been replaced by cured, lean salt pork, olive oil, or nothing at all. They used to be (and still are, but to a lesser extent) the favorites of young blades who, on the spur of the moment and generally late at night, had to have a *spaghettata*—a blend of midnight snack and spaghetti fest and convivial exchange of late news. These sauces generally come from central Italy and the beginning of the South.

SPAGHETTI AL GUANCIALE
Spaghetti with Lean Salt Pork

In this recipe, so simple it can be made on the spur of the moment, freshly ground pepper combines with salt pork (and it must be lean) to make a year-round favorite that really lifts the spirit.

SAUCE
    ¼ pound lean salt pork, sliced and diced
    ½ cup olive oil
    1 tablespoon coarsely ground pepper
    3 to 4 tablespoons grated Romano cheese

PASTA
    6 quarts water
    6 teaspoons salt
    1¼ pounds spaghetti

Sauté the diced salt pork in the olive oil in a small frying pan over medium heat until it is translucent.

Cook and drain the pasta thoroughly (page 20) and put it on a warm serving platter. Pour the pork bits and oil over the pasta, add the pepper, and toss thoroughly. Sprinkle with the cheese and serve.

SPAGHETTI ALLA CARBONARA
Spaghetti, Charcoal Makers' Style

This sauce also has a base of lean salt pork and lashings of freshly ground pepper but the added enrichment of beaten eggs gives it an altogether different flavor from the preceding recipe. It's almost a meal in itself.

SAUCE
- 4 slices lean salt pork
- 3 tablespoons olive oil
  freshly ground black pepper
- 3 large (4 medium) eggs
  grated Parmesan cheese (optional)

PASTA
- 6 quarts water
- 6 teaspoons salt
- 1¼ pounds spaghetti

Cut the lean salt pork into little pieces, and sauté them in the oil until the pork is translucent. Add the pepper (several good twists of the pepper mill).

Crack the eggs onto an unheated serving platter. Beat them until foamy, and add pepper (again, several twists of the mill).

Cook the pasta (page 20) and drain it the minute it's *al dente,* reserving some of the water in case you need it later. Put the drained pasta on the beaten eggs and toss well until the heat of the spaghetti has cooked the eggs, and they have coated the pasta. (If your pasta has cooled off too much, it won't cook the eggs. If your eggs aren't big enough, the dish will be a bit dry. You can remedy the latter by adding a tablespoon or so of the hot pasta water or olive oil.)

Add the lean salt pork together with its flavored olive oil. Mix again, and serve with more pepper to taste. The dish may or may not be sprinkled with Parmesan cheese—it's a matter of individual taste.

SPAGHETTI, CACIO E PEPE
Spaghetti with Romano Cheese and Pepper

This recipe needs no saucepan. It doesn't need a serving dish either, as it should be mixed on individual plates, as the Romans do. Each person can then mix his own sauce and decide on the amount of pepper to his taste.

SAUCE

    6 tablespoons grated Romano cheese
    1 tablespoon coarsely ground black pepper
  ½ to ⅔ cup pasta water

PASTA

    6 quarts water
    6 teaspoons salt
 1¼ pounds spaghetti

Cook and drain the spaghetti (page 20), saving about a cup of the pasta water to use in mixing the sauce.

Serve the pasta on 6 individual warm plates. To each plate add 1 tablespoon of the cheese and ¼ teaspoon of freshly ground pepper. Mix well. Then add 1 or 2 tablespoons of hot pasta water to each plate and mix again. The heat of the spaghetti melts the cheese, and the hot pasta water adds just enough moisture to develop the consistency of the sauce. Add the rest of the pepper to individual taste.

AGLIO, OLIO, PEPERONCINO
Spaghetti with Garlic, Oil, and Red Pepper

This is a hot sauce, best served with spaghetti, *spaghettini*, or *linguine*. It's a game of contrasts: the bite

of the pepper and the flavor of the garlic versus the
fresh taste and color of parsley.

SAUCE

>   3 red pepper pods, seeded
>   3 garlic cloves
>   ⅓ cup olive oil
>   2 tablespoons chopped fresh parsley

PASTA

>   6 quarts water
>   6 teaspoons salt
>   1¼ pounds pasta

Sauté the pepper pods and garlic in the olive oil
in a small frying pan over medium heat. When the
garlic is golden and the pepper dark brown, remove
them from the oil and turn off the heat.

Cook and drain the pasta thoroughly (page 20)
and put it on a warm serving platter or in a warm bowl.
Sprinkle with the parsley. Bring the flavored olive oil
to a high heat and pour it over the pasta. Turn and
mix, so that all the pasta is covered with the oil and the
parsley is well distributed. Serve immediately.

SPAGHETTI ALL'ORTICA
Spaghetti, "Nettle Style"

Spaghetti, "Nettle Style" is the literal translation, but
we assure you that nettles have no apparent relation to
the rare flavor of this traditional Roman sauce. It is
made with olive oil, mushrooms, and parsley, with a
touch of lemon juice for accent.

SAUCE

>   ⅓ cup olive oil
>   ¾ pound fresh mushrooms, thinly sliced
>   salt
>   3 tablespoons chopped fresh parsley
>   3 tablespoons lemon juice
>   freshly ground pepper to taste

PASTA

      6 quarts water
      6 teaspoons salt
  1¼ pounds spaghetti

While the pasta water is coming to a boil, warm in a wide frying pan some of the olive oil, just enough to cover the bottom, over medium heat. Add the sliced mushrooms, raise the heat, and sauté them quickly (2 or 3 minutes), stirring and salting them as they cook. Add half the parsley and cook 2 more minutes. Remove from heat and add the lemon juice.

In a separate, small pan, heat the remaining olive oil.

Cook and drain the pasta thoroughly, and put it on a warm serving platter. Pour the mushroom sauce over the pasta, sprinkle on the remaining parsley, and add the heated olive oil. Add pepper, a few twists of the mill, to taste. Mix well, and serve.

Sauces for Pasta: Third Group

Here comes the tomato in this third group of sauces, which we call the singing sauces, because they make the sea and the sunshine seem so close. The mood is definitely that of southern Italy. Some are variations on a theme, the differences among them being perhaps more apparent in the eating than in the reading.

Perhaps one note of advice is needed on their common cooking process: always let the pan with the flavored oil cool down a minute or two before adding tomatoes or tomato sauce. This will avoid instant and furious splattering all over you and your stove.

BUCATINI ALL'AMATRICIANA
Macaroni in the Style of Amatrice

This way of serving thin macaroni in a fairly robust sauce originated in the little mountain town of Amatrice in central Italy, and features tomatoes and lean salt pork. In some places, *bucatini* are also called *perciatelli*.

SAUCE
- 4 tablespoons olive oil
- 1 red pepper pod, seeded
- 4 slices lean salt pork
- 3 cups peeled plum tomatoes
- 1 teaspoon salt
- 6 tablespoons grated Romano cheese

PASTA
- 6 quarts water
- 6 teaspoons salt
- 1¼ pounds thin macaroni

Put the water on to boil for the *bucatini*.

Pour the olive oil into a large frying pan over medium heat and add the pepper pod to the oil. Dice the lean salt pork, add it to the pepper and oil, and continue cooking over medium heat.

Remove the pepper when it has turned a dark brown (it should have seasoned the oil enough by this time, but if you like a really hot sauce, let the pepper linger longer). Continue cooking the salt pork until its fat is translucent and its lean a pale pink.

Add the tomatoes, crushing them as they go in. Bring the sauce to a boil, and then lower the heat to a simmer. Keep it at a simmer about 20 minutes, or until the liquid has reduced, the color darkened, and the consistency thickened.

Taste for salt; if the salt pork has done its job, 1 teaspoon should be enough.

While the sauce is simmering, cook the macaroni until *al dente* (page 20), stirring from time to time. Drain the pasta, and put it in a deep platter, cover with the sauce, and turn gently. Serve, and let each person choose his own amount of cheese.

PENNE ALL'ARRABBIATA
Macaroni in Hot Tomato Sauce

The literal translation of the name is "angry" *penne*. *Penne* are short macaroni that are sometimes labeled *mostaccioli* in the United States. This sauce, which isn't angry at all, just pleasantly hot, is spiced with red pepper and garlic.

SAUCE

- ¼ cup olive oil
- 3 garlic cloves
- 3 red pepper pods, seeded
- 3 cups peeled plum tomatoes
- 4 tablespoons Romano cheese

PASTA

- 6 quarts water
- 6 teaspoons salt
- 1¼ pounds macaroni

Heat the olive oil in a flame-proof casserole big enough to hold the cooked pasta. Add the garlic and pepper pods. When the garlic is golden and the pepper pods are a deep brown, discard them and turn off the heat. Add the tomatoes, crushing them as you stir them in. Raise the heat to a boil, and then reduce it to a simmer. Simmer the sauce for about 20 minutes, or until the tomato juice has reduced, the color has darkened, and the sauce generally thickened.

Cook and drain the pasta (page 20), and put it into the casserole with the sauce. Add the cheese. Increase the heat, and turn the pasta over and over until it is coated with piping hot sauce. Serve immediately.

PASTA AL POMODORO E BASILICO
Pasta with Tomato and Basil Sauce

This is a perfect summer dish when made with garden-fresh ingredients, but is also heartening in winter when you have to use canned goods. The sauce is classic with macaroni (*mostaccioli, ziti, rigatoni*), and rather special and more delicate with homemade *fettuccine*.

SAUCE

      8 tablespoons unsalted butter
     12 fresh plum tomatoes, or 3 cups canned
      6 fresh basil leaves
    1½ teaspoons salt
      6 tablespoons Parmesan cheese

PASTA

      6 quarts water
      6 teaspoons salt
    1¼ pounds of macaroni, or 1 5-egg batch homemade
        pasta cut for *fettuccine* (page 27)

Melt the butter in a big frying pan over medium heat. Remove from heat. Add the tomatoes.

If you use fresh plum tomatoes: peel them, and cut them into chunks before adding to the butter. If you use canned tomatoes, crush them gently with a wooden spoon as you stir them in.

Break the basil leaves into the pan, add the salt, raise the heat, and when the whole combination starts to boil, lower the heat to a simmer. Let it bubble along about 20 minutes, or until the juice has cooked away a bit, and the color darkened. Stir occasionally during the simmering process. If the sauce hasn't simmered enough, it will sink to the bottom of the dish instead of coating the pasta when mixed.

Cook and drain the pasta (page 20), and turn it out on a deep platter or wide, shallow bowl, cover with the sauce, and sprinkle with the Parmesan cheese. Turn the pasta with a serving fork and spoon to get the sauce to coat it. Serve immediately.

MACCHERONI CO' A POMMAROLA 'N COPPA
Macaroni with Neapolitan Sauce

The title of this recipe is Neapolitan dialect for macaroni with a scoop of tomato sauce on top. Possibly

Naples's most beloved tomato sauce, it is really something special when made in season with very ripe fresh plum tomatoes.

SAUCE

    5 fresh basil leaves
    1 garlic clove
    1 onion
    4 tablespoons olive oil
1½ pounds fresh peeled plum tomatoes, or 3 cups canned
1½ teaspoons salt
    pepper to taste
    6 tablespoons grated Parmesan cheese

PASTA

    6 quarts water
    6 teaspoons salt
1¼ pounds macaroni

Mince the basil, garlic, and onion practically to a paste. Sauté gently in the olive oil until golden. Chop the tomatoes (whether fresh or canned) coarsely. Add them to the olive oil. Cook until the natural juices have boiled down to a good, thick sauce consistency. Pass through a food mill, and keep warm. Add the salt, and freshly ground pepper (5 or 6 twists of the pepper mill).

Cook and drain the pasta thoroughly (page 20) and serve it in individual plates with a scoop of sauce on top. Sprinkle with the Parmesan cheese.

VERMICELLI ALLA MARINARA
Thin Spaghetti, Sailors' Style

Plum tomatoes are the name of the game in this meatless Neapolitan tomato sauce lightly flavored with garlic and red pepper. It's called "Sailors' Style," perhaps because it is as common in Naples as the sailors of the famous gulf.

SAUCE
- ¼ cup olive oil
- 1 garlic clove, peeled
- 1 red pepper pod, seeded
- 3 cups peeled plum tomatoes
- ½ teaspoon oregano
- 1 tablespoon chopped fresh parsley
- 1 teaspoon salt, or to taste
- 4 to 6 teaspoons grated Parmesan cheese (optional)

PASTA
- 6 quarts water
- 6 teaspoons salt
- 1¼ pounds thin spaghetti (*spaghettini* or *vermicelli*)

Heat the olive oil in a small frying pan over medium heat along with the garlic and red pepper. When the garlic is golden and the pepper deep brown, remove them: they've done their flavoring job. Cool the pan and then add the tomatoes, crushing them slightly as you stir them in. Add the oregano and bring the combination back to a boil, reduce the heat to a simmer, and cook about 20 minutes, or until the sauce has thickened. Add the parsley and salt.

Cook and drain the pasta (page 20) and put it on a serving platter. Cover with sauce, and gently turn the pasta over and over. Sprinkle with cheese if you wish, and serve at once.

Sauces for Pasta: Fourth Group

With this fourth group of sauces, you are definitely South and so close to the sea you can taste it. These are the seagoing cousins of the third group, and fish is generally the defining flavor.

SPAGHETTI ALLA PESCATORA
Spaghetti, Fishermen's Style

This sauce is from the island of Lipari off the coast of Sicily, where the use of fresh plum tomatoes together with newly picked garlic and lots of parsley creates a new flavor, which is salted by anchovies.

SAUCE

> 3 tablespoons olive oil
> 4 garlic cloves
> 2 red pepper pods, seeded
> 3 cups fresh, ripe, peeled plum tomatoes
> 3 anchovy fillets, minced
> ¼ cup coarsely chopped fresh parsley

PASTA

> 6 quarts water
> 6 teaspoons salt
> 1¼ pounds spaghetti

Heat the olive oil in a big frying pan over medium heat. Make 2 crosscuts at the top of each garlic clove so that as they cook they open up like flowers. Add the garlic and all the other ingredients except the parsley, and boil the mixture for about 5 to 6 minutes, stirring frequently. Add the chopped parsley, and continue cooking, still over medium heat, for another 5 minutes. Remove the now-limp garlic and pepper pods before serving.

Cook and drain the pasta, and put it in individual warmed plates. Pour the sauce on each helping, and serve.

SPAGHETTI AL TONNO E POMODORO
Spaghetti with Tuna-and-Tomato Sauce

This quick tuna-and-tomato sauce, livened with fresh parsley, is served frequently with spaghetti, but it's just as good with macaroni.

SAUCE

> 1 garlic clove
> ½ red pepper pod, seeded
> 2 to 4 tablespoons olive oil
> 1 6½-ounce can tuna
> 2 cups peeled plum tomatoes
> 1 tablespoon finely chopped fresh parsley

PASTA

>   6 quarts water
>   6 teaspoons salt
> 1¼ pounds spaghetti

Sauté the garlic and the red pepper in the olive oil in a frying pan over medium heat. (If your tuna isn't packed in olive oil, drain it and use 4 tablespoons olive oil; if it is, use it and add only 2 tablespoons of olive oil.) As soon as the garlic is golden and the pepper pod dark brown, discard both.

Allow the pan to cool a moment or so, and add the tuna. Raise the heat again, and mash the tuna with a fork. Add the tomatoes, breaking them up a bit as you stir them in. After everything has come back to a boil, lower the heat and simmer about 15 minutes, or until some of the juices have evaporated and the sauce has thickened, darkened, and blended. Stir occasionally during the simmer. Add the parsley just before removing the sauce from the heat.

Cook and drain the pasta thoroughly (page 20), put it in a serving bowl or deep platter, and cover with sauce. Stir and toss gently, and serve immediately.

VERMICELLI CON SARDINE
Thin Spaghetti with Fresh Sardines

This delicate sauce flavored lightly with fresh sardines and tomatoes depends on the fish market and the season. When the catch is right, rush, don't walk, to make this sauce. But do not try to make it with canned sardines.

SAUCE

>   1 garlic clove
>   ½ red pepper pod, seeded
>   3 tablespoons olive oil
>   3 cups plum tomatoes (fresh and peeled, if possible)
>   1 tablespoon chopped fresh parsley
>   pinch of oregano
>   ½ pound fresh sardines

PASTA

   6 quarts water
   6 teaspoons salt
1¼ pounds *vermicelli* or *spaghettini*

Sauté the garlic and pepper pod in the olive oil over medium heat until the garlic is golden and the pepper a deep brown. Discard them and add the plum tomatoes (mashing them as you stir them in) and the parsley and oregano. Cook over fairly high heat for 10 minutes.

Clean and fillet the fresh sardines. Add them to the sauce and cook for 5 minutes. If the sardines haven't fallen apart by themselves by that time, mash them into small chunks.

Cook and drain the pasta thoroughly (page 20), and put it on a serving platter. Cover with the sauce, stir, and serve.

VERMICELLI ALLE VONGOLE
Thin Spaghetti with Clam Sauce

Thin spaghetti appears this time in a delicate sauce of tiny clams and tomatoes. *Vongole,* the small clams of the Mediterranean, are distant cousins of cherrystone clams, but their taste and texture more closely resemble the baby clams the Japanese export in cans. In short, the smaller the clams, the closer to the original taste your sauce will be.

SAUCE
   2 pounds fresh cherrystone clams, or 1 10-ounce can baby clams
   4 tablespoons olive oil
   1 garlic clove
   2 cups peeled plum tomatoes
   1 teaspoon salt
     freshly ground pepper to taste
   1 tablespoon chopped fresh parsley

PASTA
   6 **quarts water**
   6 **teaspoons salt**
1¼ **pounds** *vermicelli*

If you use cherrystone clams: wash them thoroughly, and sauté them in a wide frying pan with 1 tablespoon of the oil over high heat. Stir the clams around until they open their shells. Take them from the heat, and cool slightly. Remove the meat from the shells. Filter the clam juice and oil in the pan through a very fine sieve, and set aside. Chop the clams coarsely.

Brown the garlic in a saucepan with the remaining 3 tablespoons of oil, and remove it when well browned. Add the clams and sauté them quickly. Add the tomatoes, clam juice, salt, and pepper (2 or 3 twists of the mill), and boil gently without a cover for 15 minutes, or until the juices have evaporated a bit, the color darkened, and the sauce thickened. Add the parsley. Cook another minute, and serve.

If you use canned clams: sauté the garlic in the 4 tablespoons of oil, and discard it when well browned. Drain the clams, saving the juice they're packed in. Add the tomatoes, 5 tablespoons of clam juice, salt, and pepper (2 or 3 twists of the mill). Cook uncovered for 15 minutes, or until nearly sauce consistency. Add the clams, and cook gently for another 5 minutes. Add the parsley, and cook another minute.

Cook and drain the pasta thoroughly (page 20), put it on a serving platter, and cover with sauce. Toss gently and serve.

VERMICELLI ALLE VONGOLE IN BIANCO
Thin Spaghetti with White Clam Sauce

SAUCE

    2 pounds fresh cherrystone clams
    4 tablespoons olive oil
    1 garlic clove
    ¼ cup dry white wine
    1 teaspoon salt
    freshly ground pepper to taste
    1 tablespoon chopped fresh parsley

PASTA

    6 quarts water
    6 teaspoons salt
    1¼ pounds *vermicelli*

Prepare the clams as in the preceding recipe.

Flavor the olive oil with the garlic over medium heat, discarding the garlic when golden. Add the cleaned and chopped clams, their juice, and the dry white wine. Cook over medium high heat for 2 to 3 minutes, or until the wine has evaporated. Add the salt, pepper (2 or 3 twists of the mill), and the chopped parsley, and simmer for 5 minutes.

Cook and drain the pasta thoroughly (page 20), put it on a serving platter, and add the clams in the white sauce. Toss gently, and serve. Please, no cheese.

Sauces for Pasta: Fifth Group

The sauces in the fifth group have nothing in common either with the other groups or among themselves. They are then not a family but rich, old family friends. They are more elaborate, in the sense that if most of the others can be made on the spur of the moment, these take some planning. Each one could well figure on the gastronomic coat-of-arms of its native city: *regaglie* for Rome, *pesto* for Genoa, *ragù* for Bologna.

Ideally, both the Roman and Bolognese sauces should be cooked in Italian terra-cotta pots on top of the stove, as should any long-cooking sauce, but we've found that the American-made equivalent of terra-cotta just can't take the direct heat. So we recommend enameled cast iron or very heavy stainless steel. Also, for beauty's sake alone, we aim for the prettiest heavy casserole possible when a pasta dish (or rice, for that matter) is served from the pot in which its sauce is cooked.

RIGATONI CON LE REGAGLIE
Rigatoni with Giblets

Regaglie is the all-inclusive word for the chicken's giblets: heart, liver, gizzard. This much-loved Roman dish puts *regaglie* to marvelous use in a sauce of tomatoes, onions, and mushrooms, with *rigatoni,* the big macaroni.

At first reading, the recipe looks like a real production, but if done in 4 steps, and if you have the pots (4 of them), it shouldn't take any more time than is necessary to bring the pasta water to a boil and cook the *rigatoni.*

SAUCE

- 3 tablespoons olive oil
- 1 medium onion
- ½ celery stalk
- ½ small carrot
- 2 cups peeled plum tomatoes
  salt to taste
  freshly ground pepper to taste
- 1 to 1½ cups chicken livers, hearts, gizzards (the equivalent of the giblets from 5 average chickens, or 1 pound mixed)
- ½ pound fresh mushrooms
- 8 tablespoons unsalted butter
- ⅓ cup grated Parmesan cheese

PASTA

> 6 quarts water
> 6 teaspoons salt
> 1¼ pounds *rigatoni*

First step and first pot: put the pasta water on to boil in a big pot.

Second step: put the olive oil in a heavy stove-to-table casserole. Mince the onion, celery, and carrot. Sauté them until golden in the olive oil over medium heat. Then add the plum tomatoes, breaking them up as you stir them in, salt (approximately 1½ teaspoons), and pepper (2 or 3 twists of the mill). Bring to a boil, and then reduce the heat, simmering the sauce gently about 15 minutes, or until it has cooked down a bit, its color darkened, its flavors blended.

Third step: the preparation of the *regaglie*. In a small pot (your third) boil the gizzards in salted water to cover for 5 minutes. Then skin them and chop them to bits (less than ¼ inch) with the livers and hearts. Cut the mushrooms into thin slices. Melt the butter in a big frying pan (your fourth and last pan), and sauté the *regaglie* and mushrooms quickly (about 5 minutes) over medium heat.

Cook and drain the pasta, and put it into the pot with the tomato sauce, which is still simmering. Stir well, and add the cheese. When that's well distributed, stir in the now-cooked giblet-mushroom mixture with its butter. Raise the heat, stir again until the bits are well distributed throughout and the cheese has melted. Serve from this pot.

LINGUINE AL PESTO
Linguine with Pesto

Linguine (flat spaghetti) with a pounded basil-nut-garlic sauce is perhaps Genoa's best-known contribution to pasta. *Pesto* means pounded, and in this case a mortar and pestle are used to crush a combination of nuts and fresh basil with cheese until, when mixed with olive oil, the juices become a sauce.

SAUCE

    2 cups loosely packed fresh basil leaves
    2 medium garlic cloves
    1 teaspoon salt
    3 ounces pine nuts
    1 tablespoon grated Parmesan cheese
    1 tablespoon grated Romano cheese
    ¾ to 1 cup olive oil
    6 tablespoons unsalted butter

PASTA

    6 quarts water
    6 teaspoons salt
    1¼ pounds *linguine*

Mix together the basil, garlic, and salt, and chop them to fine bits. Crush the pine nuts with a rolling pin or meat pounder, and add them to the garlic and basil. Chop some more, and then put everything into a large mortar. Pound and grind the mixture with a pestle until a good thick paste is formed. Add the cheeses, and grind some more until the paste is homogeneous. Add the olive oil a tablespoon at a time, working with the pestle until the paste has absorbed as much of the oil as it can. Depending on how moist the cheeses and the basil leaves are, you may need to use a little more or a little less oil to reach a thick sauce consistency. This *pesto* may be made with more or less garlic, depending on taste, but the proportions above produce a flavor compromise in which the basil and garlic and pine nuts share equally.

Cook and drain the pasta (page 20), reserving a small amount of the water, and put it on a warmed serving dish or 6 individual warmed dishes. Add 1 tablespoon butter per person to the pasta, and toss lightly. Then add 1 heaping tablespoon *pesto* per person, and toss again. If the *pesto* has thickened, you can dilute it with a tablespoon of the reserved hot pasta water before serving.

RAGÙ I: SUGO ALLA BOLOGNESE
Bolognese Meat Sauce I

And here it is, the classic meat sauce from Bologna. Even if the name has a French echo, the beef, pork, veal, chicken livers, tomatoes, and dry red wine form a chorus with the unmistakable accent of Emilia-Romagna. Nearly all the regions of Italy have their own variations on the theme, such as the use of dry white wine instead of red. This master sauce is served on all sorts of commercial pasta and rice, but it is traditional with home-made *fettuccine* and *lasagne*.

This recipe makes enough for 18 servings of pasta, or *lasagne* for 12. *Ragù* can be made ahead of time and stored 3 or 4 days in the refrigerator, or it can be frozen in well-sealed plastic containers.

> 1 slice lean salt pork
> 3 small onions
> 3 small carrots
> 3 celery stalks with leaves
>   olive oil
>   hearts, livers, gizzards, necks from 3 chickens
> 1 pound lean twice-ground beef
> 1 pound mixed twice-ground beef, veal, pork
> 1 cup dry red wine
> 4 to 5 teaspoons salt, or to taste
>   freshly ground pepper to taste
> 8 cups peeled plum tomatoes, or 2 2-pound cans
> 1 small can tomato paste, plus same measure hot water

Chop the salt pork, onions, carrots, and celery over and over until they're nearly a paste. Sauté gently until golden in a big heavy pot, the bottom of which you cover with olive oil. Chop finely the chicken livers and hearts, skin and chop the gizzards, and regrind the meats if they aren't already twice ground. When the onion, carrot, celery, and salt pork are golden and limp, put in all the meats, and the chicken necks, and brown thoroughly. Work the meats over with a wooden spoon, breaking up any possible lumps to insure a smooth sauce, and when the meats are well browned, add the wine, and let it evaporate. Add the salt and a good grind of pepper, and then the tomatoes, tomato paste, and water. Bring to a boil, cover, and lower the heat. Simmer for 2 hours.

Remove the chicken necks, taste the *ragù* for salt, adding some if necessary. Simmer another hour without cover to reduce the liquid.

If the *ragù*, because of the quality of the ground beef, turns out to be fattier than it should be, you can skim off the fat at the end of cooking, or chill the *ragù* and then easily slip off the congealed fat. The less fat in your sauce, the better your pasta dish.

RAGÙ II
Bolognese Meat Sauce II

This recipe for 6 generous servings of the traditional Bolognese meat sauce is cooked in exactly the same way as the big one for *lasagne* or many portions of pasta. The difference is that unexpectedly the ingredients for the smaller batch are not exactly one-third those required for the recipe serving three times as many people. When used with *pasta all'uovo* cut either in wide *fettuccine* or less wide *tagliatelle* or narrow *tonnarelli*, it makes as superb a *primo piatto* as *lasagne*.

SAUCE

    1 slice lean salt pork
    ½ small carrot
    1 small onion
    1 celery stalk with leaves
    ¼ cup olive oil (or enough to cover the pot bottom)
    1 chicken neck, gizzard, heart, liver
    1 pound twice-ground beef, or mixed veal, pork, beef
    ½ cup dry red wine
    4 cups peeled plum tomatoes
    1 tablespoon tomato paste
    ½ cup water
    2 teaspoons salt, or to taste
    3 to 4 tablespoons grated Parmesan cheese

PASTA

    6 quarts water
    6 teaspoons salt
    1 5-egg batch *Pasta all'uovo* (pages 15 to 19), or 1¼ pound packaged egg noodles

Cook exactly as *Ragù I* (pages 50 to 51).

If using homemade pasta, see pages 18 to 19 for cutting and drying.

Cook and drain the pasta (page 20), and serve with *ragù* and a generous sprinkling of Parmesan cheese.

MINESTRE
Soups

Depending on your mood, the weather, and the market, *minestre* (soups in general) make a great alternative to pasta as a first course. Like pasta, *minestre* can appear in many shapes and tastes.

There are the *minestrine*, the light soups like *pastina in brodo* (little pasta shapes in broth), that are designed for light dinners or to precede hearty second courses. These are usually made with a fairly delicate broth—homemade, canned, or made with the humble bouillon cube—combined with a variety of pasta or rice.

Then there are the ordinary, everyday soups that usually hide under the generic term *minestre*. They are made with a broth base also, meat or chicken or vegetable, and frequently combine rice or pasta with a vegetable, such as *riso e indivia* (rice-and-endive soup).

Finally, there are the big vegetable soups that are called *minestroni* (big soups) or *zuppe*. They can be filling enough to make a dent in the healthiest appetite, and reduce the cook's work for the remaining courses. One famous example is Milan's *minestrone*, with its infinite variety of fresh and dried vegetables.

In and around these three basic types of soup— perhaps above and beyond them—is the extra-special soup, a Sunday soup whose makings take a little extra time to prepare. Under this heading, we put the broth honored with little stuffed pasta shapes such as *cappelletti* or *tortellini*. We think Italy's many fish soups— *zuppe di pesce*—also fall in this extra-special category. A proper *zuppa di pesce* is so glorious it can stand alone, followed only by a salad, to make a perfect meal.

Some people say they steer clear of soup because it has to be made in quantity, or it uses too many pots, or is too complicated, or takes all day. Others think that just because it is a soup, it is for winter only. But that's not necessarily so.

Hot or cold, thick or thin, a good *minestra* fills the basic requirements of a first course: it sets the pace for the rest of the meal, and reflects the market's offerings.

BRODO DI CARNE
Beef Broth

Plain beef broth takes about 10 minutes to organize and 3 hours to simmer. It can be made with fresh beef brisket, the small end of a bottom round roast, or soup cuts. If made in quantity, broth freezes well in plastic containers. It can be kept in the refrigerator for 3 or 4 days. The King of *brodo* (it's masculine in Italian) is that which comes with a *Bollito misto* (pages 116 to 117).

1 to 1½ pounds beef
3 teaspoons salt
1 celery stalk with leaves
1 carrot
1 small onion
2 to 3 plum tomatoes, or ½ tablespoon tomato paste
1 to 2 soupbones
2 egg whites (optional)

Put the beef and all the other ingredients in cold water to cover (3 quarts should be enough; if not, add a bit more). Bring to a boil slowly, uncovered, over low heat. When the liquid first boils, scoop off any froth that forms, lower the heat to a simmer, cover the pot, and cook for about 3 hours. The meat should be tender, the broth a light, clear brown, and flavorful.

Strain the broth, saving the meat for future use and throwing out the now overcooked vegetables and the bones. If the broth is fatty, you may chill it and then remove the congealed fat, or just take it off immediately with a spoon or bulb baster.

If you want a really clear broth, beat 2 egg whites lightly, bring the defatted broth to a boil, and mix in the egg whites, beating with a wire whisk. Boil until the particles have been absorbed by the cooked egg whites, or for about 3 minutes. Turn off the heat, and when the broth has settled, scoop off the now speckled egg whites with a slotted spoon and pour the broth through a sieve lined with 2 layers of cheesecloth.

When using broth for making rice or *pastina in brodo*, we estimate 2 cups per person, plus a little more for the pot. The amounts of broth specified in any one recipe reflect this estimate. If you have big soup lovers at table, you may want to be more generous. (In a pinch, American canned chicken and beef broths, separately or combined, are good substitutes. Even bouillon cubes, 1 to a cup of water, lend themselves gracefully to soup in the Italian manner.)

BRODO DI POLLO
Chicken Broth

Chicken broth, like beef broth, is used in making many soups, as well as for rice dishes and for basting meats as they cook.

    1 3-pound fowl
    1 celery stalk with leaves
    1 onion
    1 carrot
    3 to 4 plum tomatoes
    3 teaspoons salt
    5 peppercorns
    1 soupbone
    3 quarts cold water
    2 egg whites (optional)

Put everything into a big pot over a low heat, add the water, and bring it to a boil slowly. Once the pot boils, scoop off the froth that forms, cover, and reduce the heat to simmer. Cook for at least 2 hours, but 3 is even better. Strain, using a colander or sieve lined with 2 layers of cheesecloth to catch the bits of vegetable and bone marrow. Skim off excess fat with a bulb baster, or chill thoroughly and remove congealed fat from the top with a spoon.

If you want a very clear broth, use beaten egg whites for clarifying as described in the preceding recipe for beef broth.

As for the boiled fowl you now have on your hands, use your imagination: cut it in bits for a soup or salad, or put it through the meat grinder for use in filling pasta, such as *Cannelloni* (pages 97 to 98) or *Cappelletti* (pages 100 to 102).

STRACCIATELLA
Broth with Beaten Egg

Stracciatella is translated literally as "torn to rags," because when eggs, flavored with cheese and nutmeg, are beaten and dropped into boiling broth, they shred as they cook. Raggedy is certainly the way they look.

Classic *stracciatella* is made with a chicken-beef broth (pages 53 and 55), as fat-free as possible. To achieve the same taste using canned broths, the proportion should be 1½ quarts of chicken broth to ½ quart of beef broth.

There are a number of versions of this soup, and the second most commonly found uses bread crumbs instead of flour, but we find the results less delightful. For an even lighter soup, leave out the flour entirely.

3 eggs
1 tablespoon flour
6 tablespoons grated Parmesan cheese
   nutmeg
2 quarts chicken-beef broth

Beat the eggs well, adding the flour and half the Parmesan cheese and a dash of nutmeg as you beat. Bring the broth to a boil, add the beaten eggs, stirring constantly with a wire whisk for half a minute or so to make sure all the eggs have been cooked by the broth. Remove from the heat, pour into a soup tureen, and if the eggs tend to cling together again, whisk once more. Serve with a sprinkle of the remaining cheese on each dish.

PASTINA IN BRODO
Pasta Bits in Broth

Probably the simplest of all broth soups, this dish leaves a lot of leeway to the cook. The broth can be homemade beef (pages 53 to 55) or chicken broth (page 55), or it can be made with 12 cups of water and 12 bouillon cubes (8 chicken and 4 beef is a good combination).

The pasta shapes are cook's choice. If you use *tubettini,* small shells or bows, the amount indicated, 2 cups, is good. If you use noodle flakes, 1 cup is sufficient. Either way, it's ½ pound of pasta. In Italy, when the larder lacks *pastina,* ½ pound of spaghetti or *linguine* is wrapped up in a clean dish towel and crushed into tiny bits, thus producing instant *pastina.*

> 12 cups broth
> 2 cups small pasta
> 3 to 4 tablespoons grated Parmesan cheese

Preparing *pastina in brodo* is about like cooking any pasta: bring the broth to a good boil, add the *pastina,* and bring the pot back to a boil. Cook uncovered until the pasta is done. Ladle out into individual soup plates, sprinkle with the Parmesan cheese, and serve.

To make it for 1 person, follow this rule of thumb: about 2 heaping tablespoons of *pastina* per 2½ cups of broth.

RISO IN BRODO
Rice in Broth

Rice in broth, another light soup, is made exactly like *pastina in brodo.*

> 12 cups broth
> 2 cups rice
> 3 to 4 tablespoons grated Parmesan cheese

Bring the broth to a boil, put in the rice, and when the pot boils again, stir the rice, and reduce the heat a bit. Cook until the rice is done, stirring from time to time to prevent sticking. Serve with a sprinkling of the cheese on each bowl.

MARIOLA
Broth with Omelet Bits

This broth-base soup with the pretty name comes from Calabria. It is filled with small squares of thin herb-seasoned omelets.

> 4 large eggs
> 6 tablespoons fine bread crumbs
>   salt to taste
>   freshly ground pepper to taste
> ¼ teaspoon marjoram
> 2 tablespoons chopped parsley
> 1¼ quarts chicken broth (page 55)
> 3 tablespoons grated Parmesan cheese

Beat the eggs thoroughly. Sift the bread crumbs and add them, along with the salt, pepper, parsley, and marjoram, to the beaten eggs.

Melt a bit of butter in a heavy frying pan over a medium-high heat and pour in just enough egg mixture to make a very thin omelet. As soon as it's solid on the underside, turn it, and as soon as the second side is cooked, remove it to a plate. Keep on making thin omelets until you've used up everything.

When the omelets are cool, cut them in about ½-inch squares.

Bring the broth to a boil, drop in the omelet squares, and serve after the broth has come back to a boil. Sprinkle with the Parmesan cheese.

CAPPELLETTI IN BRODO
Cappelletti in Broth

Cappelletti (little hats) are small squares of pasta, filled with a delicate mixture of meats and cheese, seasoned with nutmeg and parsley. When folded they do look like little hats. A specialty of the Emilia-Romagna kitchen, *cappelletti* are cooked in either chicken or beef broth, or a combination of the two. They can then be

served in the broth, or drained and served with cream
and cheese or a bit of sauce.

In Italy, you can find fresh *cappelletti* hand- or
machine-made in pasta shops. In America, they can be
found packaged, frozen, in Italian specialty stores and
some supermarkets. If you make your own, you'll get
the delicate taste of the traditional *cappelletti* (see pages
100 to 102 for directions on filling and folding).

   3 quarts broth
   1 batch *cappelletti*, or 2 boxes frozen
   4 to 6 tablespoons grated Parmesan cheese

Bring the broth to a boil, put in all the *cappelletti*
by the handful, bring the broth back to a boil, and cook
gently for 10 to 15 minutes, or until the pasta is tender.
(Frozen *cappelletti* take a bit more time than the homemade ones.) Serve in soup plates with the broth and a
generous sprinkling of the Parmesan cheese.

RISI E BISI
Venetian Rice-and-Pea Soup

Risi e bisi is Venetian dialect for rice-and-pea soup so
thick you can almost eat it with a fork, a sensational as
well as a substantial first course.

   2 slices *prosciutto*, or 2 slices lean salt pork
   1 small onion
   3 tablespoons chopped fresh parsley
   3 tablespoons olive oil
   3 tablespoons unsalted butter
   1 10-ounce package frozen peas, or 1 pound fresh
   1 cup rice, long or short grain but not quick-cooking
   1 quart chicken broth (page 55)
     grated Parmesan cheese

Cut the *prosciutto* in tiny squares (if unavailable, substitute lean salt pork), mince the onion, chop the
parsley.

   Put the oil and butter in a big, heavy pot over
medium heat and add all the chopped ingredients.

Sauté until the onion is translucent and limp. Add the peas and enough water to cover (about ½ inch), and cook for 5 minutes. Add the rice and broth, and bring to a boil. Reduce the heat, and simmer about 15 minutes, stirring frequently, or until the rice is tender. The soup is now very thick. If you prefer a thinner (and less traditional) soup, add an extra cup or two of hot broth at this time.

Serve with a sprinkle of Parmesan cheese on each portion.

RISO E INDIVIA
Rice-and-Endive Soup

Another of those deceptive dishes, this soup is easy on the palate, yet filling and soothing on any day.

    1 bunch curly endive
    1 garlic clove
    ½ cup olive oil
    1 tablespoon tomato paste, or 2 peeled plum
      tomatoes
    2½ quarts hot water
    2 teaspoons salt
    1 cup long-grain rice
      grated Parmesan cheese

Break the endive apart and wash thoroughly. Shake as dry as possible and chop fine. Sauté the garlic in olive oil in a big soup pot over medium heat. When the garlic is golden, not browned, discard it, and add the tomato paste (or cut-up tomatoes). Stir and cook until blended. Add the chopped endive, and cook 2 or 3 minutes, until wilted. Raise the heat, add the water, salt, and rice, and bring to a boil. Then lower the heat and cook gently, stirring occasionally, about 12 to 14 minutes, or until rice is done. Serve with a sprinkling of Parmesan cheese.

There is a nice variation for this one: substitute hot chicken broth (page 55) for the water, and eliminate the garlic and tomato from the flavored olive oil. Just heat the olive oil, add the endive, and cook 2 or 3 minutes. Add hot broth and rice, and bring to a boil. Continue cooking 12 to 14 minutes as above, and serve.

RISO E INDIVIA AL POMODORO
Rice-Endive-Tomato Soup

Fresh tomatoes make the real variation in this rice-and-endive soup, which is also flavored lightly with the classic *battuto* of onion, herbs, and pork.

BATTUTO
- 1 slice lean salt pork
- ½ onion
- ½ celery stalk
- 1 small carrot
- 4 sprigs parsley
- 2 tablespoons olive oil

SOUP
- 10 fresh, ripe plum tomatoes
- 1 bunch curly endive
  salt to taste
- 1 quart hot water
- 1 cup long-grain rice
  grated Parmesan cheese (optional)

Make a *battuto* by mincing up the lean salt pork with the onion, celery, carrot, and parsley. Sauté the mixture until golden in the oil in a soup pot over medium heat. Once the bits are golden, turn off the heat.

Plunge the tomatoes into boiling water for about 3 minutes, drain them, and when they're cool enough to handle, peel them. Cut them open and remove the seeds. To save all the juice possible, do this over a plate, letting the juice and seeds fall in the plate to be strained into the soup pot after the chunks of tomato go in.

Add the cut-up tomatoes to the soup pot, turn the heat to medium high, and cook and stir for about 10 minutes.

Wash and chop the endive, and add it to the pot, which is still on medium-high heat, and cook for 3 or 4 minutes. Add the hot water, bring back to a boil, add the rice, and continue cooking until the rice is done (about 12 minutes). Taste for salt (the pork adds some), and add some if necessary. Serve hot. Optional: add a sprinkle of cheese to each dish.

RISO E FAGIOLI
Rice-and-Bean Soup

Rice-and-Bean Soup is another member of the same large family of winter *minestre* that combines a vegetable and its broth with either pasta or rice to make what some of our friends call Italian soul food.

> ½ cup olive oil
> 1 garlic clove (optional)
> 1 onion
> 1 celery stalk
> 1 tablespoon chopped fresh parsley
> 3 peeled plum tomatoes, or 1 tablespoon tomato paste
> 2 cups cooked kidney or shell beans, or 1 20-ounce can and its liquid
> 2½ quarts hot water
> 1 cup rice
> 3 to 4 tablespoons grated Parmesan cheese

If using dried beans: put ½ pound in water to cover, bring to a boil, cook 2 minutes, turn off the heat, and let stand an hour. Then bring back to a boil, reduce heat, and simmer until the beans are tender.

If using canned beans: when you add them to the flavored beginnings of the soup, add the liquid as well.

Put the oil in a generous soup pot and sauté the garlic until golden (if you want to use it), and discard it. Mince the onion, celery, and parsley together, and cook them in the olive oil until the onion is translucent. Add the tomatoes (or tomato paste), and cook on a low heat for 10 minutes. Add the beans and some of their liquid, not much more than ¼ cup, together with the hot water. Raise the heat, and cook 2 or 3 minutes to flavor the beans. Crush a few beans against the side of the pot with a wooden spoon to make the soup thicker. Add the rice, stir, and boil gently for approximately 15 minutes, or until the rice is plump and cooked. Serve with a sprinkle of Parmesan cheese.

MINESTRONE ALLA MILANESE
Vegetable Soup, Milanese Style

This is the big soup made with a garden of fresh vegetables, a *battuto* of seasoning herbs and vegetables, and a dried vegetable or two. The various ingredients go into the pot according to their cooking times: the ones that take the longest go first, i.e., fresh shell beans, when you are lucky enough to find them in season. The dried vegetables used to be a staple in *minestrone,* and they were soaked for hours prior to cooking time, but today's cook can easily resort to canned kidney or shell beans or chick-peas. Both yesterday's and today's cooks vary the vegetables according to the seasonal market, so feel free to add leeks, fresh tomatoes, purple cabbage, small green beans, etc., when you find them.

Naturally, there are many versions of this *minestrone.* We have adopted the one most commonly used, whose ingredients are readily available on the American market year round. The very, very original Milanese version also included thin strips of pork rind cooked with the *battuto.* Today's cooks reach for the same effect by doubling the original amount of salt pork in the *battuto.*

BATTUTO
- 1 celery stalk with leaves
- 1 onion
- 1 carrot
- 2 slices lean salt pork
- 1 sage leaf
- 3 tablespoons olive oil, to cover the bottom of the pot

SOUP
- 2½ quarts hot water
- 3 teaspoons salt, or to taste
- 2 celery stalks
- 2 carrots
- 3 potatoes
- ¼ cauliflower
- 2 medium zucchini
- ¼ small cabbage
- ¼ head escarole
- ¼ head curly endive
- 1 cup fresh spinach leaves
- ½ small onion
- 3 peeled plum tomatoes
- 1 cup green peas
- 1 cup rice or small macaroni
- ½ cup canned chick-peas and their liquid
- ½ cup canned kidney or shell beans and their liquid
- 6 slices Italian bread
- 3 to 4 tablespoons grated Parmesan cheese

You begin a *minestrone* with a *battuto:* this time you chop to a paste your seasonings, celery, onion, carrot, and sage, along with the lean salt pork. Chop all these coarsely, and then keep chopping (using either a knife or half-moon chopper) until everything is reduced to a paste. Blenders don't seem to do too well with this combination of pork and celery, so they are not recommended. When the *battuto* is ready, sauté it in the olive oil in a big soup pot. Once the *battuto* is golden, the *minestrone* is on its way.

Add to the pot the hot water and the salt, raise the heat to high. Chop the celery, carrots, and 2 of the potatoes into ¼-inch bits, break the cauliflower into small pieces, preserving as much as possible the individual flowerets. Put these 4 vegetables to boil in the flavored water for 10 minutes, while you prepare the other vegetables: slice the third potato with a potato peeler into paper-thin slices, and add them to the pot. Chop the zucchini in half, then quarters, and then slice these into ½-inch bits. Cut the cabbage into thin slices and then into ⅛-inch bits. Break the escarole, endive, and spinach into ½-inch pieces. Slice the onion into slivers. Add these, the tomatoes, and the peas to the boiling pot, lower the heat, and let bubble along for about 15 minutes. If you wish, add 1 cup of rice at this time, to make a northern variation, or a cup of small macaroni to make a southern version.

At the end of 15 minutes, or when all the vegetables are done, add the chick-peas and beans, mashing some of them as you stir them in. Cook for another 15 to 25 minutes, depending on how thick you wish your soup. The real *minestrone* has a nice, thick consistency, although some prefer it thinner.

Serve hot in winter with a slice of toasted (even better, fried) Italian bread in the bottom of the soup plate and a sprinkling of Parmesan cheese on top. Serve at room temperature without the bread in summer.

MINESTRONE ALLA CALABRESE
Vegetable Soup in the Style of Calabria

A southern Italian variation of *minestrone*, Calabrian vegetable soup uses a variety of summer vegetables, and seasons them with sweet yellow peppers.

BATTUTO
- 4 slices lean salt pork or *prosciutto*
- 2 tablespoons chopped fresh parsley
- 1 celery stalk
- 1 small carrot
- ½ garlic clove
- 4 fresh basil leaves
- 4 tablespoons olive oil

SOUP

> 1½ to 2 quarts hot water
> 1 teaspoon salt
> 1 pound mixed summer vegetables: peas, green beans, ripe plum tomatoes, zucchini, spinach, carrots, celery, potato
> 1 large yellow sweet pepper
> ½ cup rice
>   grated Parmesan cheese

Make a *battuto* by chopping the salt pork (or *prosciutto*, if available), parsley, celery, carrot, garlic, and basil until everything is reduced to a paste.

Heat the oil in a big soup pot, add the *battuto*, and sauté over medium heat until golden. Add the hot water and salt, and bring to a boil.

Meanwhile, chop the summer vegetables into pieces no bigger than ½ inch. If using a potato, slice it as finely as possible (a peeler does a good job). Add all these when the soup pot reaches a boil, and simmer for about 15 minutes.

If the soup seems terribly thick at this point, add a cup or so of hot water. Taste for salt, and add some more if necessary.

Core a yellow sweet pepper, and cut it into long, very thin strips. Add to the simmering soup.

When the carrot bits (or the vegetable that takes longest to cook) are tender, add the rice, and boil gently another 15 minutes, or until the rice is done.

Serve with a good sprinkling of Parmesan cheese.

PASTA E BROCCOLI
Pasta-and-Cauliflower Soup

Another favorite Roman soup, made of pasta and cauliflower (which in Rome is usually called broccoli), this is an easy way to start a winter's meal.

    1 small cauliflower head
  ½ cup olive oil
    1 garlic clove
      freshly ground pepper to taste
    1 tablespoon tomato paste
 2½ quarts hot water
    1 potato sliced paper thin
    2 teaspoons salt
  ½ pound of *linguine* or spaghetti broken into bits
    3 to 4 tablespoons grated Parmesan cheese

Break the cauliflower into its flowerets, cutting the bigger ones in half or quarters so that all the pieces are about ½ inch in size.

Put the oil in a soup pot along with the garlic, a dish of salt, a few grinds of pepper, and the cut-up cauliflower. Stirring gently, cook over medium heat until the vegetable bits are well oiled and flavored. Add the tomato paste, hot water, the potato slices, and the 2 teaspoons salt, and bring to a good boil.

Break the pasta into 1- or 2-inch lengths as you put it in the pot. Continue boiling until the pasta is well cooked, has absorbed some of the water, and the cauliflower, garlic, and tomato have lent their flavors to the pasta. (This, like Pasta-and Chick-pea Soup, below, is one of those dishes in which it is permissible to have the pasta cooked beyond the *al dente* stage.)

Before serving, seek out the garlic clove, and discard it. Serve with a sprinkling of Parmesan cheese.

PASTA E CECI
Pasta-and-Chick-Pea Soup

Pasta and chick-peas combine in this hearty soup. Flavored with rosemary, salt pork, and garlic, *pasta e ceci* is a sustaining dish for a cold day. Traditionally, the pasta used in this recipe was the *rimanenze*, the remainders of various cuts of pasta, long and short, all mixed together. It is a good way to use remainders and also gives the soup a different, varied texture.

2 slices lean salt pork
4 whole garlic cloves
2 to 3 peeled plum tomatoes, or 1 tablespoon tomato paste
1 sprig fresh rosemary, or 2 teaspoons dried
3 cups cooked chick-peas, or 1½ 20-ounce cans
2 quarts hot water
   salt to taste
½ pound small macaroni or broken-up long pasta
   grated cheese (optional)

If using dried chick-peas: put 2 cups in 4 quarts of cold water with a scant ¼ teaspoon of baking soda. Soak overnight. The chick-peas will have absorbed some of the water, so add enough more water to cover the peas as well, and bring to a boil. Then reduce the heat and simmer slowly 2 or 3 hours, until cooked through. Proceed as with canned chick-peas, using the cooking liquid and adding enough hot water to make 2 quarts all together.

Chop the lean salt pork to a paste. Sauté it in the olive oil in a big soup pot over medium heat. Cook until translucent. Add the garlic, tomatoes, rosemary, and 2 cups of chick-peas and their liquid. Mash the remaining peas, and add them. Pour in the hot water, and bring to a gentle boil for 10 minutes.

Raise the heat, and taste to see if the liquid is salty enough. Add some more salt, if needed, and put in the pasta when the pot has come to a good boil. You can use *tubettini*, small elbows, or a combination of *tubettini* and macaroni, or you can break up spaghetti or *linguine* into 1- or 2-inch lengths. Once the pot is boiling again, lower the heat and cook slowly, stirring from time to time, until the pasta is tender.

When you serve *pasta e ceci,* look out for those 4 garlic cloves, and discard them. Some people like this soup with a sprinkling of Parmesan or Romano cheese, but many prefer it just as it is.

PASTA E FAGIOLI
Pasta-and-Bean Soup

Nearly every region in Italy has its own version of this soup. It's made with shell or kidney beans and small macaroni (*tubetti*, elbows, squares, or broken-up spaghetti or *linguine*, as you wish). When made with fresh beans in the summer, it adds a whole new dimension to the first course.

BATTUTO
>   2 slices lean salt pork
>   1 small onion
>   1 medium garlic clove
>   1 celery stalk
>   3 tablespoons olive oil

SOUP
>   3 to 4 peeled plum tomatoes, or 1 tablespoon tomato
>   paste
>   2 quarts hot water
>   2 teaspoons salt
>   2 cups shell beans, fresh or dried
>   2 cups small pasta
>   3 to 4 tablespoons grated Romano or Parmesan cheese

Like so many of these filling soups, this one starts with the *battuto*. Put the slices of salt pork on a chopping board. Top them with the onion, garlic, and celery, and chop, then mince until the pile has turned to a paste.

Put the *battuto* in a big soup pot with the olive oil over medium heat. Sauté until golden, then add the tomatoes (or tomato paste), and cook again for about 3 minutes, or until the tomatoes have blended a bit and softened. Add the hot water, salt, and beans, and bring to a good boil.

If using fresh beans: when they are in season, buy fresh shell beans, which are the ones with the pink and white speckled pods; 1½ pounds gives you enough for this soup, and the flavor is so delicious you'll wish for fresh *fagioli* year round. Fresh beans can cook right in the pot with the water as indicated above.

If using dried beans: see page 62 for directions.

If using canned shell beans: be sure to get the ones put up without sugar. There is no precooking or long cooking. One 20-ounce can makes about 2 cups. Add the liquid in the can plus about 1½ quarts of hot water as a substitute for the 2 quarts of plain hot water you add with the fresh beans.

Once the water, salt, and beans are boiling, reduce the heat, and cook until the beans are tender (if fresh) or heated through (if canned). Then crush a few beans against the side of the pot, add the pasta, and continue cooking until it is well done. By this time the soup is really so thick you may want to add a little more water. Taste for salt, and add some if necessary. Serve with a sprinkling of the Romano or Parmesan cheese.

QUADRUCCI E PISELLI
Pasta Squares and Peas in Broth

Tiny pasta squares (noodle flakes) and new peas in chicken broth make this a delicate Roman *minestra*. If made with homemade egg pasta and the smallest of new peas, this soup is fit for a banquet.

BATTUTO
> 1 slice lean salt pork
> 1 celery stalk
> ½ carrot
> 1 onion
> 3 tablespoons unsalted butter

SOUP

> 1 10-ounce package frozen tiny peas, or 1 pound fresh
> 1 2-egg batch homemade pasta, or ½ pound noodle flakes
> 2½ quarts hot chicken broth (page 55)
> 3 to 4 tablespoons grated Parmesan cheese

Pile the celery, carrot, and onion on the strip of salt pork, and chop the whole thing to a paste (*battuto*). Melt the butter in a big soup pot, add the *battuto*, and cook over medium heat until golden and limp. Add the peas, and cook for 2 or 3 minutes. Add the hot broth, and bring to a boil for 8 minutes. Then add the pasta squares, and continue boiling until the pasta is cooked. Homemade pasta takes about 5 minutes, commercial pasta about 8. Stir the soup, which is now medium thick, and sprinkle in the Parmesan cheese so that it melts without lumping. Cook 1 minute more, and serve.

If making your own pasta, roll it out as for *fettuccine* (page 27), flour it well, and dry it about 15 minutes before cutting. Cut 10 or 12 strips the width of *fettuccine*, move them apart from the roll of pasta, and cut them again, at ¼-inch intervals, at right angles to the first cut, thus making tiny squares. Keep on cutting, first the long, folded strips, and then the squares. Spread out to dry on a dish towel until time to use, up to 5 or 6 hours if you wish.

ZUPPE DI PESCE
Fish Soups

Perhaps because the average Italian lives so close to the sea (or a well-stocked mountain lake), he understands more than others the value of its gifts: fish is highly honored on the Italian table.

Almost every sea village, if not every fisherman,

boasts its own special way to concoct a *zuppa di pesce*, but by and large they all follow the same basic rules.

Remember that even if it is called fish soup, the dish is more fish than soup.

Use as many different kinds of fish as possible, including rock fish and sea eel, and choose fish for varying flavors, texture, and color.

Use the fish, once cleaned and scaled, in its entirety: heads, tails, bones all go in. Remember that Italian parsimony has produced yet another proverb, "Tutto fa brodo," or literally, "Everything makes soup." In the case of fish, everything *is* the soup. Be thereby warned that the most finicky should stay away from fish soup, or if they must, they may remove the fish heads and tails, and cook them separately, but not in the sight of a real lover of *zuppa di pesce*.

Use the largest available pot, so that the fish will fit in it in the least number of layers, with the liquid used just barely covering the fish.

Be sure that the pot has a cover, so that the fish can cook by combined poaching, steaming, and boiling, a very gentle process.

Be careful that the fish, whole or in chunks, is cooked, but not so much as to fall apart. When adding the fish to the pot, start with the firm-fleshed kind, and finish with the most tender.

When all the rules are followed, you can be assured of a feast, a celebration of the bounty of the sea. *Zuppa di pesce* should be approached with uninhibited joy, enthusiasm, and a healthy disregard for etiquette, so a large napkin, the lobster kind, and a finger bowl are recommended.

As for the preparation of the fish involved, most of it is simple and well known on this side of the ocean. But, since squid and mussels seem to be less familiar on the American table, here are basic suggestions on how to clean them.

To clean squid: cut the tentacles from the head

just below the eyes. Discard the mouth, which is hidden in the center of the tentacles, and save the tentacles. Hold the body of the squid under running water, and peel off the thin outer skin. Squeeze out the insides as you would a tube of paste, pulling the head off at the final squeeze. Discard both head and insides. Pull out the transparent center bone, and wash the body, which is like an empty sack. Slice the body into little rings or squares. If the tentacles are bigger than a mouthful, cut them in half or quarters accordingly.

To clean mussels: scrub the mussels with a stiff brush, pull off any bits of hemp or algae that may remain, and squeeze them hard to make sure they're tightly closed and alive and well. If opened slightly, the live ones will fight back and close; if they are wide open and sandy and won't shut, throw them away. Rinse carefully under running water.

CACCIUCCO
Tuscan Fish Soup

A somewhat elaborate *zuppa di pesce* from Livorno, Tuscany, this soup starts with a *battuto* of seasoning vegetables and lots of fresh plum tomatoes; red wine is used instead of the usual white wine; and lobster or jumbo shrimp complete the varied list of fish included.

SOUP

- 3 garlic cloves
- 1 red pepper pod, seeded
- ½ cup olive oil
- 1 carrot
- 1 celery stalk
- 4 sprigs parsley
- 1 onion
- 1 cup dry red wine
- 1½ pounds fresh plum tomatoes
- 1½ teaspoons salt
  freshly ground pepper to taste
- 2 cups water

FISH

    3 to 4 small squid
    ¾ pound medium shrimp
    2 to 3 small whole fish, such as mullet, porgy, rosefish
    1 small whole sea bass
    1 whole red snapper
      fillet of fresh halibut, or 1 slice of haddock
    1 small lobster, or 6 jumbo shrimp
    6 slices Italian bread
    1 garlic clove

   Clean and cut the squid. Clean and shell the shrimp,
reserving the shells. Clean and scale the larger fish, and
cut off and reserve the heads. Clean the small fish, but
keep them whole.

   Put 3 garlic cloves, the red pepper, and the olive
oil in a large saucepan over medium heat. Add a *battuto* (page 24) of the carrot, celery, parsley, and onion,
and sauté it until golden. Add the cut-up squid and
cook for 5 minutes. Add the wine, and when it is almost
evaporated, add the fresh tomatoes, peeled and cut into
chunks. Add the salt and a few grinds of pepper, and
bring to a boil. Then lower the heat to a simmer, and
cook for 10 minutes.

   Remove the squid from the tomato sauce, and set
them aside, and add to the sauce in their place the
shrimp shells, reserved fish heads, and the small fish.
Add the water, bring to a boil, and cook over medium
heat for 20 minutes, or until the small fish are really
falling apart.

   Turn the heat off, and with a wooden spoon stir
and mash the fish, and then put the whole mixture
through a coarse sieve into a big, top-of-the-stove casserole. Put in the large fish (the sea bass, red snapper,
and halibut or haddock) cut into chunks, the shrimp,
and the squid. Bring to a boil, and add the lobster cut
in chunks (or the jumbo shrimp, whole and unshelled).
The soup should be thick by this time, and should just
barely cover the fish. If not, add a bit of boiling hot

water to do so. Lower the heat to a simmer, and cook until the fish flakes but is not overcooked.

Toast the Italian bread, and rub both sides of the slices gently with a clove of garlic. Put a slice in the bottom of each soup plate and cover it with various pieces of fish and a ladle or two of soup.

Serve immediately, and relax and enjoy one of the most delicious of *zuppe di pesce*.

ZUPPA DI PESCE ALLA ROMANA
Roman Fish Soup

Anzio, a fishing town forty miles south of Rome, and Civitavecchia, a port sixty miles to the north, quarrel over which of the two is the creator of this soup. Rome, halfway between, has appropriated the *zuppa*'s name, and has gotten away with it.

FISH
- ½ pound small squid
- ½ pound mussels
- ½ pound medium shrimp
- 1 whiting
- 1 small red snapper or rosefish
- 1 slice halibut
- 1 porgy or scup

FLAVORINGS
- ¼ cup olive oil
- 1 garlic clove
- 1 red pepper pod, seeded
- 1 cup dry white wine
- 1 cup peeled plum tomatoes
- 1 teaspoon tomato paste
- 2 to 3 teaspoons salt

Clean the squid and mussels and peel the shrimp. Clean and scale the fish yourself, or have it done at the market, but be sure to leave the heads and tails on.

Heat the olive oil in a big soup pot over medium heat. Add the garlic and the pepper pod. When the garlic is golden and the pepper a deep brown, discard them, and add the squid. Cook for 4 minutes, or until their color has changed to pink and lavender. Add the wine, and cook until it has almost evaporated. Cut the tomatoes into chunks, and add them with their juice and the tomato paste to the pot. Bring to a boil, and cook 10 to 15 minutes, or until the squid are tender. Cut the rest of the fish into good-sized chunks, and add them to the pot with enough water just to cover. Bring to a boil, reduce the heat to low, and add the shrimp and the mussels along with the salt. Cover the pot, and continue cooking 10 minutes, or until the fish barely flakes, the mussels open, and the shrimp are tender. Taste for salt, and add as needed.

Scoop the fish out with a slotted spoon, and serve in individual soup plates, giving everyone a little bit of everything. Pour a ladle or two of soup over the fish.

Zuppa di pesce can be served with a slice of fried or toasted bread in the bottom of each plate, but the real fisherman's way is to dunk hot, crusty bread in the soup.

If the idea of fish heads in your soup disturbs you, there is an alternative way to go about this recipe: cut off the heads and tails and put them in a second pot. Add a stalk of celery, ½ onion, a small carrot, 1 bay leaf, water to cover, and a teaspoon of salt. Bring to a boil, reduce the heat, and cook for half an hour. Strain and set aside for use in the final *zuppa*. When all the fish are in the pot, add the fish stock instead of water to cover.

BRODETTO D'ANCONA
Fish Soup in the Style of Ancona

Fish soup from the Adriatic town of Ancona varies from its Roman cousin in its use of onion to flavor the base, vinegar instead of wine, and baby clams instead of mussels. This recipe calls for 5 to 6 pounds of varied fish, fresh if possible (but frozen is not to be ignored).

FISH

    2 or 3 small squid
    1 pound shrimp (big ones)
    1 pound cherrystone clams (smallest possible)
    a selection of:
        1 merluzzo or whiting
        1 porgy or scup
        1 fillet fresh cod
        1 mullet
        fillet of haddock
        slice of fresh tuna or swordfish
        slice of halibut
        fillet of sole or flounder

SEASONINGS

    1 large onion
    1 garlic clove
    ½ cup olive oil
    ½ cup wine vinegar
    2 cups peeled plum tomatoes
    2 to 3 teaspoons salt, or to taste
    freshly ground pepper to taste
    4 or 5 sprigs parsley, coarsely chopped

Clean the squid and peel the shrimp. Clean and scale the fish, but leave the heads and tails on. Cut into good-sized chunks.

Cut the onion in half, and then slice each half in the thinnest possible slivers. Add them to the garlic and olive oil in a big, heavy soup pot, and sauté over medium heat. When the garlic is golden discard it. When the onion slivers are translucent, add the cut-up squid, and cook and stir until their color changes. Add the vinegar, and when that has evaporated, add the tomatoes (mashing them in the pot), fish chunks, clams, shrimp, salt, and 2 or 3 twists of the pepper mill. Add enough water just barely to cover fish. Bring to a boil, reduce the heat, and cook for about 20 minutes, or until the clams are opened and the meatiest fish is cooked. Taste for salt, and adjust if necessary. Sprinkle in the parsley, and cook another 1 or 2 minutes.

Serve with slices of crusty, hot Italian bread. When serving the soup, try to give a goodly variety of fish chunks, shrimp, and clams to each plate first, and then ladle out about a cup of broth per plate.

ZUPPA DI PESCE ALLA SICILIANA
Sicilian Fish Soup

Sicilian fish soup is flavored with herbs, black olives, wine, and olive oil, and is cooked in a casserole in the oven. This recipe calls for 3½ to 4½ pounds (after cleaning) of fresh fish. Your choice is determined by the season and the market, but you should aim for 6 or 7 varieties. The weight uncleaned runs to about 5½ or 6 pounds.

FISH

        1 or 2 small porgies
        1 whiting
        1 flounder
        1 cod fillet
     ½ pound shrimp
     ½ pound squid
        1 pound mussels

SEASONINGS

        1 onion
     ¼ cup chopped fresh parsley
        1 cup Sicilian or Greek black olives
        1 garlic clove
        5 peppercorns
     ½ red pepper pod, or dash of Tabasco (optional)
        1 bay leaf
     ½ cup olive oil
        3 teaspoons salt
     1½ cups very dry white wine
        6 slices Italian bread

Preheat the oven to 350°.

Clean the fish, but leave the heads and tails on. Cut into chunks and put in the bottom of a big (6- to 8-quart) ovenproof casserole with a good cover. Leave the shells on the shrimp, and put them on top of the fish. Clean and cut the squid and distribute all the pieces over the shrimp. Scrub the mussels and put them on top of all the other fish.

Cut the onion into fine slivers and sprinkle them over the fish along with the chopped parsley and black olives. Add the garlic, peppercorns, red pepper, or Tabasco if you wish, and sink the bay leaf in the middle of everything. Pour on the olive oil and tip the casserole gently back and forth to let the oil coat the fish. Sprinkle with the salt, add the wine.

Cut a round of brown wrapping paper just a little bit bigger than the casserole and place it between the cover and the casserole to seal in the vapors while cooking. Bake for half an hour.

While the casserole bakes, deep-fry bread slices in olive oil or toast them to a golden brown. Serve in the bottom of soup dishes, with *zuppa di pesce* ladled over them.

ZUPPA DI COZZE
Mussel Soup

"Mussel soup" is only a literal translation that in no way can indicate the delicate and exciting flavor of the dish. For those lucky enough to find fresh, clean mussels, it's a treat any day of the week.

Clean the fish, but leave the heads and tails on.

- 4 pounds fresh mussels
- 5 tablespoons olive oil
- 1 garlic clove
- 2 red pepper pods, seeded
- 1 cup peeled plum tomatoes or 3 tablespoons tomato paste diluted in ½ cup warm water
- ½ cup dry white wine
- 1 teaspoon salt
- 4 tablespoons chopped fresh parsley
  Italian bread

Scrub the mussels (page 73) and rinse carefully under running water.

Put the olive oil in a big soup pot, and add the garlic and red pepper pods. Sauté over medium heat. Discard the garlic and pepper when golden and brown, and add the tomatoes and wine. Cook for 4 minutes, raise the heat, and add the mussels. Stir them around a bit, add the salt, cover, and cook for about 5 minutes, or until all the shells have opened. If by any chance there are any unopened mussels, discard them. Add the parsley, stir, and serve in big soup plates (with a few extras for discarded shells) with slices of hot Italian bread to dip in the soup. Or, you may want to fry the bread in olive oil and serve a slice at the bottom of each soup plate.

RISO
Rice

Rice, as a separate first course for the typical Italian dinner, is handled as carefully, specially, and diversely as any *pasta asciutta*. At one time, it was strictly a northern dish, but today good risotto (rice dish cooked on top of the stove and served with a sauce) appears all over the country.

In Italy, rice comes labeled according to usage, either for *minestra* or *risotto,* and it takes anywhere from 25 to 45 minutes to cook. American rice, as far as we know, isn't labeled for soup *per se,* but rice called fancy or long-grain does well in both *risotto* and soup. The kind that fails is instant rice, the parboiled-before-you-touch-it variety. Somehow, it just doesn't absorb enough liquid from a heavenly sauce, nor does it give out enough rice flavor. So, when possible, stick to the long-grain rice that shows up on the regular rice shelf or in the Armenian or Greek food section of your local supermarket. Like pasta, a good rice, if properly cooked, holds its shape as it is cooked and becomes tender but firm.

As for the sauces, they've been developed according to the specialties in the province where they originated. Venice is famous for its fish with rice, Milan for *risotto* with butter and chicken broth, Sicily for rice with tuna and tomatoes, Bologna for rice with *ragù*. In some dishes, the sauce and the rice are cooked together. In others, they are combined after each has been cooked separately. Some are simple, some take a little more time. All are happy alternatives to *pasta asciutta* or *minestra*.

RISO AL BURRO E PARMIGIANO
Rice with Butter and Parmesan Cheese

This simplest of rice dishes is very like *risotto alla milanese* but less rich, more everyday.

- ¼ pound unsalted butter
- 2 cups long-grain rice
- 5 cups water
- 2 teaspoons salt
- 6 tablespoons grated Parmesan cheese

Melt half the butter in a good-sized pot with a tight-fitting cover. Add the rice, 4½ cups of the water, and the salt, and bring to a boil. Stir well, cover, and reduce the heat to low. Cook the rice, still covered, approximately 12 minutes, stirring 2 or 3 times. Check to see if it is getting too dry, adding a bit of the remaining water if necessary. When the rice has absorbed all the water and is cooked but not mushy, stir in the remaining butter and the cheese. Serve immediately.

RISOTTO ALLA MILANESE
Rice, Milanese Style

Cooked in broth, flavored with saffron and Parmesan cheese: this is a stunning way to treat rice.

8 tablespoons unsalted butter
1 onion, minced
1 tablespoon marrow
2 cups long-grain rice
4 to 5 cups clear chicken-beef broth
⅛ teaspoon saffron
6 tablespoons grated Parmesan cheese

Using a wide, capacious pot (a 6-quart, 2-handled, stainless steel Dutch oven, for example), melt the butter over medium heat and sauté the minced onion until golden and translucent. Be sure the onion is really finely minced. Scoop out a tablespoon of marrow from a soup bone and add it to the pot, breaking it up as it starts to melt. Add the rice and just enough broth to cover, about ½ cup.

The broth may be canned: use 3 cups (with a fourth handy) of chicken broth mixed with 1 cup of beef. If you make your own chicken broth (page 55), put in 2 beef bones to enrich the flavor.

Keep the rice on medium heat, stirring constantly. As the broth is absorbed, add more, about ½ cup at a time. When the rice has absorbed all 4 cups of broth, taste for tenderness. If it is still hard, add an additional ½ to 1 cup of broth. Keep on cooking and stirring until tender but not mushy. Stir in the saffron. This comes either powdered or in little threads. These threads should be broken up in 2 tablespoons of warm broth so that their color begins to run before they are added to the rice. When the rice is evenly colored and flavored by the saffron, stir in 4 tablespoons of the grated Parmesan cheese. This is such a heavenly dish it deserves freshly grated Parmesan. Serve in 6 individual portions and sprinkle with the remaining cheese.

RISOTTO AI FUNGHI
Rice with Mushrooms

This handsome variation of *risotto alla milanese* uses either dried Italian (not Chinese) mushrooms or fresh ones, as well as all the ingredients of the parent recipe. Prepare the *risotto* as in the preceding recipe, and while it is cooking add the mushrooms prepared as below.

If you use fresh mushrooms, this dish can be described as family style, for fresh ones cost a great deal less than the dried variety, and of course are more readily available at most markets.

1 ounce dried mushrooms, or 7 ounces fresh
2 tablespoons unsalted butter (for fresh mushrooms only)

If using dried mushrooms: soak them a few minutes in lukewarm water until limp. If soaked too long, they lose flavor and aroma. Drain them, and squeeze out any remaining water gently with a paper towel. Dice the mushrooms and add them to the rice a few minutes after it has begun to cook.

If using fresh mushrooms: clean and slice the mushrooms, and sauté them in the unsalted butter. As soon as the mushrooms start giving up their juices add them, butter and all, to the already cooking *risotto*.

RISOTTO AL RAGÙ
Rice with Bolognese Meat Sauce

This *risotto* is considered by some to be even more delicious than *pasta al ragù*.

2 cups long-grain rice
4 cups water
4 tablespoons unsalted butter
2 teaspoons salt
1 to 1½ cups Ragù I (pages 50 to 51)
4 tablespoons grated Parmesan cheese

Put the rice, the water, half the butter, and the salt in a big pot with a good cover. Bring to a boil uncovered, lower the heat, stir well, and cover. Simmer approximately 10 minutes, or until nearly done and almost all the water has been absorbed. Add the *ragù* and the rest of the butter. Continue cooking uncovered over low heat until the rice is tender, about 3 or 4 minutes. Stir in half the cheese, and serve in 6 individual plates. Sprinkle with the rest of the cheese.

RISO E SCAMPI ALLA VENEZIANA
Rice with Shrimp, Venetian Style

This *risotto* uses the broth in which the shrimp are cooked to add flavor. The shrimp may be either fresh or frozen. If using the latter, buy those frozen in their shells or the thawed-out ones usually marked "Previously Frozen" that also have their shells.

        1   medium onion
        4   fresh basil leaves
      ½   garlic clove
        4   or 5 sprigs parsley
        1   pound fresh or frozen shrimp, unshelled
        5   cups water
        1   teaspoon salt
        8   tablespoons unsalted butter
      ¾   cup olive oil
    1½   cups long-grain rice
            salt to taste

Mince the onion, basil, garlic, and parsley, and put them with the shrimp in boiling, salted water. Cook for 5 minutes, or until the shrimp are tender. Scoop out the shrimp, peel, and set them aside. Drop the shells back into the cooking water. Bring to a boil, and simmer gently for 15 minutes. Strain through a cheesecloth-lined sieve.

Examine the shrimp, and remove any black veins. Sauté the shrimp 3 minutes in a large saucepan containing the butter and olive oil. Add the rice and ½ cup of the strained shrimp broth. Cook over medium heat, adding more broth, ½ cup at a time, as it is absorbed. When the rice is cooked, after about 20 minutes, check for salt, and add as needed.

RISO CON SEPPIE
Rice with Squid

The squid in this rice dish are enhanced by tomatoes and dry, white wine. The squid may be fresh or frozen. The frozen ones usually come in 3-pound boxes, uncleaned. Defrost at room temperature 3 or 4 hours, and proceed as with fresh squid. Incidentally, the smaller the squid, the better the taste and texture.

- 1 3-pound box frozen squid, or 3 pounds fresh
- 4 tablespoons olive oil
- 2 garlic cloves
- 2 red pepper pods, seeded
- 1 cup dry white wine
- 4 cups peeled plum tomatoes
  salt to taste

RICE

- 4 to 4½ cups water
- 2 teaspoons salt
- 2 teaspoons unsalted butter
- 2 cups long-grain rice

Clean the squid and slice the bodies into little rings. If the tentacles are bigger than a mouthful, cut them in halves or quarters.

Warm the oil in a heavy Dutch-oven-type pot that has a cover, add the garlic and pepper pods, and sauté over medium heat until the garlic is golden and the pods dark brown. Remove them, and put in the cut-up squid. Cook for 3 or 4 minutes, or until the squid have changed color to pink and lavender. Add the dry white wine and continue cooking until the wine has evaporated. Cut the tomatoes into bite-sized chunks, and add them, juice and all, to the squid. Bring the pan to a boil, reduce the heat, cover, and simmer about 45 minutes, or until the squid are tender, the tomatoes reduced to a sauce. Taste for salt, and if it is needed, add about 1 to 1½ teaspoons.

Combine 4 cups of water, the salt, and the butter in another saucepan, bring to a boil, and add the rice.

Stir, and when the mixture comes back to a boil, cover, lower the heat, and cook about 12 minutes. Stir a couple of times during cooking, adding more water if needed, and when almost cooked, add the squid and sauce, and stir well. The rice should be *al dente,* bitable, cooked but firm.

Serve in a big, deep platter.

RISOTTO CON PEOCI
Rice with Mussels

Peoci is Venetian dialect for mussels. The dish is lightly flavored with olive oil, a bit of onion, and cooked in fish broth to get the real, traditional flavor.

FISH BROTH
- 1 pound fish heads, tails, bones
- 1 teaspoon salt
- 4 peppercorns
- 1 small onion
- ½ carrot
- 1 celery stalk
- 1 bay leaf
- 1 tablespoon wine vinegar
- 5 cups water

RISOTTO
- ½ cup olive oil
- 1 medium garlic clove
- 2 pounds mussels
- 4 tablespoons butter
- 1 small onion, minced
- 2 cups rice
- 4 cups fish broth
    salt to taste

Ask your fishman for a pound of heads, tails, and bones. Put them in a soup pot with all the flavorings and the water, bring to a boil, lower the heat, and simmer about 20 minutes. Strain through a cheesecloth-lined sieve, and save the broth for cooking the rice.

In another big pot, put about 3 tablespoons of the olive oil (or enough to cover the bottom), the garlic, and well-cleaned mussels. Bring to a high heat, stir with a wooden spoon, and keep cooking until the mussels open. When the mussels are cool enough to handle, fork out their meat, and put it aside in a pan or bowl, discard the shells, and strain the olive oil and mussel juices over the mussels.

Melt the butter in a 4- or 5-quart pan, add the rest of the olive oil, and the minced onion. Cook over medium heat until the onion is translucent. Add the rice and ½ cup of broth and cook over medium heat, adding ½ cup of fish broth as needed to keep the rice just barely covered with liquid. After about 15 minutes, when the rice has plumped up and is nearly cooked, it's time to add the mussels and their juices. Keep on stirring, still over medium heat, until the rice is tender. Taste for salt, add some if needed, and serve.

RISOTTO CON TONNO
Rice with Tuna

This *risotto* is quick and simple, and delightful as a summer first course, a real success at any table. Children love it. But don't wait for either summer or children to make it: it works just as well in the fall, winter, and spring for everyone.

    1 small garlic clove
    3 tablespoons olive oil
    2 cups peeled plum tomatoes
    4 fresh basil leaves
    1 6½- to 7½-ounce can light tuna, packed in olive oil

RISOTTO

        salt to taste
    2   cups long-grain rice
    4   cups water
    2   tablespoons unsalted butter
    2   teaspoons salt

Using a good-sized frying pan, sauté the garlic in the olive oil over medium heat until the garlic turns golden. Discard the clove, and turn off the heat a minute. Add the tomatoes, basil, and tuna fish. (If you can't get tuna packed in olive oil, look for light tuna packed in vegetable oil. White tuna packed in water simply isn't the right taste or texture for this dish.) Simmer about 15 minutes (mashing up the tuna and tomatoes with a fork occasionally) or until the juices are reduced, the color darkened, and the flavors blended. Taste for salt, and add some if needed.

Put the rice, water, butter, and salt in another pan, bring to a boil, stir, cover, and reduce the heat. Cook about 10 minutes, stirring a couple of times. By this time the rice is practically dry, almost cooked. Add the tuna sauce, and continue stirring and cooking uncovered until the rice is tender and done.

RISO CON TONNO IN BIANCO
Rice with White Tuna Sauce

Tuna, a bit of butter, and some Parmesan cheese: this is a simplified version of the preceding sauce.

       2   cups long-grain rice
     4½   cups water
       4   tablespoons unsalted butter
       2   teaspoons salt
       1   6½- to 7½-ounce can light tuna, packed in oil
       3   to 4 tablespoons grated Parmesan cheese

Put the rice, water, half the butter, and the salt in a big pan, and bring to a boil. Stir, cover, reduce the heat, and simmer for about 8 minutes, stirring a couple of times.

Drain the tuna (discarding the oil if it isn't olive oil; reserving it if it is) and break it in bits with a fork. Add it to the cooking rice, continuing to stir on and off for about 5 minutes, by which time the rice should be cooked and tender. If the tuna was packed in olive oil, add the reserved oil; if not, add the last 2 tablespoons of butter. Sprinkle on the cheese. Mix well and serve.

RISOTTO CON FRUTTI DI MARE
Rice with Shellfish

The name of this recipe can be translated literally as "rice with fruits of the sea," that is, rice with shrimp, baby squid, mussels, and small clams. Ideally, it is made with *vongole,* Mediterranean clams, for which we substitute the Atlantic counterpart, cherrystone clams. If you can't get mussels, you can substitute sea scallops.

- ½ **pound small squid**
- 4 **tablespoons olive oil**
- ½ **cup dry white wine**
- 1 **pound mussels, or ¾ pound scallops**
- 1 **pound small cherrystone clams**
- ½ **pound medium shrimp**

RISOTTO
- 4½ **cups water**
- 4 **tablespoons coarsely chopped fresh parsley**
- 3½ **teaspoons salt**
- 2 **cups long-grain rice**
- 2 **tablespoons unsalted butter**

Clean and cut up squid and put them in a big frying pan with 2 tablespoons of the olive oil. Cook over medium heat, stirring constantly for 3 or 4 minutes, or until the color of the squid changes to pink and lavender. Add the wine, let it evaporate, and then reduce the heat to a simmer and cook for 20 minutes.

In the meantime, scrub and clean the mussels (page 73) and wash the clams. Put the remaining 2 tablespoons of olive oil in a good-sized pot and drop in the mussels and clams. Cover and cook on high heat, stirring a couple of times, about 10 minutes, or until all the shells are opened. Turn off the heat, and let cool enough to handle. Separate the mussels and clams from their shells. Let the juices drip back into the pan they were cooked in, discard the shells, and put the meat in with the squid.

Peel and devein the shrimp, and add them to the squid, mussels, and clams. Put the shrimp shells in the pan in which the mussels first cooked, add ½ cup of the water, bring to a boil, and simmer about 15 minutes. Then strain this broth through a cheesecloth-lined sieve into the frying pan with the squid and shellfish. Add the parsley, with 1½ teaspoons of the salt, and simmer about 5 minutes.

If you substitute fresh scallops for the mussels, be sure you use small ones. Add them to the shrimp and squid when you put in the parsley, as they should cook only a short time if they are to remain flavorful and tender.

Put 4 cups of the water, the rice, butter, and the remaining 2 teaspoons of salt in a big pot, and bring to a boil. Stir, cover, and reduce the heat to simmer. Cook about 8 minutes, stirring a couple of times. Uncover, and add the squid and shellfish with their sauce. Keep on cooking and stirring over low heat until the rice is tender and flavored with the fish. Serve immediately.

LASAGNE, TIMBALLI, PASTA CON RIPIENI, ECCETERA
Lasagne, Filled Pasta, and Associates

Geographically speaking, this tribe of first courses comes from all over Italy. Although somewhat more elaborate to prepare than other first courses, these recipes frequently can be made well in advance, so that the effort involved isn't all that demanding. Anyway the results are definitely worth a little work.

As for filled pasta—homemade pasta cut in different shapes and enclosing a filling of meat and/or cheese—we have selected a few of the most familiar. A complete list of such creations would prove one thing: that when confronted by a piece of homemade pasta, Italian cooks can't resist the temptation to invent a filling, a shape, and a name. The differences are regional or so subtle (contemplate, for example, *ravioli: bauletti, marubini . . . ; tortellini: anolini, agnolini . . .*) that we had to stop short in compiling our list and retreat, famished, to the kitchen. The following recipes are just an introduction to the unending, wonderful possibilities of filled pasta.

BESCIAMELLA
White Sauce

Here is the basic white sauce used for layering *lasagne*, covering *cannelloni*, and making casseroles in general. This recipe makes enough for a large (12 to 14 servings) *lasagne*, and is of medium consistency, a factor controlled by adding more or less flour as you wish.

    8 tablespoons unsalted butter
    ¾ cup quick-mixing flour
    4 cups milk
    1 teaspoon freshly grated nutmeg
    ¾ teaspoon salt
      freshly ground pepper to taste

Melt the butter in a heavy saucepan over low heat. Add the flour all at once, and stir rapidly with a wire whisk until blended. When you use the quick-mixing flour that has a granular feeling, lumps never form. With ordinary flour, lumps are a good possibility.

Heat the milk to scalding (just under a boil, when

a skin has formed on the top), and add it all at once to the butter-flour mixture, stirring vigorously with a whisk. Continue cooking over medium heat, stirring constantly, until the sauce has thickened and is smooth, about the consistency of a thin pudding. Add the nutmeg, salt, and a few grinds of pepper.

Cool the sauce for about 15 minutes before using. It becomes firmer as it cools.

LASAGNE, PAGLIA E FIENO
Yellow and Green Lasagne

Lasagne, paglia e fieno (Straw-and-Hay) is made with two kinds of egg pasta, one straw yellow and the other hay green. The pasta is layered with Bolognese meat sauce, white sauce, *mozzarella,* and Parmesan cheese. A recipe for a real feast, this one serves 12 to 14 easily. Naturally, *lasagne* can be made using only one color of pasta: a 5-egg batch of *pasta all'uovo,* or a 3-egg batch of *pasta verde* for *lasagne verdi.* This is one of those dishes that is great fun for two cooks. But if you are making *lasagne* by yourself, with a bit of planning, you can make the *ragù* a day ahead, the pasta on the morning of the day needed, and the *besciamella* (white sauce) just before layering it, and it all goes together simply. *Lasagne,* once layered, can sit in the refrigerator before baking 5 or 6 hours without damage, but then it does take a bit more than 30 minutes to heat it through and get all the cheese melted. So allot your time accordingly.

    6 quarts water
    6 teaspoons salt
    ½ cup grated Parmesan cheese

PASTA ALL'UOVO (pages 15 to 19)
    2¼ cups all-purpose flour (approximate)
    3 eggs
      pinch of salt

PASTA VERDE (pages 19 to 20)
    2¼ cups all-purpose flour
     2 eggs
     5 ounces fresh or frozen spinach
    ½ teaspoon salt

FILLINGS
    1 recipe *Ragù I* (pages 50 to 51)
    1 recipe *Besciamella* (pages 91 to 92)
    2 pounds shredded whole-milk *mozzarella*

After the *ragù* is done, the *besciamella* is cooling, the cheeses are grated and shredded (when preparing the *mozzarella,* grate it as coarsely as you can or, if you prefer, cut it into thin slices, and then mince), the pasta is drying (up to 15 minutes), you are ready to begin assembling your *lasagne.*

Preheat the oven to 350°.

Cut both types of pasta into rectangles the size of a postcard or just a bit bigger. Bring the 6 quarts of water to a boil, add the 6 teaspoons of salt. Drop in the rectangles one by one to a total of no more than 10 at a time, and take them out the minute they're *al dente,* which takes about 3 or 4 minutes. With a big, perforated spoon in one hand and a fork in the other you can lift out and drain the pasta easily. Rinse in cold water, and spread out on dish towels. Don't stack the pieces because they tend to stick together. Keep on cooking the pasta pieces in batches of about 10 until all of it is cooked.

Ladle a thin layer of *ragù* into the bottom of a large oven-proof casserole (14" × 10" × 3" is a good size). Cover with pieces of yellow pasta, a layer of sauce, 5 or 6 generous tablespoons of *besciamella.* (If you wish to be Roman, instead of *besciamella* use *ricotta,* 2 pounds of it.) Sprinkle with *mozzarella.*

Repeat the layering, alternating yellow and green pasta until the casserole is filled. Finish with a layer of grated *mozzarella,* sprinkle with Parmesan cheese, and bake for half an hour (at 350°), or until all the cheeses

have melted. Cool about 15 minutes before cutting, so
that the sauce and the cheeses and the *besciamella* cling
together and the *lasagne* can be cut in slices without
falling apart. If there is any *lasagne* left after the feast,
transfer it to a smaller casserole and reheat the next
day. It won't have lost its character.

TORTA VERDE DI RICOTTA
Ricotta-and-Spinach Pie

This 1-crust pie, filled with spinach, *ricotta*, and Parmesan cheese, can be served hot or cold as a first
course.

FILLING
- 1 10-ounce package frozen spinach, or 10 ounces
  fresh
- 1 pound *ricotta*
- 1 large egg
- ½ teaspoon freshly grated nutmeg
- 8 tablespoons grated Parmesan cheese
- ⅓ to ½ cup flour
- 1 teaspoon salt
- 4 tablespoons unsalted butter

PIE CRUST
- 1 2-crust batch pastry dough

Preheat the oven to 350°.

The filling has just the same ingredients as the
recipe for *Gnocchi verdi* (pages 104 to 105) and is mixed
exactly the same way.

Once you have made the filling, mix a batch of
pastry dough, enough for 2 pie crusts. (To tell the
truth, we frequently use a packaged mix for ours.) Roll
it out just a bit bigger than a 10½-inch pie pan, using
all the dough to get one nice, thick crust, and crimp the
edge.

Spread the filling in the unbaked crust. Sprinkle
the top with the rest of the Parmesan cheese, and dot

with butter. Bake about 40 minutes (at 350°), or until the crust is light brown and the filling is puffed and toasty. Cool a few minutes before eating or you'll burn your tongue.

AGNOLOTTI

These squares of pasta, filled with meat, cheese, and spinach, seasoned with nutmeg, take a bit of time and practice to make, but are a lovely opener for any meal. Since the meat in the filling, as in most fillings for pasta, should be cooked before it's sent through the meat grinder, this is a delicious way to use a bit of leftover meat from an earlier meal.

PASTA
        3 medium eggs at room temperature
        2 cups all-purpose flour
     ¼ teaspoon salt
        5 quarts water
        5 teaspoons salt

FILLING
        2 or 3 slices pork loin, or beef or veal, cooked or
           uncooked
        5 ounces (½ package) frozen chopped spinach
     ½ teaspoon salt
        1 large egg
        1 teaspoon freshly grated nutmeg
        8 tablespoons grated Parmesan cheese
           freshly ground white pepper
        3 or 4 tablespoons unsalted butter

If you are using uncooked meat, cut off any extra fat, melt a tablespoon of butter in a small frying pan, and sauté quickly over medium heat until done on both sides. Do not overcook.

When cool, cut the meat in half or thirds for easy handling, and put it through a grinder, using the smallest grind. Cook the spinach in a small amount of boiling salted water, drain it thoroughly, and put it through the grinder. Place the meat-spinach mixture in a medium-sized bowl, add the egg, and stir to mix everything well. Add the nutmeg, 3 tablespoons of cheese, and 2 or 3 twists of the pepper mill. If you haven't got white peppercorns, a pinch of black will do. Stir the mixture again and set it aside to fill pasta squares for 6 servings, about 15 to a serving.

The pasta for *agnolotti* is made in the same fashion as any homemade pasta (pages 15 to 19), but because it must stick together, it is just a little moister than usual, and it must be filled and sealed before it dries out at all.

So, when you have rolled out 2 big sheets of pasta (or 3 to 4 pairs of matching strips with the pasta machine), cover all the pasta sheets but one with a dampened, well-wrung-out dish towel. On the uncovered pasta, drop little dabs of filling in even rows, positioning the filling so that each dab is the center of a 2″ × 2″ square. Cover this sheet of pasta with another, and with your fingers press the two together around each bit of filling. (If the edges are not well pressed together, cooking water can seep in and make a very watery and unsatisfactory *agnolotto*.) If by any chance the pasta has dried too much before cutting, it won't stick together with pressing. So, dampen (with a wet finger) around the mounds of filling before putting on the top sheet of pasta.

Cut between the 2″ × 2″ squares with a sharp knife or pastry cutter, so that the mounds of filling are the center of each square, and the squares themselves become individual pillows. Put the cut *agnolotti* on a flour-dusted cookie sheet until time to cook. They can dry an hour or so before cooking.

Bring the water to a boil, salt it, put in the *agnolotti* a few at a time. They float to the top immediately and crowd for position, so keep the pot boiling but cover it, and cook for about 10 minutes, or until the pasta pillows are tender at the edges. Remove them with a slotted spoon, and drain thoroughly.

Serve immediately, with butter and the remaining tablespoons of Parmesan cheese, or with Tomato Sauce (pages 210 to 211) or *Ragù II* (pages 51 to 52).

CANNELLONI RIPIENI ALLA TOSCANA
Cannelloni, Tuscan Style

Cannelloni are another of the incredibly mouth-watering combinations of egg pasta cut in rectangles and rolled up with a delicate filling, this time of meat, chicken livers, eggs, and spinach. They are then smothered with *besciamella* and baked in an oven. When two people are making this dish, one does the pasta, while the other does the filling and the *besciamella* (the amount of which, by the way, you may double, according to your taste).

½ recipe *Besciamella* (page 91)

PASTA

    3 medium eggs at room temperature
2¼ cups all-purpose flour
  ¼ teaspoon salt
  5 quarts water
  5 teaspoons salt

FILLING

  ½ pound ground beef
  ½ pound chicken livers
  ½ package frozen spinach, or 5 ounces fresh
  1 teaspoon salt
  7 to 8 tablespoons unsalted butter
  ½ cup dry white wine
  4 eggs
  ¾ cup grated Parmesan cheese

Roll out the pasta as you would for *lasagna* (pages 92 to 94), dry it 15 minutes, cut it in 4″ × 5″ rectangles, and then dry no more than half an hour before cooking, or cook it immediately to the *al dente* stage.

Remove from boiling water and spread out on the dish towels to dry a bit.

For the filling, you can use already cooked beef or veal if you wish, or fresh, lean chopped meat. Put it through the meat grinder with the chicken livers. If you use fresh spinach, remove the stems and discard them. Cook fresh or frozen spinach in a small amount of boiling water with ½ teaspoon of salt, drain thoroughly, and squeeze out as much water as possible. Send it through the meat grinder with the livers and beef for a second grinding.

Melt 3 tablespoons of the butter in a frying pan over medium heat. Add the meats and spinach, cook and stir quickly for 3 minutes. Add the white wine and cook until it evaporates. Add ½ teaspoon of salt, and cool a minute or so. Scoop out the meat and spinach mixture (leaving the melted butter and juices in the pan) and mix well with the eggs and half the Parmesan cheese.

Put a couple of spoonsful of filling on each pasta square and roll up, letting one side overlap slightly. Keep on filling and rolling until all the rectangles are used.

Preheat the oven to 350°.

Prepare half a recipe of *besciamella* and cool slightly.

Butter a shallow casserole (better yet, individual casseroles with room for 3 or 4 *cannelloni*), put in the *cannelloni*, seam-side down. Spoon over them the reserved butter and juices from the frying pan, cover with *besciamella*, dot with butter, and sprinkle with the remaining cheese. Bake (at 350°) until the cheese has melted and turned golden and the *cannelloni* are hot all the way through, about 20 minutes.

MANICOTTI
Pasta Rolls Filled with Ricotta

Similar to *cannelloni*, these rolls of egg pasta are filled with *ricotta* and spinach, and served with tomato sauce. The pasta, the filling, and the sauce may all be prepared ahead of time.

PASTA
- 1 3-egg batch *Pasta all'uovo* (pages 15 to 19) as in the preceding recipe for *cannelloni*
- 5 quarts water
- 5 teaspoons salt

SAUCE
- 1 recipe Tomato Sauce (pages 210 to 211)
- 3 tablespoons unsalted butter
- 4 to 5 tablespoons grated Parmesan cheese

FILLING
- 1 pound *ricotta*
- 1 egg
- 4 tablespoons grated Parmesan cheese
  nutmeg
- ½ teaspoon salt
- 1 10-ounce package chopped frozen spinach, cooked and drained

Prepare the pasta as for *cannelloni*, dry 15 minutes, and cut into 4″ × 4″ squares. Cook them, and cool and dry on a clean dish towel.

Prepare the tomato sauce.

Preheat the oven to 350°.

Mix together the *ricotta*, egg, Parmesan cheese, nutmeg, salt, and spinach. Spread 2 to 3 tablespoons of the filling diagonally on each square so as almost to reach the 2 corners at each end of the diagonal. Fold the other 2 corners one over the other and press together gently.

Butter and oven-proof casserole large enough to accommodate the rolls, and put a thin layer of tomato sauce on the bottom. Cover with filled pasta rolls, fold-side up. Put 1 tablespoon of tomato sauce (more if you wish) on each *manicotto*. Dot with butter, and sprinkle with Parmesan cheese. Bake (at 350°) for about 15 minutes and serve.

CAPPELLETTI ALLA PANNA
Cappelletti with Cream Sauce

Homemade pasta, cut in squares, filled with a mixture of meat, poultry, and *mortadella,* is folded to look like little hats, or in Italian *cappelletti*. With a slightly different filling and cut of pasta, they are known as *tortellini*.

Delicious when cooked and served in either beef or chicken broth, or a combination of both, *cappelletti* are positively superb when served in a cream-and-cheese sauce. Here are directions for both the filling and the pasta for about 100 *cappelletti,* enough to serve six to eight persons worthy of such a treat.

FILLING
- 4 tablespoons white meat of turkey or chicken
- 2 slices *mortadella*
- 2 tablespoons unsalted butter
- 4 tablespoons ground veal
- 4 tablespoons ground pork
- 1 tablespoon finely chopped fresh parsley
- 3 tablespoons grated Parmesan cheese
- 1 teaspoon freshly grated nutmeg
- ½ teaspoon salt
  freshly ground white pepper to taste
- 1 egg

PASTA
- 3 large eggs at room temperature
- 2¼ cups all-purpose flour
  salt

TO COOK THE PASTA
- 3 quarts broth

SAUCE
   1 recipe Cream Sauce (page 27)

   THE FILLING: cut a small slice of turkey (or chicken) breast, and chop it into ¼-inch bits. Chop up the *mortadella* also, discarding any pieces of garlic or peppercorn. Melt the butter in a saucepan over medium heat, and add all the meats and chopped parsley, stirring everything around as it cooks quickly (2 to 3 minutes). When the poultry meat has whitened, and the veal and pork have cooked to a toasty color, scoop them out and grind them twice in a meat grinder, so that they are smooth and pasty.

   Put the meat mixture in a bowl and add the cheese, nutmeg (if using preground from a can, be sure it is still fragrant, and use only ½ teaspoon), the salt, 3 or 4 twists of the pepper mill, and the egg. Mix well.

   Remember that in this recipe it's cook's choice: if you don't have turkey, substitute chicken; you can use beef instead of veal; you can use white meat of poultry and *mortadella;* but the combination of all the meats is pretty special, and we recommend it.

   THE PASTA: make your *pasta all'uovo,* and roll it first as thin as for *fettuccine,* and then continue rolling until it's almost paper thin (#2 on the pasta machine, if you have one).

   At this point, you'll want to work quickly because this pasta must be folded before it dries out and becomes fragile. Naturally the more helping hands, the better the work goes, and once stuffed, *cappelletti* can sit for hours. So once you've rolled your pasta, cut it into 2″ × 2″ squares. Put a tiny dab of filling on a square of pasta. Fold on the diagonal, pressing along the edges to seal. If the dough doesn't seal with pressure, dampen the inner edge with a drop of water on your fingertip and press again.

   Now you have a stuffed triangle. Take the two corners of the base and wrap them around the tip of your finger. Press the corners together so that they stick. If they don't, moisten the corners where they overlap each other and press again. Fold the third corner, which sticks up, back on itself, and there is your first *cappelletto*. Keep on filling, sealing, pressing, and turning, until all the squares have turned into what look like little hats.

To cook *cappelletti*, bring the broth to a boil and put in all the little hats by the handful, bring the broth back to a boil, and cook gently for about 10 to 15 minutes, or until the pasta is tender.

THE SAUCE: meanwhile, make the cream sauce by putting the butter to melt with the cream on a platter in a warm oven. When the butter has melted, add the Parmesan cheese and stir. Keep the sauce warm until the *cappelletti* are cooked. Drain them thoroughly, saving the broth for future use, and put them on the warm platter with the cream sauce. Turn them over and over gently until they are well coated with sauce. Serve immediately.

TIMBALLO DI MACCHERONI
Baked Rigatoni

This is a big, baked dish of *rigatoni,* covered with butter and cheese, layered with *mozzarella* and *mortadella,* lightly spiced with nutmeg. The beauty of this recipe is not only a prepared-ahead-of-time pasta but a delightful double crust contrasting beautifully with the pasta and the melted cheeses. If your *mortadella* is too highly flavored with garlic, you may enjoy substituting thin strips of cooked ham.

PASTA
- 1 pound *rigatoni*
- 6 quarts water
- 6 teaspoons salt
- 2 tablespoons unsalted butter
- 3 tablespoons grated Parmesan cheese

CRUST AND FILLING
  4 tablespoons unsalted butter
  ½ cup bread crumbs (approximate)
  1 egg
  1 pound whole-milk *mozzarella*
  ¼ pound thinly sliced *mortadella*
  3 or more tablespoons grated Parmesan cheese
  1 teaspoon grated nutmeg

Boil the *rigatoni* in salted water, and when very well cooked, drain thoroughly and put in a big bowl with the butter and the Parmesan cheese. Toss gently, over and over, until the butter and cheese coat the pasta.

Preheat the oven to 375°.

Butter an oven-proof casserole, and add about ¼ cup of the bread crumbs. Tilt the dish back and forth and around to get the crumbs to cling to the butter. Pour out and save the excess crumbs. Beat the egg and pour it in the buttered bowl, and tilt the bowl back and forth to get as much egg as possible to cling to the sides. Then put in more crumbs, tilt again, and you'll have made the basis for a double crust on the sides and bottom of the casserole.

Grate the *mozzarella* coarsely, or slice it thinly and then dice it. Cut the *mortadella* into thin strips.

Make a layer of *rigatoni* in the bottom of the casserole, sprinkle with shredded *mozzarella,* strips of *mortadella,* some of the Parmesan cheese, and a dash of nutmeg. Dot with butter. Repeat this layering process until everything is almost used up, reserving enough Parmesan cheese and bread crumbs to sprinkle the top layer. Dot with butter, and bake (at 375°) until the casserole is thoroughly hot and the crust a golden brown.

Cool at least 15 minutes and turn out onto a platter. Cut like a cake and serve. Baked *rigatoni* is good at room temperature, also.

GNOCCHI
Dumplings

A first course that defies proper description (it certainly is neither pasta, nor rice, nor soup) is *gnocchi*. If their name stops you cold (it sounds like knee-o-key), their taste will turn you on. Almost every Italian region has its own version, and in some of them it is part of the local folklore. In Verona, the humble *gnoccho* is as much at home as Romeo and Juliet, and in Rome, Thursday is the day prescribed for *gnocchi*. Once eaten, *gnocchi* are supposed to leave you with a beatific smile on your face, similar to that of a simpleton, who, wouldn't you know, is called a *gnoccho*.

Because they represent very well all other Italian *gnocchi* we have chosen the Florentine *gnocchi verdi,* which are light, soft, vaguely cheesy, and green with spinach, and the Roman *gnocchi di patate,* which are made with potatoes and flour and served with sauce.

GNOCCHI VERDI
Green Dumplings

These little dumplings of *ricotta* and minced spinach are seasoned with Parmesan cheese and nutmeg and served with melted butter. They can be made several hours before cooking time if covered with plastic wrap and put in the refrigerator.

- 1 10-ounce package frozen spinach, or 10 ounces fresh
- 1 pound *ricotta*
- 1 large egg
- ½ teaspoon freshly grated nutmeg
- 1 teaspoon salt
- 8 tablespoons grated Parmesan cheese
- ¾ cup flour
- 4 tablespoons unsalted butter

Barely cook the spinach (if using frozen, it's done by the time the ice has melted; if using fresh, remove the stems and boil until limp). Drain it, pressing with a spoon against the side of the strainer to remove all water possible. Mince the spinach finely.

Put the *ricotta* in a medium-sized bowl, add the spinach, and mix well. Add the unbeaten egg, the nutmeg, 1 teaspoon salt, and stir. Fold in 4 tablespoons of the Parmesan cheese and ½ cup of flour. Spread some flour, about ¼ cup, on a plate. Take ½ teaspoon of the mixture at a time, and roll it with the palm of your hand around the plate (or in between the two floured palms of your hands) until you have a little soft ball about the size of a cherry.

If this is your first experiment with *gnocchi*, test 1 or 2 in boiling water before rolling them all. If the *gnocchi* disintegrate on cooking, add another 2 tablespoons of flour to your mixture. The amount of flour is governed by how well drained the spinach is and how big the egg. Its use is to firm up the very soft cheese mixture and help the egg bind everything together.

Keep on rolling little balls in the flour until the mixture is all used. *Gnocchi* must not be stacked; line them up on a wax-papered cookie sheet until cooking time.

To cook *gnocchi*, bring 5 quarts of water to a boil, and salt it with 5 teaspoons salt. Drop the *gnocchi* in 1 by 1 until they cover the bottom of the pot. When done, they rise to the top. Remove with a slotted spoon, drain off all the water, and put them in a warm dish. As you remove the cooked *gnocchi* from the pot, add some more uncooked ones to it. When all are done, dot with butter, and sprinkle with the rest of the Parmesan cheese.

This recipe makes between 70 and 80 *gnocchi*. Ten or so per person is a reasonable helping for a first course. If you want to double the recipe you may, but don't double the flour—use only up to ¾ of a cup.

GNOCCHI DI PATATE
Potato Dumplings

Potato *gnocchi* or dumplings, served with tomato sauce, are a Roman favorite.

    4 pounds baking potatoes
 1¼ teaspoons salt
    1 large egg
 ½ cup flour (approximate)

Boil the potatoes in salted water until they are really cooked. Drain thoroughly, peel, put them back in their pot, and mash them to an even, smooth consistency. When they are tepid, beat in the egg. Then slowly add the flour by sifting in a bit at a time and mixing well each time. Since the amount of flour you need is dictated by the quality of the potatoes and how much they can absorb, you may want to use a little more or a little less flour in order to achieve a workable dough that is both elastic and smooth.

Turn out the dough on a floured surface and cut it into egg-sized pieces. Roll these pieces with the palm of your hand until they become finger-sized rolls about like an ordinary breadstick. Cut the rolls into 1-inch or 1½-inch lengths. Shake each piece in your hand as you would dice before rolling, and cast them on the lightly floured surface. The pieces are now *gnocchi* waiting for a finishing touch, and you have a choice of: (1) pressing the center of each *gnoccho* with your finger, making a single dent; or (2) rolling each *gnoccho* over the surface of a grater so that it's covered with many tiny indentations. Both systems are valid, the purpose being to give the *gnocchi* the best possible surface for a coating of sauce.

Once all the *gnocchi* are rolled and dented, let them rest while you put 6 quarts of water on to boil. When it boils, salt it with 6 teaspoons of salt. Once it reaches a second rolling boil, add the *gnocchi* a few at a time. They are cooked as soon as they surface, and should be scooped out with a slotted spoon, drained well, and put in a warm serving dish. Continue the operation until all are cooked. Serve with *sugo d'umido* (pages 120 to 123) or *Burro e parmigiano* (pages 26 to 27).

POLENTA

Polenta is impossible to ignore when you are talking about Italian food. It could be translated literally as "a cornmeal dish," but that wouldn't do it justice. Traditionally, *polenta* was, and to a certain degree still is, a major staple of the northern Alpine regions, appearing as first course, second course, side dish, bread, and dessert. This kind of wide usage seemed so inordinate to southern Italians that they nicknamed the blond northern cornmeal eaters *polentoni:* made of *polenta.* The Northerners replied, calling the Southerners *terroni:* made of *terra,* earth, referring to their tanned complexion. All in good jest, sometimes . . .

Polenta is made with cornmeal boiled in salted water, and, by itself, like macaroni without a sauce, is our idea of nothing at all. With a sauce, and the Northerners have many, *polenta* is as kind to the spirit and appetite as any good dish of pasta.

There is a variety of second courses, either meat or fish, that function best as sauce for *polenta* to their mutual advantage. One of the most traditional and most loved is *polenta e osei, polenta* with a sauce of tiny wild birds. While this sauce is particularly kind to the *polenta,* it is not so to the birds, since in great measure it is responsible for the decimation of the Italian aviary population. Thus, we have left it out of our collection, and have selected instead other traditional sauces whose ingredients are available on these shores:

In addition to being served with a sauce as a first
and second course combined, *polenta* can also be served
fried and grilled (page 110).

POLENTA

The real enemy of *polenta* is lumps, practically impossible to get rid of once they appear. Experienced *polenta* makers have developed the art of sprinkling
cornmeal into boiling water with one hand while stirring with a long wooden spoon in the other. For beginners, almost inevitably, this system produces not
only the dreaded lumps but a considerable amount of
embarrassment since there is no known use for lumpy
polenta. However, American cornmeal mixes easily in
cold water, and doesn't lump when that mixture is
added to hot water. Hence, the following, untraditional
method for 6 to 8 servings:

2 cups cornmeal
10 cups water
3 teaspoons salt

Bring 5 cups of water to a boil in a big pot over
high heat. Mix the cornmeal in the other 5 cups of cold
water, stirring rapidly. When smooth, pour the cold
mixture slowly into the boiling water. Add the salt.
Bring back to a boil, stirring constantly, lower the heat
to almost a simmer, and let bubble slowly 50 to 60
minutes, stirring constantly. When cooked, *polenta* is

very thick, smooth, and creamy. Pour on a platter, cool slightly, and serve (below).

POLENTINA

While Northerners hold to the traditional firm *polenta,* Southerners, in spite of name-calling, have adopted *polenta* but in a form with a more porridge-like consistency called *polentina,* made with less cornmeal:

    1⅓ cups cornmeal
    10 cups water
     3 teaspoons salt

Mix and cook exactly as *polenta.* When cooked, *polentina* is easily spooned up. A favorite sauce for *polentina* is *sugo d'umido,* the sauce from a pot roast (pages 120 to 123).

How to Serve: Polenta when cooked is a very thick affair that is poured on a *polenta* board, a slab of wood used as a serving platter (and only for this purpose), and allowed to cool a bit. With the back of a spoon, make a series of indentations or one long one down the center of the cooling surface to catch the sauce. Pour some of the sauce over the entire *polenta.* Put the remaining sauce in a serving dish. Country-style eaters then serve themselves, all eating from the common board, so to speak, spooning on more sauce as they wish. City-style diners are served *polenta* in individual dishes with a scoop of sauce on top, with the remaining sauce passed around.

Polentina is served in its spoonable condition in soup plates with the sauce on top.

POLENTA FRITTA
Fried Polenta

1 recipe *Polenta* (page 108)
vegetable oil for frying

Cook and cool the *polenta*. Slice into ½-inch-wide slices, and cut these in half for easy handling. Bring the frying oil to high heat, put in the *polenta* slices, as many as fit the pan, and fry until golden and crisp on both sides. Drain and cool for a moment. Serve plain, sprinkled with grated Parmesan cheese or marmalade as a snack.

POLENTA E FORMAGGIO ALLA GRIGLIA
Grilled Polenta and Cheese

1 recipe *Polenta* (page 108)
1 pound cheese (mozzarella or Muenster)

Cook and cool the *polenta*. Slice into ½-inch slices. Top them with thin slices of cheese and put under a hot broiler until the cheese has melted and the *polenta* is heated through. You can get about the same results by putting the cheese-topped slices in a 400° oven for 20 minutes. Serve slightly cooled, or you'll burn your mouth.

SECONDI PIATTI
Second Courses

Second courses, like everything else that appears on the table, are controlled by the season as well as your mood and shopping habits. In Italy, where daily shopping is usual, the menu is often decided at the market, depending on the day's bargain or the sales pitch.

In maintaining an Italian kitchen in America, we try to keep on hand the various staples called for to flavor almost any meat or fish: tomatoes, seasoning vegetables, herbs, salt pork, and olive oil. Then we let the store's offering dictate the week's shopping. By and large, Italians use less meat than most Americans, use as much fish as is available, and frequently make a *frittata,* which is made of eggs, do the work of either one.

In organizing the recipes for this chapter, we've simply put them in the usual order: beef, veal, lamb, pork, poultry, eggs, fish, and the *frattaglie,* the assortment that includes liver, brains, and tripe, which we call the "in between" cuts.

MANZO
Beef

Beef on the hoof, on the hook, or on the table, has always been one of the luxuries of the Italian economy. Most edible beef was, and still is, imported. Of the native breed, the female is revered for her milk-producing qualities; the male is honored for his work in the fields, where he has assumed the social position of the horse in more northern, beef-eating countries. In Italy you close the barn door after the ox has gone, and the metaphorical cart is always put before the ox. No poet has been inspired by a beefsteak, but no Italian child exists who has not had to memorize these lines from a romantic sonnet:

> *I admire you, humble ox,*
> *Because you imbue my heart*
> *With a feeling of vigor and peace...*

That is why beef, either expensive and imported, or the native kind, toughened and flavored by a life of work, is highly respected on the Italian table, and is treated with maximum regard and parsimony.

There isn't much of the animal, tongue to tail (insides included), that is not boiled, braised, broiled, fried, or stewed. No matter how it is cooked, what's important is to *farlo fruttar di più,* to make it stretch as far as possible to feed as many mouths as possible.

Of the cooking processes, broiling is the least common, because it produces no fringe benefits. With boiling you get a delicious and abundant broth, and the meat—that is, the part not totally consumed on the spot—is used in another and preplanned fashion another day. The term "leftover" doesn't exist in the Italian kitchen. Leftovers in Italy are those portions of food not fit for human consumption, and hence tossed to cats and dogs or other domestic animals.

In braising, the sauce is as important as the meat itself, and is used partially with the meat but mostly with pasta or for cooking other meats and vegetables.

Stewing glorifies what in other kitchens are considered to be poor cuts. If you have tasted *stufatino in umido* (shinbone stew) or *coda alla vaccinara* (oxtail stew, cowhand's style), you'll have to agree.

For pan-frying, beef is cut thin, and then pounded, floured, breaded, and egged so that two Italian customers are easily satisfied with the amount that would serve one American.

Those portions of beef that cannot be sliced, or are too small to appear as a chunk in a stew, or are just remainders on the butcher's block, are ground, mixed with other ingredients, and used for stuffing vegetables. Even if in the final presentation, beef is a minor ingredient, the dish itself is usually considered as meat, and as such we include it in this chapter.

BOLLITO DI MANZO
Boiled Beef

Beef brisket boiled with seasoning vegetables gives you the benefit of its broth to use in a first course. The meat is sliced and served with either *Salsa verde* (pages 213 to 214) or Tomato-and-Onion Sauce (pages 211 to 212). If anything remains on the platter, it is usually ground up and turned into *polpette* (meatballs) or stuffing for pasta or vegetables such as zucchini.

    3 pounds fresh beef brisket
    3 teaspoons salt
    1 celery stalk
    1 carrot
    1 small onion
    1 small bay leaf
    3 plum tomatoes
    4 or 5 peppercorns

Put the beef and all the other ingredients in cold water to cover. Bring to a boil slowly, uncovered, over low heat. When the water first boils, scoop off the froth that forms, lower the heat to a simmer, cover the pot, and cook for about 3 hours. The meat should be tender, the broth a clear, light brown.

Remove the meat from the broth and put it on a warm platter for slicing and serving.

Strain the broth, and use it with *Pastina* (pages 56 to 57) or rice or *Cappelletti* (pages 101 to 102) as a first course. Extra broth may be frozen and kept for weeks in the freezer.

BOLLITO MISTO
Mixed Boiled Meats

Northern Italy's long-simmered boiled dinner makes the broth that is traditionally used with *cappelletti*, the four meats being invariably served with *salsa verde* (green sauce of capers and parsley) or *mostarda di Cremona* (hot spiced fruit pickles). This recipe makes enough for 8 generous servings.

- 1½ pounds beef brisket
- 1 3-pound chicken, or half a fowl
- 1½ pounds small beef tongue
- 4 celery stalks with leaves
- 2 carrots
- 2 onions
- ¼ medium-sized turnip
- 4 plum tomatoes
- 4 teaspoons salt
- 10 peppercorns
- 1 teaspoon marjoram
- 1 teaspoon thyme
- 2 bay leaves
- 1 small *cotechino* sausage
  whites of 2 eggs (optional)

Put the meats with the exception of the *cotechino* into a big pot, at least 8 quarts. Add the 5 vegetables and enough cold water to cover everything. Add the salt and peppercorns. Put the pot on a high heat, bring to a boil, and scoop off any froth that forms. Add the herbs, reduce the heat, and simmer for 2 hours. If using a chicken instead of a fowl, add it after approximately 1 hour's boiling so that it won't be overcooked and fall apart.

Prick the skin of the *cotechino* on all sides and

put it on to boil in abundant cold water. When it boils, reduce the heat, and simmer 2 hours.

When it's time to serve, remove the meats and chicken from the pot, saving the broth. Remove the *cotechino* from its pot, and throw away that water. Cut the chicken in the usual pieces of leg, wing, half breast, etc. Skin the tongue, and slice it very thin, slightly on the diagonal. Slice the beef and *cotechino*. Put all the meats and chicken on a large, well-heated platter, baste with a bit of hot broth, and serve with *Salsa verde* (pages 213 to 214).

Strain the broth into another big pot. If you wish to clarify it, beat the egg whites slightly, bring the strained broth to a boil, add the beaten egg whites, and let them boil, beating with a whisk, for about 2 minutes, or until the little particles floating in the broth have been caught by the egg whites. Pour through a cheesecloth-lined sieve into another pan.

Use about half the broth for cooking *Cappelletti* (pages 100–102) or any other *minestra* for a first course. The rest may be saved in the refrigerator a couple of days, or frozen in the freezer for weeks.

BRASATO
Braised Beef

This is the Milanese way to cook a nice piece of top or bottom round or boneless chunk, using the usual seasoning vegetables plus dry red wine to make a dark, smooth sauce. It's most frequently served with peas, whose sweetness and color make a lovely contrast to the beef.

    2 to 3 pounds lean beef
    4 slices (or 4 ounces) lean salt pork
    1 celery stalk
    1 onion
    1 carrot
    2 to 3 tablespoons olive oil
 1½ teaspoons salt
    1 cup red wine
    1 tablespoon quick-mixing flour
    1 cup water

Cut 2 slices of the salt pork into small cubes. With a sharp, pointed knife make small slits around the beef, and fill them with the cubes of pork. Tie the meat up with butcher's string like a small package so that it will hold its shape during cooking.

Chop the other 2 slices of pork into bits, add the seasoning vegetables (the celery, onion, and carrot), and keep mincing until everything is reduced to a fine paste (*battuto*).

Heat the olive oil in a Dutch-oven-type pot (with a cover) that is just big enough to hold the meat. Add the *battuto,* and cook until golden. Add the meat, and brown it thoroughly on all sides over high heat to seal in the juices. Add the salt, and then add the wine, and when its vapors no longer tingle your nose, add the flour diluted in the water. Stir, and cover well (slide a piece of brown wrapping paper between cover and pot to seal in the steam). Reduce the heat to the lowest simmer possible, and cook for 2 hours. Turn the meat around once in a while, and check the liquids occasionally to make sure they haven't by any chance evaporated too much. If they have, add a little warm water.

If your beef is boneless chuck, use only the 2 slices of lean salt pork needed for the *battuto* and omit the larding altogether.

When tender and well cooked, remove the string, slice the beef into thin slices, cover with the sauce, and serve hot.

STRACOTTO DI CREMONA
Pot Roast in the Style of Cremona

Stracotto means cooked and cooked and cooked. It's a
northern Italian pot roast, originally from the Piedmont, but the best we ever ate was in Cremona, which
is to the east in Lombardy. Traditionally, it would be
cooked in a top-of-the-stove earthenware pot taller than
it is wide, with a very tight cover. After the first 3 to
4 hours simmering, the heat would be turned off and
the *stracotto* left to cool. The next day the pot would
be uncovered, the sauce stirred, and half a glass of red
wine added, Barbera usually, but at any rate a full-
bodied dry red wine. The *stracotto* would then be
covered and brought back to simmer for another 3 to
4 hours. This process was repeated for 3 days. By that
time, as an old Cremonese friend used to say, just a
whiff of *stracotto* was the equivalent of a meal. Above
and beyond the time consumed in its making, the essential elements are simply a nice piece of pot roast, seasoning vegetables, spices, and dry red wine—all of
which blend to an incredible richness. This recipe will
serve 8 to 10 people.

> 1 3-pound boneless chuck or bottom round
> 2 to 4 slices lean salt pork
> 6 whole cloves
> 1 medium onion
> 1 medium carrot
> 1 celery stalk
> 1 quart dry red wine, or 2 cups wine and 2 cups water
> 1 2½-inch stick of cinnamon
> 3 tablespoons olive oil, or enough to cover the pot bottom
>   flour
> 1 teaspoon salt
> ½ teaspoon ground pepper
> 2 tablespoons tomato paste (diluted in 1 cup water)

If your meat is very streaked with fat, use only
2 good slices of salt pork. If it is fairly lean, use 4

slices. Cut the salt pork slices crosswise into little strips. Make a whole series of slits in the roast on all sides, and stuff them with the strips of pork. Stick in the cloves at random. Then tie the piece of meat with butcher string as you would a sausage or a neat parcel.

Put the roast in a bowl just wide enough to fit it snugly and deep enough to hold the marinade. Mince the onion, carrot, and celery as finely as possible, and sprinkle over the meat. Add the wine and the cinnamon, and marinate at least 8 hours. The Cremonese advise 24 hours, but we found American meat needs at most only half that time.

Remove the meat from the marinade and drain it well. Put the olive oil in a stewpot that has a good cover. Flour the meat, patting it well to get it evenly covered. Add the meat to the oil, and brown slowly over medium heat. Once browned, salt and pepper the meat. Scoop the minced vegetables out of the marinade and add them to the pot. When these are browned, add the marinade. Add the tomato paste diluted in warm water and, if necessary, enough more warm water to cover. Bring the pot to a boil, reduce the heat to a very low simmer, and cover. Put a piece of heavy brown paper between the pot and its cover to seal it well. Cook very, very slowly for at least 4 hours. Uncover the pot, stir the sauce gently, and continue cooking uncovered until the sauce has reduced and thickened. The sauce should be smooth, like a fine gravy. The meat should be tender enough to cut with a spoon.

Use half the sauce with pasta (*rigatoni* or *fettuccine*) as a first course, and the rest with the meat for a second course. Serve with whipped potatoes or slices of hot Italian bread in order to take full advantage of the sauce.

MANZO IN UMIDO
Beef Pot Roast

Glorified pot roast of beef is the best way to describe this dish. It involves a lean piece of eye of the round, cooked ever so slowly in its own juices flavored with tomatoes and seasoning vegetables. The resulting sauce is famous with any kind of pasta as a first course. The meat, sliced thin, is enough to serve 8 at least, but is so delicious that 6 usually devour the whole thing.

- 1 3- to 4-pound eye of the round
- 3 to 4 tablespoons olive oil
- 2 teaspoons salt, or to taste
  freshly ground pepper to taste
- ½ cup dry white wine
- 4 cups plum tomatoes

BATTUTO
- 2 slices lean salt pork
- 1 medium onion
- 1 medium carrot
- 1 celery stalk, with leaves
- 4 sprigs parsley
- ¼ garlic clove

Though the eye of the round is a fairly solid piece of meat, it's best to tie it as you would a sausage, because in the long, slow cooking process it becomes so tender it's inclined to fall apart a bit. After it's tied, put it with the olive oil in a stewpot over medium heat, and brown it slowly and thoroughly on all sides. When the meat is a rich, dark brown, remove it to a warm platter in a warm place.

Make a *battuto* by chopping the lean salt pork to bits, adding the onion, carrot, celery, parsley, and garlic, and continuing to chop until the whole pile is well minced. Put the *battuto* in the stewpot, and cook it gently until golden in color and limp. Put the meat back in the pot, and keep on browning it for another 5 minutes or so. Add the salt and 3 or 4 grinds of pepper, and turn the meat over. Add the wine, and when it has evaporated, add the tomatoes cut into chunks or, if you wish, mashed through a sieve or food mill. If the liquids don't cover the meat, add enough warm water or stock to do so. Bring to a boil, lower the heat, and cover the pot. Simmer very gently for 2 to 3 hours, or until the meat is tender, and the sauce has thickened. Throughout the simmering, stir the pot occasionally, and turn the meat over to make sure it doesn't get stuck to the bottom of the pot. Remove the meat to a hot platter in a warm place.

Strain the sauce through a sieve, and spoon off any excess fat that rises to the top as it cools. Reheat the sauce, slice the meat, and pour about half the sauce over it, and serve. The other half of the sauce can be passed around for those who wish more, or can be used with a first course of pasta, rice or *Polenta* (page 108).

STUFATINO IN UMIDO
Shinbone Stew

Here is a stew that includes the succulent marrow of the shinbone as well as the meat. Long stewing with tomatoes and seasoning vegetables produces a hearty red sauce, to which potatoes are added at the end.

>   3 good-sized shinbones
>   3 to 4 tablespoons olive oil
>   1 cup dry wine (red, preferably)
>   1½ teaspoons salt, or to taste
>   3 cups peeled plum tomatoes
>   6 medium boiled potatoes, peeled and cut into chunks

BATTUTO
>   1 slice lean salt pork
>   1 onion
>   1 garlic clove
>   1 carrot
>   1 celery stalk

Cut the meat away from the bones (it comes to about 2 pounds), saving the bones. Discard only the fat, and chunk the meat. Make a *battuto* (page 24) of salt pork, onion, garlic, carrot, and celery. Put enough olive oil into a stewpot to cover the bottom, sauté the *battuto* until almost golden, add the meat and the bones, and continue cooking until the meat is well browned, the *battuto* a golden brown. Add the wine (dry red is preferable to dry white). When the wine has evaporated, add the salt and tomatoes, mashing them a bit as they go in. Add enough water to cover (barely) the meat chunks, stir well, bring to a boil, and then reduce the heat to simmer. Cook until very tender, about 2 hours. During cooking, stir occasionally, and when the marrow is soft, poke it out of the bone so that it will melt into the sauce.

Once the meat is cooked, remove the bones. If the sauce has boiled away too much, add a little warm water. Add the potatoes, stirring them in gently, and simmer 10 minutes. Serve hot.

CODA ALLA VACCINARA
Oxtail Stew, Cowhands' Style

This classic dish from Rome's Trastevere section, oxtail in a thick tomato sauce, is seasoned with garlic, onion, and dry wine, and served with chunks of celery added in the final minutes of cooking. Your wine can be red, but the *trasteverini* always use white.

> 3 pounds oxtails, in small pieces
> 3 to 4 tablespoons olive oil
> 1 cup dry wine, preferably white
> 4 cups peeled plum tomatoes
> 2 to 3 teaspoons salt, or to taste
>   beef broth (pages 53 to 55)
> 1 bunch celery

BATTUTO
> 2 slices lean salt pork
> 1 onion
> 1 celery stalk
> 1 garlic clove

Make a *battuto* by chopping the salt pork with the onion, celery, and the garlic, and then mincing them down to a paste. Sauté the *battuto* until golden in the olive oil in a big stewpot, and then add the oxtail pieces. (Frequently the most uniform are found in ordinary supermarkets, packed in frozen 3-pound packages; fresh ones can be obtained from Italian meat markets.) Over medium heat, stir, turn, and cook the oxtails until they are thoroughly browned all around. Add the wine, and when it has evaporated, add the plum tomatoes, mashing them a bit with a wooden spoon against the side of the pot. Add the salt. Bring to a boil, reduce the heat to a simmer, cover, and cook gently 2 to 3 hours, or until the meat practically falls off the bone. Stir occasionally during cooking, and if the sauce gets too dense, add ¼ to ½ cup of broth (homemade or made with bouillon cubes) or water to thin it. Taste for salt, adding some more if necessary.

Wash and chop the remaining celery into 2-inch chunks. Add to the oxtails, raise the heat, and cook another 10 to 15 minutes or so, or until the celery has lent its flavor to the sauce and is tender but still sort of crisp.

Serve with generous amounts of hot Italian bread, capacious napkins, and finger bowls for those who really clean the bone by taking it in hand.

INVOLTINI IN UMIDO
Beef Birds in Tomato Sauce

The Chinese would call these "wrapplings," the French "alouettes," Americans "birds," but, whatever you call them, these thin slices of beef, lined with *prosciutto*, filled with chopped celery, wrapped like a package and cooked in a sauce, taste absolutely delicious.

2 to 2½ **pounds top or bottom round roast**
¼ **pound** *prosciutto*
2 **celery stalks**
2 **tablespoons chopped fresh parsley**
   freshly ground pepper to taste
3 **cups plum tomatoes**
1 **medium onion**
1 **carrot**
2 to 3 **tablespoons olive oil**
   salt to taste
½ **cup dry wine, red or white**

Cut thin slices from a top round roast (or bottom round, but it will be a little chewier), and pound them well to make them even thinner and more tender. Cut the slices into 4″ × 4″ pieces, or as near to that size as possible, saving the trimmings. Cut the *prosciutto* to match the meat pieces, and save those trimmings. Chop 1 stalk of celery, 1 tablespoon parsley, and the meat trimmings all together, adding a twist of the pepper mill, until the whole pile is of paste consistency. On each piece of meat, put a slice of *prosciutto* and about 1 tablespoon of celery-meat paste in the middle. Roll the slice up on the diagonal, then fold over the ends, one at a time, making a little packet that you can either skewer with a toothpick or tie with cotton thread to hold it shut during cooking.

Peel and cut up the plum tomatoes and put them through a sieve. Mince the onion and carrot with the remaining celery and parsley, and sauté until golden in a wide frying pan in just enough olive oil to cover the bottom. When the minced vegetables are golden, add the meat packets, and brown them gently all around. Add salt to taste. Add the wine, and when it has almost evaporated, add the strained and peeled tomatoes. The liquid in the pan should just cover the meat. If it doesn't, add a bit of hot water. Bring the pan to a boil, cover it, reduce the heat, and simmer for about 1 hour, stirring occasionally, until the sauce has been reduced and concentrated, and the meat is very tender.

FETTINE IN PADELLA
Pan-Cooked Beef Slices

In padella means in the pan. Recipes cooked *in padella* are simple and take practically no time or thought. Beef slices cooked in this way are tasty and just different enough from the ordinary steak to warrant recognition with a recipe of their own.

>   12 small or 6 large slices bottom round (about 1½ pounds)
>   3 tablespoons unsalted butter
>   salt to taste
>   freshly ground pepper to taste
>   2 lemons
>   2 to 3 tablespoons hot water

You can buy bottom round already sliced, or use a 3- to 4-pound roasting piece and slice it yourself to make enough for 2 meals. The first slices of the round will be large and long, and the end slices will be short. Either way, make them no thicker than ⅛ of an inch. Pound the slices to make them tender and even thinner.

Melt the butter in a big frying pan over medium heat. Put in as many slices as fit comfortably, brown them quickly on both sides. Salt and pepper lightly. Remove the slices the minute the juices start to flow on their second side and place them on a warm platter in a warm place. Repeat until all the slices are cooked.

Add the juice of ½ lemon to the pan's sauce, scrape the bottom and sides with a wooden spoon to collect any bits stuck there, and add a little hot water and any juice from the platter to extend the sauce. Put the cooked slices back in the sauce if they've cooled, or pour the hot sauce over the cooked slices if they haven't. Serve with wedges of lemon.

FETTINE ALLA PIZZAIOLA
Beef Slices in Pizza Sauce

Here thin slices of beef round (top or bottom) are cooked in a sauce of tomatoes seasoned with a touch of oregano and parsley. Not so incidentally, mashed potatoes are a perfect complement to this dish.

1½ to 2 pounds top or bottom round
4 tablespoons olive oil
1 garlic clove
2 cups peeled plum tomatoes
1½ teaspoons salt, or to taste
1 teaspoon oregano
1 tablespoon chopped fresh parsley

Slice the beef in the thinnest possible slices (they should be no thicker than ⅛ inch), and then pound them to make them even thinner, bigger, and more tender.

Heat the olive oil over medium heat. Brown the meat slices quickly in the oil, turning them as soon as possible and removing them to a warm platter the minute both sides are barely done.

Slice the garlic clove in half, sauté it until golden in the olive oil, and discard it. Add the plum tomatoes, mashing them as they go in. Add the salt and oregano, and cook over medium heat for about 15 minutes, or until thickened to sauce consistency. Put the meat slices and their now-accumulated juices back in the sauce. Add the parsley, stir gently, and simmer another 5 minutes.

COTOLETTE ALLA CALABRESE
Beef Cutlets, Calabrian Style.

Thin slices of beef or veal dipped in egg and bread crumbs, golden-fried, and served with a sauce of sweet peppers and tomato: these are the principals in this southern Italian dish. Like the Neopolitan *pizzaiola,* meat cooked this way is grand with whipped potatoes.

SAUCE

    1 tablespoon chopped fresh parsley
    1 garlic clove
    3 tablespoons olive oil
    1 to 1½ cups peeled plum tomatoes, with juice
    2 big sweet peppers
    ½ teaspoon salt, or to taste

MEAT

    1½ pounds bottom round beef or veal
    ½ cup flour
     2 eggs, beaten
    ¾ cup sifted bread crumbs
     2 tablespoons butter
     2 tablespoons olive oil
    ½ teaspoon salt, or to taste

Mince the parsley and garlic together, and sauté them in the olive oil in a medium-sized frying pan over medium heat. Add the tomatoes, mashing them with a fork as they go in, and simmer about 10 minutes.

Peel the peppers either by blanching them in boiling water for 10 minutes and stripping off the thin outer skin with a paring knife, or by roasting them over an open flame (page 8). Cut first in strips, then chop coarsely and add to the simmering tomato sauce.

Simmer another 5 minutes, taste for salt on a piece of bread and, if needed, add a dash or two.

Cut the meat into thin slices no thicker than ⅛ inch. Pound them with a meat pounder or the flat of a big butcher knife to tenderize them even more. Dip them in the flour, and pat well on both sides. Dip them in the beaten egg, and then in the sifted bread crumbs, gently patting on as many crumbs as will adhere. Let them sit about 5 minutes.

Heat the butter and oil in another frying pan over medium heat, and fry the slices on both sides. Put them into the simmering pepper-tomato sauce. Scrape the pan well, add the butter and oil and scrapings to the sauce, and let the meat simmer another 5 minutes. Salt to taste.

POLPETTE DI MANZO
Beef Meatballs

These delectable meatballs are made of twice-ground beef, seasoned with parsley, Parmesan cheese, and nutmeg, rolled in bread crumbs and fried in oil. They can be served with lemon wedges or Tomato-and-Onion Sauce (pages 211 to 212). The same mixture makes the filling for zucchini or cabbage leaves (pages 130 to 131).

       2 pounds twice-ground beef
       2 eggs
       3 tablespoons chopped fresh parsley
       1 teaspoon freshly grated nutmeg
    2½ teaspoons salt
       4 tablespoons grated Parmesan cheese
       3 slices day-old Italian bread
       1 cup unseasoned bread crumbs
          vegetable oil for frying
          lemon wedges (or Tomato-and-Onion Sauce)

Put the twice-ground meat in a large bowl, and add the eggs, parsley, nutmeg, salt, and cheese. Wet the bread, squeeze out the water, and shred it into the meat mixture. If the crusts are too crusty and don't shred easily, discard them. Mix everything well but not too harshly. Form the mixture into balls about the size of a large egg. Flatten them a bit so that they are not more than 1 inch thick in the middle. Roll the *polpette* in bread crumbs, patting them gently to get them well covered.

Pour the frying oil in a pan to a depth of ½ inch (half the thickness of the *polpette*). When the oil is bubbling hot, put the *polpette* in, and cook them until they are nicely browned and crisp on both sides. Remove them and drain on paper towels. Serve with wedges of lemon, or simmer them in Tomato-and-Onion Sauce for about 10 minutes more, and then serve.

ZUCCHINE RIPIENE
Stuffed Zucchini

Zucchini stuffed with meat, flavored with parsley, Parmesan cheese, and nutmeg, and poached in Tomato-and-Onion Sauce, a dish which sometimes tastes even better reheated the day after. It is an easy recipe to double for a crowd.

> 1 recipe Tomato-and-Onion Sauce (pages 211 to 212)
> ½ recipe mixture for *Polpette* (pages 129 to 130)
> 1 dozen medium (8- to 9-inch) zucchini or 3 or 4
> great big zucchini
> salt to taste

Prepare Tomato-and-Onion Sauce in a big pot with a good cover, and simmer for 10 to 15 minutes. Mix the meat stuffing.

Cut the tops and tips off the zucchini. Slice big zucchini in 2-inch-thick drums. Cut out the center and all its seeds. Cut medium zucchini in half, and core them with an apple corer (or a zucchini corer, which is a little longer) by inserting it at one end of the zucchini, turning it completely around, and then pulling it out. The core should slip out in its entirety, but if it doesn't, turn the piece around and core from the other end.

When all the pieces are cored, fill them with the meat stuffing but don't pack it in too tightly. Place the stuffed pieces in the simmering sauce. Cover. Raise the heat to medium for about 15 minutes, or until the flesh of the zucchini is tender but still firm. Taste for salt, adding some if necessary.

CAVOLI IMBOTTITI
Stuffed Cabbage Leaves

Stuffed cabbage leaves use the same two basic recipes as stuffed zucchini for their filling and sauce. They also stretch a bit of beef to make a rather special dish that is easy to double for a crowd, and is still good when reheated.

1 large cabbage head
1 recipe mixture for *Polpette* **(pages 129 to 130)**
1 recipe Tomato-and-Onion Sauce (pages 211 to 212)

Tear off and discard the tough outer leaves of the head of a big cabbage. With a sharp, strong knife, cut all around the core and lift out as much as possible, separating the leaves at their base. Take 12 to 18 of the largest leaves and plunge them into boiling, salted water just long enough to let them get limp but not cooked through. Drain, and spread on paper towels to dry off a bit.

Make the *polpette* mixture for the filling and put a rounded tablespoon of it on each leaf. Then wrap the leaf up like a neat package and tie it with cotton thread.

Make Tomato-and-Onion Sauce. When it has simmered for about 15 minutes, add the stuffed cabbage leaves and continue simmering for another 10 to 15 minutes.

VITELLO
Veal

Everyone knows that veal cuts are just about the most expensive pieces of protein to reach the table. There are times, however, when expense is justifiably set aside, and happily, most of the ways in which Italians use veal are fairly parsimonious anyway.

Italian veal, like Italian lamb, has a short professional life. Once the animal reaches 4 to 5 months of

age its meat becomes known as *vitellone* (big veal),
and as such is not as highly appreciated, nor is it as
costly. Experienced Italian cooks and shoppers recognize, or some think they do, the age of the veal by the
color of the meat: pale pink for the youngest and rosy
pink for the oldest. It isn't at all unusual to get involved
in long, erudite discussions with the butcher and a
handful of total strangers while only waiting to be
served. The color, size, age of the meat, and the recipe
planned, all undergo scrutiny.

The crucial dimension of a veal cutlet or chop is
one matter that is rarely challenged: it should be as
close to ⅛ inch thick as possible, and then should be
pounded down even thinner. About 1¼ pounds cut like
this serve 6 people. All the little pieces left after cutlets
and chops or an extraordinary roast have been cut are
sold for veal stew, a more delicate dish than its beef
cousin. Breast of veal, probably the least expensive part
of the animal, can be stuffed and rolled and cosseted
in a sauce so that it becomes a dish worthy of a feast.

COSTOLETTE ALLA MILANESE
Veal Chops, Milanese Style

Milan is famous for its traditional way of preparing veal
chops: they are pounded thin, dipped in beaten egg,
then in fine bread crumbs, and fried to a golden brown.
They're always served with a bit of lemon juice. If you
can't find the chops, you may use slices of veal round,
cut thin, and still achieve veal cutlets *alla milanese*.

    12 very thin veal rib chops
     2 big eggs, beaten
     1 to 2 cups fine bread crumbs
     6 tablespoons unsalted butter
     3 tablespoons olive oil
     1 teaspoon salt, or to taste
    1½ lemons, cut into wedges

Only the smallest veal chops should be used to
prepare this dish, as the bone should be approximately

½ inch thick and the resulting chop the same. With a sharp knife or just by pulling, loosen the meat around the handle of the chop and bend it back over the fleshiest part. Pound that part with the flat of a big butcher knife or a meat pounder to make it thinner and to get the little bent-back piece to stick to the bigger one. Dip the chops, one by one, in the beaten egg so that they are completely covered. Then dip in fine, unseasoned bread crumbs, patting them gently to get as many crumbs as possible to adhere. Let them sit about 5 minutes.

Melt the butter with the oil in a big frying pan over medium heat, and sauté the chops, turning them the minute they are golden brown on one side. Salt lightly. When both sides are nicely colored, remove to a hot serving plate, and serve with lemon wedges.

COTOLETTE ALLA BOLOGNESE
Veal Cutlets, Bolognese Style

You could call this dish a gilded lily. It's made with thin slices of veal dipped in flour, egg, and finally bread crumbs, and golden fried in butter. To crown this delicacy, the Bolognese add a thin slice of *prosciutto* and one of *mozzarella,* toast the cutlets in the oven, and before serving top them with a bit of tomato sauce.

    1¼ pounds veal cutlets, sliced ⅛ inch thick
     ½ to ¾ cup flour
      2 large eggs, beaten
      1 cup bread crumbs
      8 tablespoons unsalted butter
        salt to taste
     ⅓ pound *prosciutto,* sliced thin
     ½ pound whole-milk *mozzarella*
     12 tablespoons Tomato Sauce (pages 210 to 211)

Preheat the oven to 300°.
Pound the veal slices with a meat pounder or the flat side of a big butcher knife to make them thinner

and as even as possible. Pat them into the flour, dusting both sides. Dip in the beaten eggs, and press the slices into the bread crumbs, again patting on both sides to make as many crumbs stick as possible.

Melt the butter, and sauté the slices in it over medium heat, turning them over once the first side is golden brown. When both sides are done, remove, salt lightly, and drain on paper towels. Put a slice of *prosciutto* on each piece of veal, then a thin slice of *mozzarella*. Place in an oven (at 300°) just long enough to melt the mozzarella. Before serving, top each slice with a couple of tablespoons of Tomato Sauce.

PICCATA DI VITELLO
Veal in Lemon-and-Wine Sauce

Veal slices, pounded thin, floured, cooked in butter, and then generously covered with a white wine and lemon sauce: this is a basic recipe used for white meat of poultry as well as for veal. It gives a taste of both delicacy and sharpness that is hard to beat.

1½ **pounds veal round, sliced ⅛ inch thick**
½ **cup flour**
6 **tablespoons unsalted butter**
1 **teaspoon salt, or to taste**
½ **cup dry white wine**
juice of ½ lemon (approximate)
springs of parsley

This amount of veal usually cuts up into 6 to 10 very thin slices, some larger than others. Pound them with a meat pounder to make them uniform and even more tender. Flour them by pressing them in the flour and patting them gently to get as much as possible to adhere.

Melt the butter in a big frying pan over medium heat and add the veal slices. Turn them the minute their edges whiten, and salt them lightly. When both sides are done, pour in the wine, and let bubble until its vapors cease to tingle the nose. Add the juice of ½ lemon, and stir gently with a wooden spoon. Taste for both salt and lemon. Sometimes ½ lemon is too little for that nice tang that lemon juice should give to this sauce. If more lemon is needed, squeeze it on, stir, and cook a moment more. Serve with the sprigs of parsley, which many find adds still a third distinct flavor to the sauce and meat.

SCALOPPINE AL MARSALA
Veal Cutlets with Marsala Wine Sauce

By now the very name of this dish (either veal scallops, veal *scaloppine*, or a version thereof) has taken its place in the international vocabulary, but the original dish remains the same, far simpler and tastier than the many variations on the theme.

- 1¼ pounds veal round, sliced ⅛ inch thick
  flour
- 8 tablespoons unsalted butter
  salt to taste
  freshly ground pepper to taste
- ½ cup Marsala wine
- 4 to 5 tablespoons chicken broth (page 55)

Pound the veal slices gently with a meat pounder or the flat side of a heavy butcher knife. Pat with flour so that as much as possible adheres to both sides of the cutlets.

Melt the butter in the widest frying pan you have, and put in the slices in one layer. Salt and pepper lightly. Sauté quickly both sides, over medium high heat. As soon as both sides are done, pour in the Marsala, and cook another 2 minutes. Remove the slices to a hot platter.

Add just enough broth to the liquid in the pan to make a pourable sauce. (If you don't have real chicken broth available, use a bouillon cube in hot water.) Scrape the bottom and sides of the pan to collect any bits stuck there, stir, cook for another 1 to 2 minutes. Pour over the veal slices and serve.

If you have to sauté the meat in 2 batches, put all the cutlets back in the pan before you add the Marsala. Once you have added the wine, turn them over to get them all well coated with the sauce on both sides. Then remove them, add the broth, and proceed as above.

SALTIMBOCCA
Veal Slices with Prosciutto

The translation for this delicacy is "jump in the mouth." Tender veal slices are seasoned with fresh sage, salted by the thin pieces of *prosciutto* they're layered with, and then are cooked in butter. It's really a quick dish, tastes like a banquet, and is synonymous with Rome.

       1¼ **pounds veal round, in palm-sized slices ⅛ inch thick**
        ¼ **pound thinly sliced** *prosciutto*
            fresh sage leaves, 1 per slice of veal
         6 **tablespoons unsalted butter**
            salt to taste
            freshly ground pepper to taste

Pound the veal slices gently to make them even. Cut the *prosciutto* slices so that there is a piece to cover each piece of veal. Put a leaf of fresh sage on each veal slice and cover with *prosciutto*. Pin the ham to the veal with a toothpick inserted in and out of the length of the slice, or roll the slices up with the ham inside, and fix with a toothpick.

Put half the butter in a good-sized frying pan, melt it over medium heat, and put in the *saltimbocca* with just a touch of salt and pepper (the *prosciutto* will take care of the major salting). The minute the edges of the veal start to whiten, turn the pieces over. Total cooking time is approximately 2 minutes to a side.

When they are cooked, remove the slices or rolls to a hot platter. Over medium heat, melt the rest of the butter, stir, and scrape the edges and bottom of the pan to get all the bits off and into the butter. Pour it over the *saltimbocca* and serve.

SPEZZATINO DI VITELLO CON PISELLI
Veal Stew with Peas

This is a stew of bite-sized chunks of veal flavored with white wine and tomatoes, and combined at the end of its cooking with tiny peas.

    1½ pounds veal stew meat
     ¼ cup flour
     3 to 4 tablespoons olive oil
     1 garlic clove
     2 teaspoons salt
       freshly ground pepper to taste
     1 tablespoon minced fresh parsley
     1 cup dry white wine
     2 cups peeled plum tomatoes
     1 10-ounce package frozen tiny peas, defrosted

Cut the veal into generous bite-sized pieces and flour them lightly by shaking in a bag with about ¼ cup of flour.

Put enough olive oil in the bottom of a stewpot just barely to cover, add the garlic, sauté until golden, and then discard the clove. Add the floured veal pieces, and brown them thoroughly and slowly. Add the salt, pepper, parsley, and wine. When the wine has evaporated, add the plum tomatoes, mashing them up a bit as they go in. If needed, add enough water so that the meat is barely covered. Cover the pot and simmer on low heat for about an hour.

Stir once in a while, and if the sauce has reduced too much, add a bit of hot water or chicken broth to thin it. Taste for seasonings and tenderness. When the meat is really tender, add the defrosted peas, and cook for another 10 minutes. Serve hot with hot Italian bread.

ROLLATO DI VITELLO
Rolled Breast of Veal

A boned breast of veal, smothered in chopped flavorings of carrot, celery, sage, parsley, and layered with cheese, *mortadella,* and *prosciutto,* is rolled and cooked as gently as possible on top of the stove. This is a dish for special occasions, and can be served warm or cold.

If you don't have *mortadella,* ¼ clove of garlic in the *battuto* will add the right amount of flavor. Thinly sliced cooked ham can be substituted for the *prosciutto.*

  1 breast of veal, boned
     salt
  ¼ pound grated whole-milk *mozzarella*
  3 slices *mortadella*
  6 slices *prosciutto*
  4 tablespoons olive oil
  1 teaspoon rosemary
  1 cup dry white wine
  1 cup chicken broth (page 55)
  1 tablespoon quick-mixing flour (optional)

BATTUTO
  ½ celery stalk, with leaves
  1 carrot
  1 jumbo or 2 medium eggs, hard-boiled
  1 fresh sage leaf
  4 sprigs parsley
  ¼ shallot (or ⅛ onion)

Have the butcher bone the veal breast, and be sure he gives you the bones. Spread the veal out, smooth-side down, and pound it to an even thickness. Make a *battuto* (page 24) of the celery, carrot, egg, sage, parsley, and shallot. Salt the rough-cut (boned) side of the veal, and spread it with the *battuto,* leaving an inch bare on the long sides as well as the wider end. Cover the *battuto* with the grated *mozzarella,* then with the slices of *mortadella,* and finally with the *prosciutto.*

Starting with the smaller end of the veal breast, roll it up slowly into a big sausage. Be careful not to squeeze too hard; push the filling in place with your fingers as you roll so that it will not come out at the wide end. Temporarily skewer shut the lengthwise opening. Then tuck in and skewer each rolled end. Finally, tie up the whole roll like a sausage, using butcher's string, and remove the skewers.

Heat the olive oil over medium-high heat in a big, heavy pot (a Dutch oven would be perfect), and put in the veal roll and bones. Sprinkle with rosemary. Brown thoroughly, turning slowly, to seal in all the juices. Once it is browned, add the wine, and let it evaporate. Then cover the pot, lower the heat, and cook for 1½ hours. Check it from time to time, and turn the roll over so that it will cook evenly. Baste it with the juices in the pot; if they seem to be cooking away (you should have about ¾ inch of them in the pot), add some chicken broth.

When the meat is cooked, cool it on a platter at least 15 minutes before slicing. While it is cooling, add a bit more chicken broth to the juices in the pot, heat, scrape well to get any bits of meat from the sides and bottom, then strain into a sauceboat, and serve hot with the sliced veal roll. If you prefer a thicker sauce, add 1 tablespoon granulated (quick-mixing) flour to the strained juices and cook a moment or two over medium heat, or until thickened, before serving.

OSSOBUCO
Veal Shanks

Literally, *ossobuco* means bone with a hole, and in this case it is the small veal shinbone (shank), complete with its marrow, cooked in a bouquet of herbs and zest of lemon. The Milanese are the real patrons of this delicate dish, and they pair it with their *risotto*, one of the rare occasions when the first and second courses are served at the same time. It is a meal most people never forget.

6 to 8 pieces veal shinbone
flour
4 tablespoons unsalted butter
3 tablespoons olive oil
1 cup dry white wine
1 teaspoon salt
freshly ground pepper to taste
½ to 1 cup chicken broth (page 55)

BATTUTO

1 teaspoon rosemary
3 or 4 fresh sage leaves
1 small garlic clove
2 tablespoons chopped fresh parsley
4 slices lemon zest

Have the veal shank sawed into pieces 1½ to 2 inches thick. These pieces vary in width, so 2 small ones or 1 large make a portion. If by any chance the skin around the meat of the bone is broken, tie butcher's string around the slice before flouring and browning in order to hold the meat snugly in place.

Flour the pieces thoroughly, and brown them well in butter and oil over medium heat. Use a frying pan that will accommodate the *ossobuchi* snugly without crowding. If the pan is too big, the sauce will be too spread out and shallow to cook the veal properly.

Make a *battuto* (page 24) of the rosemary, sage, garlic, parsley, and lemon, and add to the browned veal bones. Spread the herbs around, and cook for a moment or two. Add the wine and stir. Add the salt and a few grinds of pepper. When the wine has partially evaporated, add enough chicken broth to bring the sauce to the top of the veal slices without covering them. Lower the heat, and simmer about 40 minutes, or until really tender. Serve hot with the sauce.

VITELLO TONNATO
Veal with Tuna Sauce

Vitello tonnato is a favorite Italian cold dish for a summer's day. Famous in the Piedmont and Lombardy, loved by the French, who call it *veau tonné,* and the English, who call it tunnied veal, it's easy to make. Most people prepare this roast, with its wine-and-tuna sauce, the day before serving so that all its flavors blend perfectly.

> 1 2-pound boned roast of veal
> 2 cups dry white wine
> 1 tablespoon wine vinegar
> salt to taste
> freshly ground pepper to taste
> 1 6½- to 7½-ounce can tuna
> ½ cup olive oil
> juice of 1 lemon

BATTUTO

> 1 tablespoon capers
> 1 or 2 fresh sage leaves
> 1 small onion
> 2 or 3 anchovy fillets

Make a *battuto* (page 24) of the capers, sage, onion, and anchovy fillets, and put it in a pan just big enough to hold the meat snugly. Tie the roast with butcher's string, and put it on top of the *battuto.* Add the wine, the vinegar, and as much water as necessary just barely to cover the meat. Bring to a boil, reduce the heat, and cook at a slow boil for about 1½ hours, or until the liquid is reduced to about ⅔ of the original amount. Taste for salt, and adjust if necessary. Add a few grinds of pepper.

Drain the tuna, saving the oil if it's olive oil. Put the drained tuna in with the meat, mashing it up with a spoon, and cook another 15 minutes. Remove the meat, and put it on a cool platter.

If you don't have a blender: let the tuna sauce cool slightly, and then put it through a sieve into a bowl. Add the olive oil (that reserved from the tuna if it was olive oil, plus enough to make ½ cup) and the lemon juice, and blend well.

If you do have a blender: put the tuna sauce in it, and blend at high speed. When it is smooth and homogeneous, add the oil and lemon juice, and blend at low speed. The sauce should be smooth, relatively thick, and creamy. It will thicken as it cools.

When it is cool, cut the veal into very thin slices. Pour a bit of sauce in the bottom of a deep platter. Arrange the veal slices on the sauce so that they barely overlap. Pour the rest of the sauce over them. Decorate with a few more capers, or tiny sprigs of parsley, as you wish. (Some cooks like to add a garnish of sliced hard-boiled eggs just before serving to accent the edges of the platter.) Cover with another inverted platter or aluminum foil, and refrigerate for at least 24 hours. This dish keeps well in the refrigerator for a long time—up to a week—and actually improves with time.

AGNELLO O ABBACCHIO
Lamb

Italian lambs seem to reach the slaughtering age sooner than their American or Australian cousins. They weigh in at 18 to 20 pounds at the point of sale. Knowing the frugality of shepherds in general and Italians in particular, this waste of potential poundage may appear illogical, but perhaps it can be explained by the answer we got from an old hand in the Abruzzi, "We have limited pastures, so we have to limit the flock."

"Fine," we said, "but why not slaughter the big ones and let the little ones grow?"

He considered a second whether he would answer such a stupid question, and then he told us, "Because the little ones taste better."

All this is to say that in Italy only young baby lamb (*abbacchio*) deserves the title of lamb. Once past that stage it becomes mutton.

Nonetheless, there are several dishes that can be prepared with excellent results using older lamb (*agnello*) like that available on the American market. Also in many Italo-American markets, especially around Easter, one can find true baby lamb for *abbacchio al forno* (roast lamb). What little fat there is on an 18-pound lamb is very delicate and digestible, and the cuts cook in practically no time. As the lamb grows beyond the 20-pound stage, its fat loses these qualities, and it is advisable to trim off as much as possible, cook in a very slow oven (if roasting), or cut and trim and cook on top of the stove, making good use of wine and/or wine vinegar to soften and season the meat. The best cuts, American style, are the leg, the rack or ribs, then the fore, and finally the breast and neck.

ABBACCHIO AL FORNO
Roast Lamb

Baby lamb, a traditional Easter dish, uses almost half a lamb, which should weigh no more than 6 to 8 pounds (only the fore is saved for other dishes); flavored with a whisper of garlic and a breath of rosemary, it is roasted with thin wedges of potatoes.

    1 6- to 8-pound half baby lamb
    ½ cup olive oil
    1 teaspoon rosemary
    2 teaspoons salt
       pepper to taste
    6 to 8 potatoes, cut into quarters or eighths to make
       thin wedges

BATTUTO

½ garlic clove
3 teaspoons dried rosemary, or 2 sprigs fresh
2 teaspoons chopped fresh parsley
1 teaspoon salt
  pepper (3 or 4 twists of the mill)
1 teaspoon olive oil

Preheat the oven to 400°.

Chop up all the dry ingredients of the *battuto*, mince them further, pile them up, and add 1 teaspoon olive oil to make a paste. With a sharp knife make 6 to 8 slits in the lamb and fill them with the *battuto*.

Put the ½ cup olive oil in an open roasting pan, add the lamb, and turn it over and over in the oil to coat all sides. Sprinkle with the remaining 1 teaspoon rosemary, 2 teaspoons salt, and pepper to taste. Surround the lamb with the thin wedges of potato, giving them a turn to coat them with oil, and place the pan in the 400° oven for 10 minutes. Reduce the heat to 375°, and roast for approximately 45 minutes more, or until the meatiest part of the lamb reaches 150° to 160° on the meat thermometer. Remove the lamb from the pan, test the potatoes, and if they are not done, return the heat to 400° and finish roasting the potatoes. Incidentally, during the 55 minutes roasting time, baste the lamb 3 or 4 times, and turn the potatoes with a spatula in order to get them evenly browned and roasted.

ABBACCHIO ALLA CACCIATORA
Hunters' Lamb

Here, lamb chunks are prepared the way the hunters of yesterday cooked venison, spiced with rosemary and garlic, simmered in wine and wine vinegar.

Buy the smallest lamb possible for the best of flavor and texture. Originally, this dish was made with acidulous wine, wine starting to go to vinegar, which was common in Italian households, especially in the wine-producing areas.

    3 pounds lamb fore
    2 garlic cloves
    3 to 4 tablespoons olive oil
    3 teaspoons rosemary
    2 teaspoons salt
      freshly ground pepper to taste
    ½ cup wine vinegar
    ½ cup dry white wine

Have the butcher chop the lamb into chunks, about as for stew. Cut off any extra fat, but leave the bones in, as they add flavor.

Peel the garlic cloves, split them, and sauté them in a large frying pan over medium heat in just enough olive oil to cover the bottom of the pan. When the garlic is golden, remove it and add the chunks of lamb, rosemary, salt, and pepper. Raise the heat, and brown the meat thoroughly on all sides. Add the vinegar, and right away cover the pan for a few seconds, or until you hear that the vinegar has stopped steaming. Then uncover, and stir with a wooden spoon to loosen any bits of browned meat stuck to the sides and bottom of the pan. Add the wine and stir some more. When the wine has almost evaporated, lower the heat, and cook until tender, about 15 minutes.

If your pan is not large enough to accommodate the meat in one layer, either do the browning in two pans, each containing garlic-flavored olive oil, or brown one portion at a time. When all the pieces are evenly and thoroughly browned, combine them in one pan before adding the vinegar and wine. Rinse out the pan in which you browned them with a bit of vinegar, scraping to detach all the bits that may have stuck to the side of the pan, and add to the lamb pieces to enrich the wine sauce. Cook about 15 minutes more, or until tender. Serve with the sauce.

COSTOLETTE D'ABBACCHIO A SCOTTADITO
Grilled Lamb Chops

A *scottadito* (to scorch the fingers) is a Roman way of describing cooking swiftly over the high heat of a hot, open grill. The melted fat raises the flame to sear the outside of the chop quickly, leaving the inside tender and moist.

> 12 thin shoulder lamb chops
> 4 tablespoons olive oil
>   salt to taste
>   freshly ground pepper to taste
> 2 teaspoons rosemary
> 1½ lemons, cut into wedges

Get your charcoal grill started.

Flatten the chops with a meat pounder or the flat side of a heavy butcher knife. Put the olive oil on a platter and dip the chops in it, oiling both sides. Let the chops marinate in the oil for about 5 minutes.

When the coals are red hot, remove the chops from the oil, salt and pepper them, and put them on the grill. Sprinkle them with the rosemary, and turn them the minute they are crackling brown on one side. Brown the other side, and serve with lemon wedges.

AGNELLO ALLA MARCHIGIANA
Lamb Stew in the Style of the Marche

The *marchigiani,* the people of the Marche region of central Italy, know and understand good food and wine as well as any. This, their recipe, is one of the most appetizing ways of serving lamb stew.

  2 to 3 pound lamb fore, cut into chunks
½ cup flour
  1 garlic clove
  1 sprig fresh rosemary, or 1 teaspoon dried
¼ cup olive oil
2½ teaspoons salt
    freshly ground pepper to taste
  1 cup dry white wine
  1 cup peeled plum tomatoes
  1 teaspoon tomato paste, diluted in ¼ cup warm
    water

Put the lamb chunks and flour in a paper or plastic bag, and shake well. Chop the garlic and rosemary to tiny bits, and sauté them until golden in the oil in a fair-sized pan over high heat. Add the lamb, and brown it thoroughly, turning it over and over on all sides. Add the salt, a few grinds of pepper, and the wine. When the wine has evaporated, add the tomatoes and the tomato paste diluted in warm water. When the whole mixture is back to a boil, lower the heat, and simmer for about 1 hour, or until the meat is tender. Stir occasionally while the stew is simmering.

COSTOLETTE D'ABBACCHIO PANATE
Breaded Lamb Chops

Loin lamb chops, no more than ½ inch wide, are dipped in beaten egg and bread crumbs, fried crisp, and served with lemon. Chops cooked this way are in that category of delicate foods best eaten with the hands in order to get every last tasty morsel.

  12 thin loin lamb chops
   3 eggs
 1½ to 2 teaspoons salt, or to taste
   1 cup unseasoned fine bread crumbs
   4 to 6 tablespoons olive oil
 1½ lemons, cut into wedges

It's not always easy to find thin-cut lamb chops, so either ask the butcher to cut them that way or look for the sales when the cut-while-frozen ones from Australia or New Zealand show up. They're frequently much thinner than the usual American cut. Trim off any excess fat and cut a bit of the meat away from what could be called the handle of the chop. Turn it back on the meaty end, pound with a meat pounder to thin it a bit more and to make the folded meat stick to the main part of the chop. Beat the eggs well and add the salt. Dip the chops, one by one, into the eggs, then press them into the bread crumbs, first one side and then the other. Pat them well so that as many crumbs stick as possible. Let stand a few minutes.

Heat the oil in a wide frying pan, put in the chops, and fry on both sides until they are a golden brown. Drain on paper towels and serve hot with lemon wedges.

SPIEDINI D'AGNELLO
Skewers of Lamb

The people of Umbria who grow, as well as know, sheep take the lesser cuts, cut them into bite-sized chunks, spread them with an herb paste, stick them on skewers with lean salt pork and sage, brown them, and then finish them off with a light tomato sauce.

Juniper berries are available on some specialty spice shelves, but if you can't find any, use sprigs of fresh rosemary, which give almost the same type of accent.

There's a minor problem with making this recipe, and that is finding the right size skewers to fit the amount of meat and then fit the pan you have at hand. We found that 6 8-inch skewers held the lamb involved but then wouldn't all fit in the average 10-inch round frying pan. So we used 5 long and 2 shorter ones and managed to make them fit snugly in the bottom of a 12-inch cast-iron stewpot that cooked them just beautifully.

1½ pounds boned lamb shoulder or breast
¼ pound lean salt pork, sliced
3 cups plum tomatoes, strained, or 3 cups extra-thick tomato juice
10 tablespoons chopped fresh parsley
1 onion
4 juniper berries, or 2 sprigs fresh rosemary
2 tablespoons bread crumbs
¾ cup flour
2 tablespoons grated Parmesan cheese
12 to 14 fresh sage leaves
3 to 4 tablespoons olive oil

Cut the lamb into even cubes about 1½" × 1½" × 1½"; cut the salt pork slices into 1½" × 1½" squares.

Strain any stringy pulp and all the seeds out of the plum tomatoes by putting them through a sieve or vegetable mill.

Mince the parsley, the onion, and the juniper berries (or rosemary). Mix in the bread crumbs, 2 tablespoons of the flour, and the Parmesan cheese. Add 2 tablespoons of the strained tomato (or juice), and mix again. Add another tablespoon of tomato, or enough to produce a spreadable paste.

Spread one side of a lamb cube with paste, skewer it, add a dab of paste to the top side, follow with a ½-inch bit of sage leaf, and then with a square of salt pork. Repeat until the skewers are full. Put the remaining flour on a plate and roll each skewer in it to dust lightly.

Heat the olive oil in a 12-inch heavy pan and brown the skewers on all sides. The flour and some of the paste may stick to the bottom a bit, but keep scraping gently with a wooden spoon. When the meat is well browned, add the rest of the tomato, and scrape the sides and bottom of the pan to get all the browned bits into the sauce. Bring to a boil, lower the heat, and simmer for about 15 to 20 minutes.

ABBACCHIO BRODETTATO
Lamb Stew

Lamb fore, flavored with spices, is cooked in broth that
is then transformed into a lemon-egg sauce. The Romans, in making this dish, use a stock made with lamb
and beef, but a plain beef broth is fine. As for the lamb
itself, ask the butcher to chop it in 2- or 3-inch chunks,
bone and all.

        3 pounds lamb fore, cut into chunks
      ½ cup flour
        1 small onion
        2 to 3 slices lean salt pork
        3 tablespoons olive oil
        2 teaspoons salt
          freshly ground pepper to taste
      ¼ teaspoon marjoram
      ½ cup dry white wine
        4 cups beef broth (pages 53 to 55)
        3 egg yolks
          juice of 1 large lemon
        2 teaspoons minced fresh parsley

Put the lamb and the flour in a sturdy plastic or
paper bag, and shake to coat the chunks well.

Mince the onion and the salt pork to a paste and
sauté them with the floured lamb in the olive oil over
medium heat. Add the salt, 3 or 4 twists of the pepper
mill, and the marjoram, and brown well, turning the
pieces of lamb over and over on all sides.

Add the white wine and stir with a wooden spoon
to scrape any stuck pieces away from the pan bottom
and sides. (This dish is inclined to stick, but the bits
become unglued at the addition of wine.) When the
wine has almost evaporated, add the 4 cups of beef
broth, or enough barely to cover the meat. Bring to a
boil, reduce the heat, and simmer for 40 to 45 minutes,
or until tender. While the stew is simmering, check it
once in a while, and add some water if necessary to
maintain the level of the broth. Turn off the heat and
cool to lukewarm.

Beat the egg yolks until they are pale yellow. Continue beating and add the juice of a lemon and the minced parsley.

Pour the egg-lemon mixture slowly into the cooled lamb, stirring gently so that the eggs mix with the broth evenly. Over low heat warm the meat and sauce slowly, stirring constantly, until the sauce has become very creamy and smooth. Serve hot.

MAIALE
Pork

Unlike cattle and sheep, which are raised only in some parts of Italy, pigs fare well—in fact, prosper—all over the country. Depending on climate and feed, they differ in size and taste from region to region. Most of the animal, after its demise, reaches the market cured and in an infinity of preparations. Almost every region, if not town, has its own cured pork specialty. For example, Parma is known for its *prosciutto,* cured, unsmoked ham. Bologna is the home of *mortadella,* the original bologna. The Abruzzi is famous for all sorts of sausages, Modena for its *zamponi* (stuffed pigs' feet) and *cotechino* (cooking salami). Milano and Genoa vie for honors in the preparation of their salami.

The pork cuts perhaps most frequently called for are also cured: *pancetta* or *guanciale* (unsmoked bacon). They appear in pasta sauces, stuffings, as the base for gravies, soups, and in some top-of-the-stove meat dishes.

Thus very little of the pig gets to market fresh. The most common fresh cuts are the chops and the loin roast. Italian chops are generally cut thinner than their American counterparts, but most butchers don't mind adjusting their cut to your recipe, and some supermarkets even make a policy of offering both thick and thin chops. As for pork roasts, the average is somewhat smaller in Italy and a little less fat.

Dishes that are also common on the Italian table include fresh sausage, the liver, the rind, the feet, and the knuckles. Pigs' feet and knuckles are particularly popular in the North, especially as winter dishes.

BRACIOLE DI MAIALE IN PADELLA
Pan-Fried Pork Chops

A quick, tasty way to cook pork chops is to do as they do in the Abruzzi with herbs and white wine.

- 6 thick pork chops
- 2 tablespoons olive oil
- 2 bay leaves
- 2 teaspoons rosemary
  freshly ground pepper to taste
  salt to taste
- ¼ cup dry white wine, or ⅛ cup wine vinegar diluted with ⅛ cup water

Chops for this dish should be no more than ¾ inch thick. Trim off most excess fat, leaving just a bit to aid in cooking. Put the olive oil in a pan big enough to accommodate the chops. Add them, the bay leaves, half the rosemary, and 5 twists of the pepper mill. Place the pan on medium heat and sauté slowly until the bottom side of the chops is a light golden brown. Turn them, sprinkle with the rest of the rosemary and a few more twists of the pepper mill. When both sides are golden brown, salt the chops, raise the heat, and really brown each side.

Without reducing the heat, pour in the wine (or the diluted vinegar), and cover. Lower the heat, and tip the pan back and forth to get the juices spread around. As soon as the steaming noise subsides, uncover the pan, and let the wine evaporate completely. Serve hot.

COSTOLETTE DI MAIALE PANATE
Breaded Pork Chops

This is the same sort of recipe as Veal Chops, Milanese Style: thin pork chops, dipped in beaten eggs and bread crumbs, are fried crisp and golden and served with lemon.

    12 thin (½-inch-thick) pork chops
     1 to 1½ cups unseasoned bread crumbs
     3 eggs
     1 teaspoon salt, or to taste
    ½ to 1 cup oil
    1½ lemons, cut into wedges

Have your butcher cut the pork chops so they are no more than ½ inch thick. Cut off any excess fat around the edges and pound them with a meat pounder or the flat side of a big butcher knife to make them even thinner. Put the bread crumbs (the amount depends on the size of your frying pan and how much oil the crumbs absorb) on a big plate. Beat the eggs in a shallow bowl, adding the salt. Dip the chops, one by one, in the beaten eggs, then press them into the bread crumbs. Pat them well to make as many crumbs as possible stick to the chops. Let stand a few minutes.

Heat the oil in a wide frying pan, put in the chops, and fry them on both sides to a golden brown. Drain on paper towels, and serve hot with lemon wedges.

SALSICCE IN UMIDO
Sausages in Tomato Sauce

This is a classic way to cook sausages to serve as a second course. When coupled with *polenta,* this recipe gives you a mountaineer's one-dish meal, good for any after-ski crowd.

3 to 4 tablespoons olive oil
3 cups peeled plum tomatoes
1½ teaspoons salt
12 sweet Italian sausages
    freshly ground pepper to taste

Put the olive oil in a big pan over medium heat and add the tomatoes, mashing them as they go in. Add the salt, raise the heat and, once the tomatoes are bubbling, lower the heat to a simmer.

In the meantime, prick the sausages around and about with a fork and put them in a frying pan with ½ inch of water. Bring to a boil, reduce the heat, and simmer until all the water has evaporated, and the sausages have given up some of their fat (you may want to prick them again) and are lightly browned on all sides. Add them to the simmering tomato sauce.

Cook 25 to 30 minutes, or until the sauce has really thickened, and the sausages have lent their flavor to the tomatoes. Taste for salt, adding some more if necessary, and add the pepper. Serve as a second course, or with *Polenta* (page 108) as a one-dish meal.

SALSICCE CON FAGIOLI
Sausages with Beans

This is a variation on a theme: sausages in tomato sauce are combined with a generous amount of boiled beans. For the sausage-tomato sauce, see the preceding recipe.

1 recipe Sausages in Tomato Sauce (pages 153 to 154)
4 cups shell or kidney beans
½ cup warm water

If using fresh or dried beans: boil them in salted water until cooked. Then drain them and add them to the cooked sausages in tomato sauce.

If using canned beans: be sure they have been put

up without sugar. Drain them and add to the cooked sausages in tomato sauce.

Add ½ cup warm water and simmer another 10 to 15 minutes.

Serve with hot Italian bread.

SALSICCE CON LENTICCHIE
Sausages with Lentils

Although lightly flavored with vegetables (carrot, onion, celery, tomato, and garlic), lentils remain the main character in this recipe. The sausages are an everyday addition, but if you wish to make a traditional New Year's Day dish, add a *cotechino* (northern Italian sausage) or a *zampone* (sausage-stuffed pig's foot) in place of the sausages themselves. According to folklore, lentils eaten on New Year's make you rich all year. Both *cotechino* and *zampone* are available in Italian specialty shops at Christmastime.

> 2 cups dried lentils
> 8 cups cold water
> 1 garlic clove
> 1 carrot
> 3 or 4 plum tomatoes
> 1 onion
> 1 celery stalk, with leaves
> 3 to 4 teaspoons salt, or to taste
>   freshly ground pepper to taste
> 12 sweet Italian sausages, or 1 *cotechino*, or 1 *zampone*

Sort through the lentils, a handful or so at a time on a plate, and remove any bits of chaff or stone. Wash them quickly by putting them in a colander under cold water. Put the lentils, water, and all the vegetables into a big pot. Bring to a boil, scoop off any froth that may have formed, add the salt and a few grinds of pepper, and reduce the heat. Simmer for about 45 minutes to 1 hour, or until the lentils are soft and the liquids have reduced to practically nothing. Check the level of the liquid toward the end of the cooking time, because a heat that is too high can reduce the liquid too quickly, in which case a little water must be added.

If using sausages: prick them liberally all around and cook them in ½ inch of water in a wide skillet. When the water has evaporated and the sausages' fat has begun to run, brown the sausages all over for another 10 minutes. Drain, add to the cooked lentils, and simmer about 10 minutes before serving.

If using cotechino or zampone: prick them as you would the sausages and put them in cold water to cover amply. Bring to a boil, reduce the heat to a simmer, and cook for 1 hour. Remove the *cotechino* or *zampone* from the cooking water, cool a bit, and then slice in ¼-inch slices. Place the slices down the center of a big platter, and surround them with boiling hot, cooked lentils.

As you serve the lentils, be sure to search for the garlic and remove it. Also remove the now limp celery stalk, and the carrot, and any piece of onion that hasn't disintegrated as the tomatoes have.

SPUNTATURE (E SALSICCE) AL SUGO
Spareribs (and Sausages) in Sauce

This is a worthwhile, versatile recipe, especially valuable for the rich tomato sauce it produces. It can be made also with the added attraction of sausages. Either way, it is great with *Polenta* (page 108) as a one-dish meal. The sauce alone is exceptional with *rigatoni,* while the spareribs with the addition of beans make a glorious second course. This recipe serves 6 to 8 generously and is easily stretched for a crowd.

3 tablespoons olive oil
1 red pepper pod, seeded
1 pound pork spareribs, cut in 3-inch lengths (not country style)
½ teaspoon salt
freshly ground pepper to taste
1 cup dry red wine
4 cups peeled plum tomatoes
6 sweet Italian sausages (optional)

Cover the bottom of a big pot with olive oil and put the red pepper pod in to cook over medium heat. When the pod is dark brown, discard it. Add the spareribs, salt, and a few grinds of pepper. Cook over high heat until thoroughly browned, and then add the wine and stir carefully. Add the tomatoes, mashing them a bit as they go in.

If you use sausages: put ½ inch water in a medium-sized frying pan, add the sausages, and prick them with a fork to let their fat flow. Cook over medium heat until the water has evaporated, the sausages have released their fat (you may want to prick them again midway in the cooking), and they are nicely browned. Add to the tomato-sparerib pot. Bring that pot to a boil, then lower the heat to simmer, and cook for at least 1 hour, stirring from time to time. This simmering can go on longer, for even 2 hours, in which case you may have to add a bit of water to maintain a good consistency in the sauce. It should be dark, thick, reduced to about half the original amount. Taste for salt, and add some if necessary. Serve hot.

SPUNTATURE (E SALSICCE) CON FAGIOLI
Spareribs (and Sausages) with Beans

The ingredients for this dish are exactly the same as in the preceding recipe, plus ½ cup of water and 4 cups of kidney or shell beans.

Proceed exactly as for *Spuntature al sugo* (pages 156 to 157), with or without the sausages, but 15 minutes before serving, add 4 cups of drained kidney or shell beans, with ½ cup of water, and simmer. The beans may be canned, or they may be prepared by boiling dry or fresh ones in salted water until cooked. In any case, be sure that the canned ones have been put up without sugar; that is, with just salted water so that they retain that special sort of nutlike bean taste. Serve with hot bread.

PORCHETTA ALLA PERUGINA
Roast Pork in the Style of Perugia

This is an old-fashioned way to prepare a nice pork loin. The final taste is very similar to that of the real *porchetta,* a full-grown pig cooked on a spit over an open fire and then sold in slices at street corner stands. We recommend, as do the *perugini,* this recipe as practical for the family kitchen.

> 1 4- to 5-pound pork loin, boned
> 1 teaspoon salt
> ¼ to ½ cup olive oil

BATTUTO
> 2 or 3 fresh sage leaves
> 1 sprig rosemary
> 2 fresh basil leaves
> 1 garlic clove
> 1 bay leaf
> 1 teaspoon salt
> freshly ground pepper to taste

Prepare the *battuto* by mincing all the ingredients together until they are practically a paste. Spread this mixture on the inner side of the loin (where the bones once were), and then tie the meat up as if it were a sausage, so that the herbs are held tightly inside. Put it in a heavy pot, just big enough to hold the roast, add enough water almost to cover the meat, and the salt, and put over a low heat. Cover and bring slowly to a boil, and then uncover and boil slowly until all the liquid has evaporated. Pour on enough olive oil to coat the loin thoroughly, and continue cooking, turning the meat over and over until a good, golden crust has formed. Slice and serve.

ZAMPETTO
Pigs' Feet

A favorite dish in northern Italy; when winter sets in, the pigs' feet are boiled in flavored, salted water until tender, and are served with *salsa verde*. Bean salad is frequently served as a *contorno,* as are other vegetables *all'agro.*

    2 little pigs' feet or 1 big one per person
    2 tablespoons wine vinegar
      salt
    1 onion
    1 carrot
    1 celery stalk
    4 to 5 peppercorns

Put the pigs' feet in a pot, cover well with water, add the vinegar, salt (1 teaspoon per quart), and the vegetables. Bring to a boil, reduce the heat, and simmer for about 1½ hours, or until tender, so tender the meat practically falls away from the bone. Serve with *Salsa verde* (pages 213 to 214) and kidney bean salad, or any vegetable *all'agro* you desire.

POLLAME
Poultry

There are probably only two basic differences between American poultry and its Italian counterpart: the Italian product is still sold in its entirety (head, feet, sometimes even feathers), and it is less fat than the American bird.

The feet are put in broth to strengthen it with natural gelatin, and the crest is used in sauce for rice or pasta. Because it's been years since either heads or feet were sold in the average American market, we've not included them in our recipes.

At the same time, the current way of selling poultry in parts lends itself admirably to buying a bit at a time for such things as pasta stuffing. You can get breast of chicken or turkey to cook in butter and wine, or gizzards and livers for sauces, without having the rest of the bird on your hands and conscience. You should also save those little packets of giblets that come inside each chicken. Rewrapped and frozen, they keep for weeks. Defrosted at room temperature, cleaned and cut, they serve in sauces for both rice and pasta.

As for the fat in both turkeys and chickens, cut it off anywhere you find it, and either throw it out or use it in some other way.

The American turkey is somewhat bigger and plumper than the Italian, so much so that it is a big item on Italy's import list, but self-basting birds are not advised for Italian recipes, as they are too rich and overpower their stuffings. The self-basting fat makes the breast fall apart when sliced for cooking in a pan.

Besides these few pointers, all we can say is that poultry is versatile, easy to prepare, and a genuine favorite in Italian cooking, North to South.

POLLO ARROSTO CON PATATE
Roast Chicken with Potatoes

This is the simplest way to cook a chicken without giving it much attention. All it needs is just the careful insertion of rosemary, basting with oil, and a hot oven to turn it crisp and golden brown on the outside, tender and moist on the inside. *Pollo arrosto* makes a Sunday dinner when cooked with roast potato wedges also treated to rosemary and oil.

BASICS
OF
ITALIAN
COOKING

HOMEMADE EGG PASTA

Turn your mound of flour into a crater and break the eggs into it.

Beat the eggs with a fork held in one hand. Use the other hand to shore up the walls of the crater.

It gradually becomes too difficult to work the newly created dough with a fork.

Put the fork aside and begin working with your hands.

Knead the dough well until it is smooth and elastic to the touch and the working surface is practically clean.

Flour the working surface and rolling pin lightly and begin to roll the pasta out.

Continue rolling until the pasta is the desired thickness, about that of a dime.

If using the pasta for *fettuccine*, dry it about 15 minutes, flour it very lightly, and fold it over and over on itself into a flat roll about 4 inches wide.

Using a very sharp knife, cut the roll of pasta into strips about ¼ inch wide, shake out, and dry.

If using a pasta machine, break off a piece of dough about the size of the palm of your hand, flour it, and send it through the adjustable rollers set at their widest distance apart.

Send the pasta through the machine again and again, reducing the space between the rollers until the pasta has reached the desired thickness.

To cut *fettuccine*, dry the rolled pasta about 15 minutes, flour lightly, and send it through the wider cutting rollers.

Complete directions for home-made egg pasta appear on pages 15 to 19.

FILLED PASTA

To make *cappelletti*, cut the pasta into 2" x 2" squares, put a dab of filling in the center of each square, fold on the diagonal, and press the edges together tightly to seal.

Wrap the stuffed, diagonally folded pasta triangle around your finger, one corner over the other, and press to make them stick together. If they don't, moisten the corners where they overlap each other and press again.

If making *agnolotti*, position the filling in even rows on one sheet of pasta so that each dab is the center of a 2" x 2" square. Cover with another sheet of pasta and with your fingers press the two together around each mound of filling. Cut between the mounds with a pastry cutter.

Complete directions for making cappelletti *appear on pages 100 to 102; for* agnolotti *on pages 95 to 97.*

HOW TO PREPARE ARTICHOKES

A good fresh artichoke should be tightly closed and firm. The circle in the cut artichoke indicates the choke.

Tear off the tough outer leaves until they snap loudly as they break away.

Peel back with a paring knife over the point where the leaves were broken off to get to the outside of the heart of the artichoke.

Cut off about a third of the top of the remaining leaves.

Pare all the way around the top to cut off any remaining fibrous parts.

Rub the peeled artichoke with a lemon to prevent blackening.

Cut the artichoke in half from top to bottom, then into quarters, exposing the choke.

Scoop out the choke with a paring knife.

As the artichokes are cut and de-choked, put them in cold water with the juice of a lemon. Drain well and pat dry before using.

1 4-pound roasting chicken
6 to 8 medium potatoes
1 lemon
2 to 2½ teaspoons salt
3 sprigs fresh rosemary, or 3 to 4 teaspoons dried
**   olive oil**

Preheat the oven to 375°.

Peel the potatoes, cut them into wedges, and soak them in cold water.

Take out the giblets and neck of the chicken and save them for future use. Wash the bird, rinsing out the cavity thoroughly. Cut the lemon in half, and scrub it around open-faced inside the cavity, squeezing it as you work so that a lot of juice coats the bird. Lightly salt the cavity and put in a few rosemary leaves. Make small slits in the body of the bird, under the wings, where the leg meets the body, in the fleshy parts of the breast. Stuff these with the rest of the rosemary leaves. Place the bird breast-down on a poultry rack in a big, shallow roasting pan. Add the drained potatoes all around. Sprinkle with olive oil, and add a bit of salt. Roast (at 375°) for ½ hour. Take the bird out, turn it breast-up, baste it with oil and pan juices 2 or 3 times, sprinkle with a touch of salt, flip the potatoes and baste them, and return the bird to the oven for another ½ hour or so of roasting. (Chickens usually are done, tender, crisp and brown on the outside, if one allows about 18 minutes per pound.)

POLLO RIPIENO ALLA ROMAGNOLA
Stuffed Chicken in the Style of Romagna

In Romagna, as in the other northern regions of Italy, little touches of flavoring are blended together with butter and wine to change the whole idea of stuffing. Incidentally, roast potato wedges, as prepared with *Pollo arrosto* (pages 160 to 161), are the usual as well as the perfect accompaniment to this chicken.

1 4-pound roasting chicken, including giblets
1 Italian sweet sausage
1 small onion
1 small celery stalk
2 tablespoons butter
3 to 4 ounces fresh mushrooms, chopped coarsely
½ to 1 cup shredded Italian bread (crusts not included)
¼ cup dry white wine
2 teaspoons salt
1 teaspoon rosemary
olive oil

Preheat the oven to 375°.

Skin the sausage. Boil the gizzard just long enough (5 to 10 minutes) so that it can be skinned easily. Send the sausage, gizzard, heart, and liver of the chicken through a meat grinder. Mince the onion and celery into tiny bits and sauté them gently in the butter over medium heat until golden. Add the ground meats and chopped mushrooms, and continue cooking until the meats have lost their rosiness. Put the shredded bread in a bowl, dampen with the wine, and add the meats with their flavorings and juices. Add 1 teaspoon of the salt and mix lightly.

Rinse the cavity of the chicken and drain well. Spoon in the stuffing and skewer or sew shut. Make slits in the joints and fill them with the rosemary. Sprinkle with a little olive oil.

Proceed as for ordinary roast chicken: cook it (at 375°) breast-down for the first half an hour; then turn it, salt it, and baste it during the last half hour or so.

POLLO ALLA DIAVOLA
Chicken, Devil's Style

Anything cooked *alla diavola* in Italy usually means it's been grilled over abundant hot coals, of which the devil himself should have enough, and the seasonings are also hot, but not so hot as to ruin the taste buds.

In this chicken's case, the flavor is heightened with red peppers, black pepper, and lemon.

2 small broilers, or 1½ medium ones
½ cup olive oil
3 red pepper pods, seeded, or 3 or 4 dashes Tabasco sauce
2 lemons
freshly ground pepper to taste
salt to taste

Start your charcoal grill.

Heat the olive oil in a small pan over medium heat, add the pepper pods, and sauté them until they are deep, dark brown. Turn off the heat, cool the olive oil, and throw away the browned peppers. (The alternative is just to add Tobasco to the olive oil to make it hot.)

Cut the chickens in half, crack the legs and wing joints loose, and spread them out, skin-side up, on a board or clean counter. Pound the chicken halves well with a meat pounder and really flatten them out.

Add the juice of 1 of the lemons to the seasoned olive oil along with 3 or 4 twists of the pepper mill. Put the chicken halves in a big bowl, pour the seasoned olive oil over them, and turn the pieces over and over to coat them well. Let stand 1 or 2 hours, turning the pieces from time to time.

When your grill is heaped with hot, hot coals, put the marinated chicken halves on to cook, skin-side down. Add salt, a bit more pepper, and grill thoroughly, turning, basting from time to time with any leftover marinade. The chicken is done when it is tender and has acquired a dark brown crust all over (some spots may well be charred).

You can use the broiler in your oven, but it never seems to get quite hot enough. If you want to try, preheat the broiler, put the chicken as close to the flame or coil as possible, and grill it, turning it frequently and basting it often.

Serve hot with lemon wedges.

POLLO ALLA CACCIATORA I
Hunters' Chicken I

Chicken prepared in the way, according to tradition, hunters cooked their venison, using wine and wine vinegar to make a sauce flavored with rosemary and a hint of garlic. For today's nonhunters, this dish is fast and easy to make on top of the stove. A large frying chicken will serve 6, because the sauce (and the inevitable bread dipped in it) is an integral part of the dish.

        1 large frying chicken
        3 tablespoons olive oil
        1 garlic clove
        2 teaspoons rosemary
     1½ teaspoons salt, or to taste
      ¼ cup wine vinegar
      ½ cup dry white wine

Fryers usually come cut in 4 pieces, but for this you should cut these in half again, so that you have 8 pieces. If you have the patience, try for 10 to 12 pieces, because the smaller the piece, the quicker the cooking and browning, and the tastier it is. Cut off any bits of fat you see.

Heat the oil with the garlic in a deep frying pan (a chicken frying pan with its high edges is ideal, but a deep cast-iron pot is almost as good). When the garlic is golden, discard it. Put in the chicken, rosemary, and salt, and brown thoroughly, turning the pieces on all sides. When the chicken is a deep golden brown, add the wine vinegar, and quickly cover the pan until the sizzling stops. Then add the wine and cook on high heat until it has evaporated (when its vapors no longer tingle the nose). Reduce the heat and simmer about 20 minutes, or until the chicken is tender. Put the pieces on a warm platter in a warm oven.

Add about 1 tablespoon of water to the juices in the pan, turn up the heat, and with a wooden spoon scrape clean the sides and bottom of the pan to detach any little bits that may have cooked on. This will turn the sauce a golden amber. Pour the sauce over the chicken and serve with Italian bread.

POLLO ALLA CACCIATORA II
Hunters' Chicken II

This somewhat fancier version of the traditional *cacciatora* uses a *battuto* of parsley, celery, and garlic, plus bay leaves as the herb seasoning.

>   1 3-pound frying chicken
>   3 tablespoons olive oil
>   2 bay leaves
>   1 cup dry white wine
>   4 tablespoons chicken broth (page 55)
> 1½ teaspoons salt
>   freshly ground pepper to taste

BATTUTO
>   1 tablespoon chopped fresh parsley
> 1½ celery stalks, with leaves
>   1 garlic clove

Cut the chicken into at least 10 small pieces. Make a *battuto* (page 24) of the parsley, celery, and garlic. Brown the chicken for 10 minutes in the olive oil over high heat in a good-sized frying pan. Add the *battuto* and continue to cook over medium-high heat, turning everything over and over so that all the chicken pieces are well browned and the little bits of vegetable don't burn or stick to the bottom of the pan. Don't worry if some do, for they will be taken care of by the next step.

Add the bay leaves and wine, and cook over high heat until the wine has almost completely evaporated. Add the broth. With a wooden spoon scrape all the little bits off the sides and bottom of the pan. Add the salt and a few grinds of pepper. Simmer for 20 minutes, or until the chicken is tender and the sauce has cooked away a bit and darkened. Serve with Italian bread.

POLLO ALLA ROMANA
Chicken, Roman Style

Cut-up chicken, sautéed until golden in olive oil, is then poached in a tomato sauce with roast peppers. It's a traditional Roman dish for celebrating Ferragosto, the Feast of the Assumption, August 15.

> 1 big frying chicken
> 4 to 6 sweet red and green peppers
> 3 tablespoons olive oil
> 1 garlic clove
> 1 red pepper pod, seeded
> 4 cups peeled plum tomatoes
> 1½ to 2½ teaspoons salt

First roast the peppers (page 8). Then cut them in long strips and set them aside to drain.

Chop the chicken into as many pieces as possible, at least 8 but aim for 12. Put the olive oil in a heavy, high-sided pot over medium heat. Add the garlic and red pepper pod, and cook until the garlic is golden, the pepper is a deep brown. Remove these flavorings and add the chicken pieces. Fry them thoroughly, until they are a rich, golden brown all around. Then remove the pieces and set them aside to drain.

Pour off most of the fat from the pan, leaving only enough to cover the bottom. Add the tomatoes, mashing them with a wooden spoon. Bring the pan to a bubbling boil, add half the pepper strips and the chicken. Add the salt and cook at least 20 minutes, or until the chicken is really tender and flavored with the sauce. Taste for salt and add the rest of the pepper strips. Keep on the heat only long enough to warm the last of the peppers.

Serve with abundant slices of Italian bread.

POLLO IN BARCHETTA
Boiled Chicken in a Boat of Rice

This easy family dinner practically cooks without supervision, is enormously comforting, and can be stretched easily to serve more than 6 people.

CHICKEN
- **1 small fowl (3 to 4 pounds)**
- **2 celery stalks**
- **1 onion**
- **2 carrots**
- **3 teaspoons salt**
- **1 clove**
- **5 peppercorns**

RICE
- **½ onion, minced**
- **2 tablespoons unsalted butter**
- **2 cups rice**
- **nutmeg**
- **3 tablespoons quick-mixing flour**
- **4 or 5 sprigs parsley**
- **½ pound fresh mushrooms (optional)**

Put the fowl in a deep pot with all the seasonings, and cover with abundant cold water (at least 2½ quarts). Bring the pot to a boil over medium heat, skim off any froth that may form, cover, and lower the heat. Simmer until tender, about 1½ hours.

About 20 minutes before the chicken is done, sauté the minced onion in the butter in another good-sized pot. When it is limp and golden, add the rice and enough broth from the cooking chicken to slosh around. As the rice absorbs the broth, add more broth plus a dash of nutmeg. Add only enough broth, however, to keep the rice just moist. Keep adding a little at a time, until the rice is plump and cooked through. Place on a warm platter, shaping it like a boat or ring, and put in a warm oven.

Remove the chicken from the broth, slip out the

bones, and place the pieces in the center of the rice boat. If two cooks are collaborating, one can do this while the other prepares the sauce.

Scoop about 2 cups of the broth into a saucepan, correct the seasonings if necessary, and add 3 tablespoons of quick-mixing flour. Heat the sauce until thickened (about 4 minutes), and then pour it over the entire platter of rice and chicken pieces. Garnish with sprigs of parsley.

This dish can be made in a more luxurious version. Simply include a handful or so of sliced mushrooms when you sauté the minced onion, and cook them along with the rice.

GALLINA IN UMIDO
Chicken Steeped in Sauce

Another family dish cooked on top of the stove, this provides grand quantities of sauce to serve with whipped potatoes.

    1 3-pound frying chicken
    2 to 3 tablespoons olive oil
    ½ cup dry white wine
    1½ teaspoons salt
      freshly ground pepper to taste
    3 cups peeled plum tomatoes, cut up

BATTUTO

    1 medium onion
    1 celery stalk
    1 carrot
    1 tablespoon chopped fresh parsley

Cut the chicken up into 10 pieces, and remove all the fat you can.

Make a *battuto* of the onion, celery, carrot, and parsley, mincing them to a paste. Cover the bottom of a medium-sized stewpot with olive oil, and add the *battuto*. Cook everything until golden over medium heat, and then add the chicken pieces and slowly brown them in the flavored oil. Add the wine, and scrape the sides and bottom of the pot to collect any bits that may have stuck. Add the salt and pepper. When the wine has almost evaporated, add the tomatoes and bring to a boil. If the liquids don't quite cover the chicken pieces, add enough warm water to do so and cover the pot. Simmer very slowly for 1 hour, stirring occasionally, or until the chicken is very tender and the sauce has thickened and has reduced to about half its original quantity.

TACCHINO RIPIENO ALLA LOMBARDA
Roast Stuffed Turkey in the Style of Lombardy

Beef, sausage, chestnuts, and giblets combine with mushrooms, sage, and rosemary to make a completely different kind of stuffing. This is a real production, and gives the American turkey a whole new appeal.

      1 10- to 15-pound turkey, with giblets
      1 carrot
      1 celery stalk
      1 small onion
      2 teaspoons salt
   $\frac{1}{2}$ pound chestnuts
      3 sweet Italian sausages
   $\frac{1}{2}$ pound twice-ground beef
      2 eggs
      4 tablespoons grated Parmesan cheese
   $\frac{1}{2}$ teaspoon nutmeg
   $\frac{1}{2}$ pound fresh mushrooms
      1 lemon
      2 fresh sage leaves
      1 to 2 teaspoons rosemary
      2 slices lean salt pork
        olive oil
      1 cup dry white wine
      1 tablespoon quick-mixing flour

Preheat the oven to 325°.
Remove the giblets and neck from the turkey and

put them in a saucepan with the carrot, celery, onion, 1 teaspoon of salt, and enough water to cover. Bring to a boil, cover, reduce the heat, and let it bubble along on a simmer until the giblets are tender, about ½ hour or so.

With a sharp paring knife make an incision through the outer shell of each chestnut. Put them in a saucepan with enough water to cover, bring to a boil, reduce the heat, and cook gently for ½ hour, or until tender. Drain, cool slightly, and peel off the outer shell and inner skin as quickly as possible. Mash up the chestnuts, but don't make a puree—little nuggets of nut are necessary for the proper texture.

Skin the sausages and send them with the beef through a meat grinder. Put in a bowl and add the eggs, the cheese, the nutmeg, and the chopped mushrooms. When the giblets are done, strain their broth and save it. Chop up the liver and the heart, and skin and chop the gizzard, and add the chopped mixture to the bowl. Add the chestnuts, and stir and mix well. Add salt to taste, perhaps ½ to 1 teaspoon.

Rinse the turkey well and wipe the cavity with wedges of the lemon, squeezing as you wipe to cover all the surface with juice. Stuff the turkey cavity and neck pouch and skewer shut. Make little slits in the skin under the wings, where the legs join the body, and a few in the fleshiest part of the white meat. Stuff each slit with a bit of sage and rosemary. Put the bird in a big roasting pan.

Put the salt pork crosswise on the breast. Cut a double piece of cheesecloth big enough to drape over the entire bird, and lay it on. Dribble olive oil over the cloth to moisten it slightly. This keeps the bird from drying out excessively in the first hours of cooking.

Put the stuffed turkey in the oven (at 325°). When the beast begins to brown (about 40 minutes), pour the wine over it, and baste thoroughly 3 or 4 times. Continue to baste frequently, and if more liquid is needed, use the giblet broth. Half an hour before the estimated cooking time is over, remove the cheesecloth and salt pork, and baste again. When the turkey is done (the leg moves easily and is about to break away from the body), put it on a platter. Add the remaining giblet broth to the juices in the pan, scraping the bottom and sides to collect any bits stuck there. You may thicken this gravy by adding a tablespoon or so of quick-mixing flour, and cooking it, stirring constantly, a moment or two over medium heat.

Serve with turkey in slices with spoonfuls of the rich stuffing and gravy.

RIPIENO PER TACCHINO ALLA LOMBARDA
*Another Stuffing for Roast Turkey in the
Style of Lombardy*

This stuffing's exotic flavor comes from prunes and pears or apples cooked with veal and turkey giblets. This recipe makes enough stuffing for a 10- to 15-pound turkey, prepared and roasted as in the preceding recipe.

- 1 dozen prunes
- 1 pound chestnuts
- 4 hard pears or apples
  turkey giblets
- 1 pound ground veal or very lean beef
- 3 tablespoons unsalted butter
- 1 cup dry wine
- ¼ teaspoon nutmeg
  salt to taste
  freshly ground pepper to taste

Put the prunes in a saucepan with abundant water and cook until soft enough to stone easily. Score the chestnuts and put them in another saucepan to boil until tender. Shell and skin them and set aside.

Peel the core the pears (or apples), and cut them into small bits. Chop the prunes and chestnuts to the same size as the pears. Skin the turkey gizzard and put it through the meat grinder with the veal (or beef), the liver, and the heart.

Melt the butter in a big frying pan, add the meats, and cook over medium heat until their color has changed from pink to beige. Add the chopped fruit and chestnuts, stir, and add the wine. Cook for 5 minutes, season with the nutmeg, salt, and pepper, and the stuffing is ready for the bird.

PETTO DI TACCHINO DORATO
Golden-Fried Turkey Breast

This is a classic way to cook the white meat of poultry. The golden and crisp outside leaves the meat moist and tender inside, and everything has its flavor heightened with lemon juice. A 7- to 8-pound breast of turkey, frozen, yields more than enough slices for 6, and the carcass serves for a good broth, while the little bits of meat remaining on it can be used for various pasta stuffings. The turkey breast slices marvelously when almost defrosted, after having been left at room temperature about 5 hours.

    12 slices turkey breast
        flour
     2 or 3 large eggs, beaten well
    ½ pound unsalted butter
     1 tablespoon olive oil
     1 teaspoon salt
    1½ lemons, cut into wedges

Remove the skin from the turkey breast and slice the meat into thin (about ⅛-inch) slices, pounding them to make them even thinner. Make small incisions around the edges to cut any membrane, otherwise the slices tend to curl while cooking.

Dust the slices with flour, and dip them in the beaten eggs.

Melt the butter in a big frying pan, add the olive

oil, and cook the turkey slices quickly over medium heat. Turn them over as soon as they are golden on one side. Sprinkle lightly with salt as soon as they are cooked, and remove to a warm platter in a warm oven. Serve with lemon wedges.

PICCATA DI PETTO DI TACCHINO
Turkey Breast in a Piquant Sauce

Thin slices of white meat of turkey cooked in a lemon-and-wine sauce are another common favorite. The same process can be used for chicken breasts or slices of veal with the same mouth-watering effect.

    1   small frozen breast of turkey
        flour
    8   tablespoons unsalted butter
    1   tablespoon olive oil
    ½   cup dry white wine
        juice of 1 lemon
    ½   to 1 teaspoon salt

Slice the breast into 12 thin slices no more than ⅛ inch thick. Pound them gently with the side of a big butcher knife or a meat pounder. Dust them with flour, patting it on to make sure it sticks. Melt the butter in a big frying pan over medium heat, adding 1 tablespoon olive oil to help prevent the butter from browning. Sauté the slices in the butter and oil, turning them when the edges get white (this takes about 3 minutes). Cook the second side another 3 minutes. Since hardly anyone but a restaurant has a huge frying pan, you'll probably have to cook two batches. Remove the first to a warm platter. When the last slices in the second batch are cooked, don't remove them from the pan. Just add the wine, and stir and cook for a moment. Then add the lemon juice and stir again. Taste the sauce on a bit of bread and, if desired, add salt. Put all the cooked slices back in the pan, and see that each one is coated with the sauce. Simmer about 2 minutes. Serve hot with the sauce.

FRITTATE
Omelets

The easiest way of translating *frittata* is as "omelet." But the very word "omelet" conjures up a host of white-clad chefs who, at the end of a long professional life, having mastered special tools and techniques, finally turn out the Perfect Omelet: puffy, golden, slightly crisp on the outside, filled or unfilled, almost a soufflé. The *frittata* is not necessarily difficult, not exactly filled, because all the additions to the eggs are mixed and blended with them, and most of the time it's not puffy. In fact, some of the time it must be spooned rather than cut.

Moreover, the Italian *frittata* is a much humbler, more peasant dish. For centuries it was the working man's lunch. A loaf of bread, slit open, was filled with a *frittata* and taken along on the job. On today's Italian table, it appears as a second course in a lunch, as part of a light supper, or is carried on picnics. Restaurants have been serving them up cold as *antipasti,* but the true followers of the *frittata* cult insist on serving them hot, at the table.

In many regions, the word is used as an exclamation: "What a *frittata!*" people say, to comment on any sort of action that ends up as a scrambled mess.

The *frittata* pan is a normal frying pan, copper, iron, or aluminum (in order of historical appearance on the market). It is usually cured by age and by the simple fact that it is never washed. Once used, and preferably while still hot, it is rubbed clean with a rag or a paper towel. An aged, well-seasoned pan is considered an heirloom. The heavy iron or aluminum omelet pan available on the American market is of course marvelous for making *frittate,* but you can be successful without one.

If you're a novice or buy a new pan, choose a wide, heavy iron or aluminum pan, fill it with fresh cooking oil, bring it to a very high heat, let it cool overnight, empty it, and wipe it dry. From then on, use it only as a *frittata* pan, with butter or olive oil as the recipe dictates. Wipe it clean each time you use it; don't soak or soap it.

If the right size pan is not available, the *frittata* can be cooked in two batches. The ingredients, other than the eggs, are usually prepared first in the pan, and then divided in half, as are the eggs. This insures for each batch the proper texture as well as the correct thickness of no more than about ¾ of an inch.

Northern Italians traditionally use butter, while the Southerners use olive oil. The Northerners tend to use more eggs and less of the other ingredients, the so-called filling. The Southerners use fewer eggs, considering them to be mainly a binder for the filling. On the average, 1½ eggs per person is the right amount if the eggs are medium-sized. Most of our recipes call for 7 large eggs for 6 people (about the equivalent of 9 medium eggs). Experiment for yourself, and adjust the number to your taste.

When you've decided how many eggs to use, you should warm them to room temperature while you prepare and cook the filling. Once beaten, the eggs can be salted before you add them to the vegetables, or you can salt them during cooking. Some *frittate* (for example, the zucchini one) taste better if salted again after cooking.

When you are ready to combine the vegetables and the eggs, raise the heat so that you'll be able to cook quickly. There should be no need to add more oil or butter, but if the vegetables look a little dry, use your own judgment and add a bit of butter or oil if it seems necessary. Then pour in the eggs, stirring right away. As the edges of the *frittata* start to solidify, lift them gently with a spatula to get the uncooked eggs down to the bottom of the pan. Once the bottom of the *frittata* is solid and golden, it should slide back and forth when the pan is shaken.

Then it's time to turn the whole thing over and cook the second side. Some champions can just flip it, and of course the smaller the *frittata,* the more easily it is flipped. The most revered way to turn it, whether it's large or small, is to slide it out, cooked-side down, onto a big plate. Cover the plate with the pan, and then turn plate and pan together, letting the uncooked side of the *frittata* plop back into the pan. Return it to high heat and cook until this second side slides back and forth. Then, once more, slide it out onto that big plate, cut like a pie, and serve.

FRITTATA DI CIPOLLE
Onion Omelet

Thin slivers of onion, flavored with salt pork (in the peasant style) or *prosciutto* (for the rich), make a new variation on the bacon-and-egg theme.

- **3 medium onions**
- **3 tablespoons olive oil**
- **2 slices lean salt pork, or 4 slices** *prosciutto*
  salt to taste
  freshly ground pepper to taste
- **7 eggs**

Slice the onions into very thin slivers (3 onions should make about 3 cups), and soak them in cold water for about 10 minutes. Drain, dry, and put them in a big, shallow, heavy frying pan with the olive oil. Chop the salt pork (or *prosciutto*) into tiny cubes and add it to the onions. Sauté over medium heat, stirring from time to time, until translucent. Sprinkle with salt and freshly ground pepper (several good twists of the pepper mill).

Beat the eggs well and add them to the onions and

salt pork. Stir the whole pan gently, raise the heat, and cook quickly. As soon as the bottom is solidified and browned, turn the *frittata* and cook the second side to a golden brown.

FRITTATA ROGNOSA
Tomato-and-Onion Omelet

The *rognosa* isn't really an omelet in the usual sense of the word, since it isn't supposed to be crisp and shapely. The perfect *rognosa* is just moist and spoonable. For years and years it has been the workingman's lunch, as a filling inside a loaf of bread called a *pagnottella*. Today it's the cook's selection for a quick snack or second course when there is no meat.

    1 large Bermuda onion
    2 to 3 tablespoons olive oil
 1½ cups peeled plum tomatoes
       salt to taste
    7 eggs

Sliver the onion by cutting it in half, eliminating the core at the bottom, and cutting each half in the thinnest possible slices the shape of new moons. If you don't have a big Bermuda, use 2 medium yellow onions, slivered and soaked in cold water for about 10 minutes, and then drained and dried. Put the onion in a big frying pan with the olive oil (just enough to cover the bottom), and sauté over medium heat until golden and translucent. Add the tomatoes, mashing them up with a wooden spoon. Bring to a boil, reduce the heat, and simmer about 15 minutes, or until the liquids are reduced and the color deepened. Salt lightly.

Beat the eggs to a froth and add them. Raise the heat to medium and stir the eggs into the tomato sauce until the whole thing starts to solidify. Stir once or twice more as the eggs and sauce unite to make a moist, almost solid *frittata*.

If your frying pan won't accommodate this many eggs, proceed by installments. Cook the tomatoes and onion to the point where they're ready for the eggs. Remove half the tomato mixture and add half the eggs, making a *frittata* for 3. Serve on a hot platter. Put the last half of tomato and onion back in the pan, add the rest of the eggs, make a second *frittata,* and serve.

FRITTATA DI CARCIOFI
Artichoke Omelet

A *frittata* makes a few artichokes go a long way. This one is eaten cold as an *antipasto* or on picnics. Hot, it is a most delicate second course.

- 3 **artichokes**
     juice of 1 lemon
- 3 **tablespoons olive oil**
- 7 **eggs**
     salt to taste

Prepare the artichokes for cooking as on pages 224 to 226. Slice them from top to stem into ⅛-inch slices. Soak them in water with the lemon juice. Drain and dry before using.

Heat the olive oil in a big frying pan, add the sliced artichokes, and cook them until tender over medium heat, stirring from time to time.

Beat the eggs, add salt to taste. Raise the heat and put in the eggs, shifting the artichokes back and forth with a fork to make sure the eggs seep down to the bottom of the pan. As soon as the bottom crust is formed, turn the *frittata.* When golden brown on both sides, it's ready to serve and eat.

FRITTATA DI FUNGHI
Mushroom Omelet

Here is another dish in which a few ingredients flavor a lot of eggs to make a very light and delicate second course.

   ½ to 1 pound fresh mushrooms
   3 tablespoons unsalted butter (approximate)
      salt to taste
   5 sprigs parsley, chopped (optional)
   7 eggs

If the mushrooms are nice and clean and white as
they come from the market, just cut off a thin slice at
the bottom of the stem, throw it away, and slice the
rest of the mushroom. The small ones slice nicely from
the top to bottom, each piece including a tiny bit of
stem. The big ones should have their stems sliced separately into tiny rounds and the tops into thin slices.

Melt enough butter to cover the bottom of the pan
and put the sliced mushrooms in to cook. At first they
will absorb the butter, and then they will give out their
own delicious liquid just as they are about done and
are ready to have the eggs added. At this point the
mushrooms are cooked but still slightly crisp. Sprinkle
with a bit of salt. Add parsley, if desired, to the mushrooms.

Beat the eggs thoroughly and pour them onto the
cooked mushrooms. Stir gently with the tip of a spatula
to get the egg to slip down and around and in between
the mushroom slices. As soon as the bottom has
browned and the top begun to solidify, turn the *frittata*
to complete the cooking. Sprinkle with a bit of salt, and
serve.

FRITTATA CON PATATE A TOCCHETTI
Potato Omelet

A Roman favorite, this *frittata* uses boiled potatoes cut
in cubes, sautéed until golden in olive oil, and seasoned
with freshly ground pepper.

   3 good-sized potatoes
   3 tablespoons olive oil
      salt to taste
      freshly ground pepper to taste
   7 eggs

Boil the potatoes, with their jackets on, until barely cooked. Drain, and when cool enough to handle, peel, and cut into ½-inch cubes.

Pour enough olive oil to cover its bottom into a heavy, wide frying pan. Add the potatoes and sauté them just until golden (but not thoroughly fried), turning the bits around with a spatula so that all sides cook. Sprinkle with salt and freshly ground pepper (several good twists of the mill).

Beat the eggs, and pour them on the potatoes. Lift the potatoes up with the spatula to make sure the eggs get down to the bottom and in between all the cubes. When the bottom has solidified and browned and the top is fairly solid, turn the *frittata* to finish cooking.

FRITTATA CON SPINACI
Spinach Omelet

Another *frittata* commonly used by workingmen for lunch on the job, this omelet of spinach with a hint of Parmesan cheese can be made with the frozen or fresh vegetable, the exact amount fluctuating with the cook and the kitchen.

> ½ pound fresh spinach, or ½ package frozen (5 ounces)
> 7 eggs
> 2 tablespoons grated Parmesan cheese
> salt to taste
> 3 tablespoons unsalted butter

Cook the spinach in boiling salted water. Drain it, squeezing it against the side of a sieve to get out as much water as possible. Chop it, if it isn't already chopped.

Beat the eggs well. Add the Parmesan cheese and a pinch of salt, and then beat in the chopped spinach.

Heat the butter in a big, heavy frying pan, and when it is melted and bubbly (not browned), pour in the eggs with their spinach and cheese. Cook over medium-high heat, lifting the sides of the *frittata* from time to time and tilting the pan to let the uncooked egg run down to the bottom. When the bottom is a golden brown and the top is fairly solid, turn the *frittata,* using either a spatula or the plate system, and cook the second side to a golden brown. Sprinkle with salt, and serve.

FRITTATÀ CON ZUCCHINE
Zucchini Omelet

Once a summer dish, this *frittata* made with the smallest of zucchini is a year-round possibility in America. Many people consider a zucchini omelet the only way to get the real flavor of zucchini.

    2 medium or 4 small zucchini
    3 to 4 tablespoons olive oil
       salt to taste
    7 eggs

Cut the zucchini into very, very thin rounds. Heat the oil in a heavy frying pan and put in the zucchini. Cook over medium-high heat until they are just wilted and slightly golden. Sprinkle with salt.

Beat the eggs well and pour them over the zucchini, stirring gently to get the eggs down to the bottom of the pan and all around the edges and in between the slices. As soon as the bottom is golden brown and solid, slide a spatula under one side, tilt the pan, and let more uncooked egg go to the bottom. When the whole pan is fairly solid, turn the *fritatta* and finish cooking. Sprinkle with salt. Serve hot or cold.

FRITTATINE AL SUGO
Little Omelets with Tomato Sauce

Omelets, thin as French *crêpes,* are stacked like layers in a cake, with basil-flavored tomato sauce in between each *frittatina*. The little extra effort that goes into mak-

ing this transforms an everyday dish into something
that seems to be a Sunday treat.

SAUCE

    4 tablespoons unsalted butter
    1½ cups peeled plum tomatoes
    4 or 5 fresh basil leaves
    1 teaspoon salt

FRITTATINE

    8 eggs
    2 tablespoons flour
    ½ teaspoon salt, or to taste
    2 tablespoons water
    2 to 3 tablespoons unsalted butter
    3 to 4 tablespoons grated Parmesan cheese

THE SAUCE: melt the butter in a large saucepan,
add the tomatoes and their juice, mashing the tomatoes
as they go into the pan. Tear the basil leaves into little
pieces and add them. Add the salt, and let the mixture
come to a boil, lower the heat, and simmer for about
15 minutes, or until reduced to sauce consistency.

THE FRITTATINE: beat the eggs well, adding the
flour, salt, and water. Melt 2 tablespoons of the butter
in a heavy omelet or frying pan. When the butter is
melted and bubbly, spoon enough beaten egg into the
pan to make a thin round about 5 inches in diameter. As
soon as its bottom is solidified and golden, turn it over.
As soon as its second side is cooked, take it out and
put it on a warm serving platter on which you have
placed 1 tablespoon of sauce. Cover the finished *frittatina* with a bit more sauce.

Continue cooking the *frittatine,* layering them as
they are done with a bit of sauce. Add the last tablespoon of butter to the pan when it is needed. When all
the beaten egg is used up (you should have made about
10 thin *frittatine*), pour the remaining sauce over the
layers. Sprinkle with cheese, and cut as you would a
cake, and serve hot.

An alternative way of serving *frittatine* is to roll

each one up as it is cooked and put it into the simmering tomato sauce.

PESCE
Fish

The first thing to know about Italian fish is that they are Mediterranean and as such don't swim the Atlantic. Even when of the same family, they are different from ocean fish, sometimes in size and variety, sometimes in color and texture, but not much in flavor if the same cooking techniques are followed in America. It is a matter of marinating, grilling, frying, seasoning, poaching in a sauce in the Italian way.

The second thing to know is that Italian recipes, regardless of fish family lineage, do wonders with almost any creature of the sea. They make especially good use of squid and mussels as well as the ubiquitous cod, one of the few fish found easily on both sides of the Atlantic. By and large, little fish are fried, medium are grilled or poached, and big fish are sliced and done in a sauce.

The third thing to know is that if you stick to these general rules of shopping, handling, and cooking, the palate will be more than pleased:

Buy fresh fish whenever possible.

Keep the heads and tails, which add to flavor (especially in soups) and to shape (when being grilled).

If using frozen fish, defrost on the least cold shelf of the refrigerator and reduce the cooking time.

Look for fish frozen whole (not fillets) with their heads and tails.

If using frozen shrimp, when possible get those with their shells still on.

In choosing squid, look for the smallest ones

you can find, for they are more tender and quicker cooking.

If grilling fish, you may use a stove broiler, which is adequate, but for ideal results use a charcoal grill.

If using dried salt cod, the whole beast (split open, dried with skin and bones) or that which is skinned, boned, and boxed, is recommended. Second choice is that which is dried, frozen, and wrapped in plastic. All dried salt cod must be soaked in cold water, which is changed from time to time, up to 24 hours or until it is soft and fleshy. The whole cod that is sold in Italian shops takes a 24-hour soaking, but it is frequently found already soaked and can be purchased by the piece. The boxed cod, more easily found in the average American supermarket, should be soaked at least 12 hours (or according to directions on the box).

In choosing recipes, we have tried to be impartial as to region of origin. We have also tried to select the most representative recipes whose ingredients could be found or duplicated easily on this side of the ocean, using either oceanic cousins of fish found in the Mediterranean basin or good counterparts.

BACCALÀ AL SUGO ALLA ROMANA
Cod in a Roman Sauce

Dried cod, soaked to fleshiness, is cooked in a tomato-and-onion sauce and accented with raisins. Leave out the raisins and serve with *polenta* for a northern variation. The Romans serve it with bread alone.

2 pounds dried cod
3 medium Bermuda onions
3 tablespoons olive oil
3 cups peeled plum tomatoes
¾ teaspoon pepper
2 tablespoons white raisins
    salt to taste

Soak the cod, skin and bone it if necessary, and cut it into 4-inch chunks.

Slice the onions into thin slivers. Sauté them in the olive oil until translucent, golden, and limp. Let the pan cool a moment, and then add the tomatoes and pepper, and simmer for 15 to 20 minutes, or until the mixture has amalgamated a bit. Add the fish chunks and the raisins, and cook over low heat for about 15 minutes, or until the fish flakes. Taste for salt, and add it if needed. Serve with *Polenta* (page 108) or generous pieces of Italian bread.

FILETTI DI BACCALÀ FRITTI
Batter-Fried Cod Fillets

Salt cod fillets, dipped in batter and deep-fried, are an old, old favorite. The batter is made with yeast and flour; the frying, ideally, is done in a big cauldron, but a good deep pan in your own kitchen will do almost as well.

2 pounds dried cod
1 recipe *Pastella II* (page 215)
    vegetable oil for deep-frying
1½ lemons, cut into wedges

Soak the cod, skin and bone it if necessary, and cut it into pieces about 5 inches long, 1½ inches wide.

Prepare the *pastella* and let it stand in a warm place at least an hour, or until it has doubled in bulk and is rather full of bubbles.

Put the frying oil in a deep pan to the depth of at least 2½ inches and bring it to high (375°) heat. Dip the cod in the batter, coating all sides well, and put the pieces in the hot oil. When they are deep golden on one side, turn them over and continue frying until they are really crisp and golden all around. Take them out with a slotted spoon and drain on paper towels. Serve hot with the lemon wedges.

BACCALÀ IN PADELLA CON PEPERONI
Pan-Cooked Cod with Peppers

The codfish fillets are poached in tomato sauce with sweet green peppers. It is a marvelous way to cook cod and members of its family such as pollock or whiting. Turbot and halibut fillets also are suitable for this dish.

> 2 to 3 pounds dried cod
> 2 medium onions
> ½ cup olive oil
> 3 cups peeled plum tomatoes
>   salt to taste
> 4 large, fleshy green peppers
> 1 tablespoon chopped fresh parsley

Prepare the salt cod as usual, soaking it in water, skinning and boning it if necessary.

Slice the onions into slivers and sauté them in the olive oil in a deep frying pan. When the onions are translucent, add the tomatoes and about 1 teaspoon of salt.

Core the peppers and cut them into long, thin (¼ inch wide) strips. Add them to the sauce. When the peppers are tender (after about 15 to 20 minutes), and the sauce has condensed, add the fish. Check for salt, adjust the seasonings, and cook for another 15 minutes, or until the fish flakes easily. Sprinkle with the parsley.

If using frozen fillets, wait until the sauce has become really thick before adding the fish, which should be defrosted and dried on paper towels before going into the pan.

BACCALÀ AL FORNO CON PATATE
Baked Cod with Potatoes

Chunks of cod fillets, layered with slivers of onions and potatoes, seasoned with parsley, rosemary, and a bit of plum tomato, make a casserole good for all seasons.

- 2 pounds dried cod
- 3 large potatoes
- 2 large onions
- ½ cup olive oil
- 2 tablespoons minced fresh parsley
- 1 tablespoon dried rosemary
-   salt
- 4 to 5 peeled plum tomatoes

Preheat the oven to 350°.

Prepare the cod by soaking it, and then skinning and boning it if necessary. Cut it into 2″ × 3″ pieces. Slice the potatoes into thin rounds. Cut the onions into the thinnest of slivers.

Put 2 tablespoons or so of the oil in a deep baking dish, just enough to cover the bottom. Put in a layer of potato rounds, then a layer of onion slivers. Sprinkle with some of the minced parsley and rosemary and a bit of salt (not too much, since the cod will have retained some of its salt), and dribble on a bit of olive oil. On top of this, make a layer of cod chunks. Mash up the tomatoes in a bowl or on a plate and distribute a few bits here and there over the cod.

Repeat the layering sequence until all the ingredients have been used up, but be sure that the last or top layer is of potato rounds. Garnish the top with the last of the parsley and rosemary, and a generous amount of olive oil. Bake (at 350°) for 45 minutes, or until the top potatoes are cooked.

BACCALÀ ALLA VICENTINA
Cod in the Style of Vicenza

A poet from Vicenza wrote about this creation, "It is a masterpiece, with a perfume of temptation: every mouthful a balsam." This really means that the cod is creamed in a delicate sauce with a whisper of cinnamon and an abundance of fresh parsley. It is baked very slowly, and is traditionally served with *polenta*.

>   2 pounds dried cod
>   flour
>   ½ cup olive oil
>   4 tablespoons grated Parmesan cheese
>   ¼ teaspoon cinnamon
>   2 cups milk

BATTUTO

>   2 large onions
>   1 garlic clove
>   4 anchovy fillets
>   ⅓ cup chopped fresh parsley
>   ½ teaspoon salt
>   freshly ground pepper to taste

Preheat the oven to 250°.

Having soaked the cod as usual, skin and bone it if necessary, and pat dry with paper towels. Cut it into squares approximately 2½″ × 2½″. Dip the squares into flour, and tap gently to shake off any extra flour.

Make a *battuto* (page 24) with the onions, garlic, anchovies, parsley, salt, and freshly ground pepper (2 or 3 twists of the mill).

Use an oven-proof casserole (cast iron is fine, but if you have an earthenware Italian casserole, that's better still). Pour into it enough oil just barely to cover the bottom. Put in a layer of the floured fish squares. Sprinkle over the fish a bit of the *battuto,* some of the Parmesan cheese, and a touch of the cinnamon. Finally, dribble over a little olive oil.

Repeat the whole process, layering until you have used all the fish and other layering ingredients. Pour the milk over the whole dish, tilting the casserole back and forth gently a couple of times to make sure the milk reaches all the layers.

Cover the casserole, and if the cover doesn't seal tightly, slip a round of brown paper between the pot and its cover, so that all the vapors are kept inside. Bake 2 or 3 hours (at 250°), or until all the liquids are absorbed. Serve hot and, to be traditional, with *Polenta* (page 108).

FILETTI DI BACCALÀ IN BIANCO
Poached Cod Fillets

This simple way of treating a nice piece of fish capitalizes on a marinade of capers, black olives, parsley, lemon juice, and olive oil. It's an ideal summertime approach to frozen fish fillets, such as halibut, ocean perch, or haddock, as well as cod.

 2 pounds fresh or frozen cod fillets
 1 teaspoon salt
 2 tablespoons minced fresh parsley
 1 tablespoon chopped capers
 ½ cup olive oil
 2 lemons
 1 cup black olives

If using frozen fish: defrost it before cooking.

Put the fish fillets in the bottom of a large frying pan, and add enough water to cover by at least ½ inch and the salt. Bring to a boil, reduce the heat, and cook gently until the fish flakes. Lift the fish out with slotted spoons and put it on a platter. Allow it to drain well and then pour off any water remaining on the platter.

While the fish is still warm, sprinkle it with the parsley and capers and dress it with olive oil and the juice of 1 of the lemons. Cover with black olives (preferably Greek or Sicilian olives packed in brine). Slice the last lemon into rounds and arrange them around the edge of the platter. Let the fish stand for at least half an hour in the refrigerator, marinating in the oil and lemon. Serve cold.

SEPPIE COI PISELLI ALLA ROMANA
Squid with Peas, Roman Style

Small squid, fresh or frozen, cooked in flavored olive oil, white wine, and parsley, are joined by peas toward the end of their simmering. A delicate dish loved by Romans, this has many variations up and down the coast of Italy.

    3 pounds fresh or frozen squid
    4 tablespoons olive oil
    1 garlic clove
    1 red pepper pod, seeded
    1 cup dry white wine
    2 tablespoons chopped fresh parsley
    1 teaspoon salt, or to taste
    1 package frozen peas, or 1 pound fresh

If using frozen squid: defrost them either at room temperature or under running cold water. Clean and cut.

Put the olive oil in a big, wide frying pan over medium heat. Add the garlic and the pepper pod. When the garlic is golden and the pepper a deep brown, remove them both and put in the squid. Cook for about 3 minutes, or until the squid have changed their color to pink and purple. Add the wine and continue cooking until it has evaporated. Lower the heat and add the parsley and salt. Simmer about 20 minutes, or until the squid are tender. Add the peas (frozen take about 10 minutes, the fresh about 15 to cook). When everything is tender to the bite, check the sauce for salt, adding more if necessary. Serve piping hot with the Italian bread.

SEPPIE ALL'UMIDO ALLA GENOVESE
Squid, Genoese Style

Squid, Genoese Style is very like the Roman versions only the sauce is more abundant, filled with tomatoes, and flavored with a bit more garlic. The dish can accommodate squid that are a little larger because you do have more sauce to go around for longer simmering.

> 1 3-pound package frozen squid
> 4 tablespoons olive oil
> 2 garlic cloves
> 2 tablespoons fresh parsley
> 2 teaspoons salt
> ½ teaspoon ground pepper
> 1 cup dry red wine
> 3 cups peeled plum tomatoes
> 1½ packages frozen peas (15 ounces), or 3 cups fresh

Clean the squid in the usual fashion and cut them into squares or rings, the tentacles in half.

Heat the olive oil in a big frying pan, add the garlic, and cook until golden. Discard the garlic, and add the squid, parsley, salt, and pepper. When the squid start to turn pink (after about 3 or 4 minutes over medium heat), pour in the wine and cook until the alcohol has evaporated and the vapors no longer tingle the nose. Add the tomatoes, mashing them with a wooden spoon against the side of the pan. Bring to a boil, lower the heat, and simmer about 15 to 20 minutes or until the sauce has reduced and concentrated a bit and the squid are tender. Add the peas and continue simmering another 10 to 15 minutes, or until the peas are cooked. Taste for salt, adding some if necessary. Serve hot with Italian bread.

SEPPIE RIPIENE
Stuffed Squid

With a little bit of patience, and dexterous fingers, nearly anyone can stuff a squid's body, which is then poached in sauce (basically wine and tomatoes) and served as a second course. If you use medium-sized squid, about 6 or 7 inches long, plan 2 to a person.

12 medium squid
 1 small garlic clove
 1 cup parsley leaves
 ¼ teaspoon oregano
 2 teaspoons salt
 1 teaspoon freshly ground pepper
 3 or 4 slices Italian bread
 4 tablespoons olive oil
 ½ cup dry white wine
 6 plum tomatoes (optional)

Clean the squid, letting the bodies dry on paper towels. Put the tentacles, garlic, parsley, oregano, salt, and pepper together on a chopping board, and chop them well. Shred the Italian bread, discarding the crusts, into a bowl. You should have about 1 cup of shredded bread. Add the chopped tentacles and herbs, and mix well. Moisten with a bit of the olive oil to make a coarse paste.

Fill the squid with the paste until they are ½ to ¾ full. Don't stuff them too tightly or they'll burst in the pan. Skewer them shut with plain round wooden toothpicks. Save any leftover stuffing.

Cover the bottom of a big frying pan with the rest of the olive oil and put in the stuffed squid in 1 layer. Brown gently over medium heat. Move the squid about a bit with a spatula or wooden spoon while they are browning to keep them from sticking. Then, if there is any, add the remaining stuffing, and sauté it for a moment or so. Add the wine, stir well, and keep on medium heat until the wine has nearly evaporated.

At this stage, if you wish tomato-flavored sauce, put the plum tomatoes through a sieve or food mill and add the resulting thick juice to the pan. Add enough warm water just barely to come up to the top of the squid. If you don't want to include the tomatoes, add water only. Stir around with a wooden spoon to loosen any bits that may have stuck to the sides and bottom of the pan. Lower the heat and simmer uncovered for 20 to 30 minutes, or until the squid are tender and the sauce has condensed. Turn the squid over a couple of times while simmering them in order to insure even cooking.

Remove the squid to a platter, pour the sauce over them, and serve.

GAMBERI ALLA CASALINGA
Shrimp, Family Style

Originally, this dish used shrimp just as they come from the sea, skin, tail, head and all to be eaten with the fingers. But for those who prefer forks, buy fresh or frozen shrimp with their jackets on, peel them, and dry them on paper towels before you begin with the seasoned olive oil.

    2 pounds medium shrimp
    4 tablespoons olive oil
    1 garlic clove
    1 red pepper pod, seeded (optional)
    2 tablespoons chopped fresh parsley
    1 tablespoon capers
      juice of 1 lemon
    1 teaspoon salt, or to taste

Clean the shrimp by shucking off the shells, breaking off the tails, and deveining if necessary.

Sauté the garlic clove (and a red pepper pod if you like a hot touch in your dish) in olive oil over medium heat until golden and then discard it (with the red pepper after it has turned a deep brown).

Cook the shrimp in the olive oil, stirring constantly until they've turned a nice coral pink. Add the parsley and capers with the lemon juice. Stir, add salt. Taste the sauce for flavor on a morsel of bread and add a bit more salt if necessary. Cook another 3 minutes, and serve.

Remember that if you keep the shrimp over high heat too long they'll lose both flavor and texture. The secret of this dish is speedy cooking, which leaves the shrimp cooked through but still firm.

FRITTO MISTO DI PESCE
Mixed Fried Fish

There's hardly a fishing town in all Italy that isn't able to come up with this combination of golden-fried fresh shrimp, small squid, and fish no more than 3 or 4 inches long. Any one of these fried by itself is grand, but the combination of the three gives a delicious contrast of taste and texture. The choice of small fish depends on your fish market, but we found that small fresh smelts are a good substitute for the tiny fish frequently found in Italian seaports.

      1½ pounds fresh or frozen small squid
        1 pound fresh or frozen medium shrimp
        1 pound fresh or frozen smelts, or other tiny fish
        1 cup flour
          vegetable oil for deep-frying
          salt to taste
        2 lemons, cut into wedges

Defrost the fish if necessary.

Clean the squid, cutting the bodies into rings and the tentacles in half. Shell and devein the shrimp. Clean the smelts. Dredge all the pieces by shaking them in a sturdy bag with the flour.

Bring the frying oil to a high heat (375°). Drop the fish in a few at a time, so that the pan is full but not overcrowded. Keep turning the pieces as they become golden and remove them with a slotted spoon when they are really crisp and thoroughly golden. Drain on paper towels on a cookie sheet and sprinkle with salt. Serve on a hot platter with the lemon wedges.

CALAMARETTI FRITTI
Deep-Fried Tiny Squid

Calamaretti floured and fried by themselves make a delightful dish usually served with a crisp mixed salad and lots of lemon.

> 3 pounds fresh or frozen tiny squid
> ½ cup flour
>   vegetable oil for deep-frying
>   salt to taste
> 2 to 3 lemons, cut into wedges

Clean the squid, cutting the bodies into rings and the tentacles in half. Dredge all the pieces by shaking them in a sturdy bag with the flour. Proceed exactly as for the preceding recipe for *fritto misto*.

PERSICO ALLA MILANESE
Ocean Perch, Milanese Style

An everyday, old-fashioned way to prepare any fish fillets, illustrated here with perch. Slices of the fish are dredged in flour, dipped in beaten egg, then in fine bread crumbs, and are fried golden in butter. This is another easy recipe for many of the frozen fish fillets found on the American market.

> 2 1-pound packages frozen ocean perch
> ½ to ¾ cup flour
> 2 eggs
> 1 cup unseasoned bread crumbs
> ½ cup unsalted butter
> 1 teaspoon salt
> 2 lemons, cut into wedges

Defrost the perch fillets, and press out as much water as possible by gently squeezing the fish between paper towels. Press the fillets into the flour, patting it on them gently so that they absorb as much as possible. Knock off any excess flour. Beat the eggs, and then dip the fillets in them and then into the bread crumbs, patting the crumbs as you did the flour. Melt the butter in a heavy frying pan, over medium heat, and sauté the fillets quickly until golden, first on one side and then on the other. Drain on paper towels, sprinkle with the salt, and serve with lemon wedges.

PESCE SPADA DORATO
Golden-Fried Swordfish

Swordfish (or halibut) steaks, cut no thicker than ½ inch, dipped in flour and egg, and then fried golden in olive oil, retain the delicacy and moistness of the fish.

> 2½ to 3 pounds swordfish or halibut
> ¾ cup flour
> 1 teaspoon salt
> 2 or 3 eggs
> 4 tablespoons olive oil
> 2 lemons, cut into wedges

If you can't have the swordfish or halibut cut to the ½-inch thickness on purchase, cut it yourself, carefully slicing through the steaks. Mix the flour and salt on a big plate and dredge the steaks well, gently patting the flour on them so they absorb as much as possible.

Beat the eggs well and dip the fish in them.

Heat the olive oil in a heavy frying pan over medium heat and fry the fish steaks to a golden brown on each side. Drain on paper towels. Serve with lemon wedges.

SOGLIOLE FRITTE DORATE
Golden-Fried Sole

The tiniest sole, no bigger than the palm of your hand, are ideal for this dish, and are most authentically Mediterranean, but fresh fillets of ocean sole are just as good and more frequently available. Don't pass this recipe up even if frozen fillets of sole are all you can find. Just defrost them slowly in the refrigerator and allow them to drain thoroughly on towels to remove all the water before you begin.

> 6 large or 12 small sole fillets
> flour
> 2 eggs
> ¾ teaspoon salt
> olive oil
> 1½ lemons, cut into wedges

Gently press the fillets into the flour, covering both sides well. Beat the eggs lightly and add the salt. Dip the fish into the beaten eggs, then fry them in about ½ inch hot olive oil. When the fillets are golden on one side, turn them and do the second side. Remove the minute both sides are a good golden color. Serve with lemon wedges.

TONNO ALLA SARDEGNOLA
Fresh Tuna, Sardinian Style

Thick slices of fresh tuna fish, flavored with herbs, seasoning vegetables, and poached in a sauce with sliced mushrooms, is a very different way of handling big fish. Since not all fish markets have fresh tuna, the same treatment can be used with the more easily found pollack, turbot, or swordfish, with absolutely beautiful results.

> 2½ pounds fresh tuna steaks
> ½ cup wine vinegar
> 4 tablespoons olive oil
> ½ pound fresh mushrooms, sliced
> 6 anchovy fillets
> 4 peeled plum tomatoes and their juice
> ¾ teaspoon salt
> ½ teaspoon freshly ground pepper
> 2 beef bouillon cubes (dissolved in ½ cup warm water)
> 1 cup dry white wine
> 2 egg yolks
> 3 teaspoons lemon juice

BATTUTO
    1 **medium onion**
    1 **carrot**
    1 **celery stalk with leaves**
    ½ **teaspoon thyme**
    2 **bay leaves**

If using fresh tuna or swordfish: soak it in enough water to cover with the wine vinegar. If using fresh turbot or pollack: proceed without the water and vinegar treatment.

Make a *battuto* (page 24) of the onion, carrot, celery, thyme, and bay leaves, and sauté until golden in the olive oil. When it is golden, add the sliced mushrooms. Mash up the anchovy fillets with a fork and add them. Add the tomatoes, mashing them up a bit, and then add the salt, pepper, and the fish. Bring to a boil and then lower the heat and simmer for about 5 minutes. Dissolve the bouillon cubes in the warm water and add them to the sauce with the wine. Cook 15 minutes, or until the fish flakes and the sauce has condensed a bit. Remove the fish to a warm platter. Beat the egg yolks, add the lemon juice to them, and then add the egg-lemon mixture to the sauce in the pan, stirring constantly. Cook for 1 or 2 minutes, or until smooth and slightly thickened. Pour over the fish and serve.

TRANCE DI PESCE ALLA GRIGLIA
Grilled Fish Steaks

Almost any of the more fleshy types of fish lend themselves well to cooking over an open grill. This simple treatment includes rosemary and parsley as the herbs, together with a bit of olive oil and lemon juice to keep the fish moist while it cooks.

3 **pounds thick slices or fillets of fish (turbot, halibut, perch, haddock, or fresh cod)**
⅓ **cup olive oil**
2 **lemons**

BATTUTO
1 **small garlic clove**
5 **sprigs fresh rosemary, or 2 teaspoons dried**
2 **tablespoons chopped fresh parsley**
1 **teaspoon salt**
  freshly ground pepper to taste

Get your outdoor grill going.

Make a *battuto* (page 24) of the garlic, rosemary, parsley, salt, and pepper.

Mix the olive oil and the juice of 1 of the lemons together in a small bowl and brush both sides of the fish slices with the mixture. Spread the fish slices out on a platter and sprinkle them evenly with half the *battuto*. Place the slices, herbed-side down, on a hot open grill. Sprinkle the up sides with some of the *battuto*. When the first sides are well browned, turn the slices carefully (using two spatulas helps to do this easily). Sprinkle again with the remaining *battuto,* and brush with the oil-lemon mixture, and cook until the second side is thoroughly browned. Serve with the remaining lemon cut in wedges.

ORATA ALLA GRIGLIA
Grilled Porgy

Seasoned with a paste of herbs, basted with oil and lemon, grilled porgy becomes a treat. Red snapper, ocean perch, or any other medium-sized fish can be substituted. Grilling over open coals is ideal, but broiling in a stove gives eminently satisfactory results.

4 pounds fish, including heads and tails
1 garlic clove
5 sprigs fresh rosemary
3 tablespoons fresh parsley
1½ teaspoons salt
   freshly ground pepper to taste
⅓ cup olive oil
2 lemons

Get your outdoor grill going, or preheat the broiler of your oven.

Clean and scale the fish, cut off the fins but leave on the heads and tails. Mince the garlic, rosemary, and parsley together, add the salt and some pepper, and also a few drops of oil to turn the minced herbs into a paste. Make 2 or 3 diagonal incisions on either side of the fish and spread some paste in the incisions as well as in the cavities.

Mix ¼ cup olive oil and the juice of ½ lemon (double this amount if more than 2 fish are involved) and baste the fish with the mixture.

When the coals of the grill are ready, put the fish on, but not too close to the coals, or place the fish under the oven broiler, also not too close. When it is nicely browned and crackling, turn it, baste again with the oil-and-lemon mixture, and finish cooking. Serve with the remaining lemon cut in wedges.

FRATTAGLIE
The "In Between" Cuts

Frattaglie aren't just "in between" cuts, they're the interior organs—kidneys, liver, sweetbreads, brains, and tripe—of all those noble beasts who've been to market. Depending on where you shop, you can find perhaps all or only a few of them. Sometimes they're very much the fashion: the elegant New York brunch features sweetbreads, the British dinner its mixed grill, a French lunch a delicate dish of brains. In Italy the presence of a dish of veal kidneys isn't merely a matter of fashion. It has traditionally made a regular, weekly appearance, although our Italian butcher has admitted that a time-honored group of menus is being ignored in this decade by the modern housewife. Yet there is hardly a reputable restaurant from the top to the toe of Italy that doesn't include one or more *frattaglie* on every menu.

In the United States we easily find calf's liver as well as beef and baby beef liver in our local markets. Tripe also is usually available. To buy pig's liver, we frequently have to go to Italian butchers, as we do also for brains and sweetbreads. Again, it just depends on market supply and demand.

We don't know why the modern housewife has begun to ignore *frattaglie,* but we do know that most of the ways of cooking them are easy, and that their taste makes any search for them well worth the effort. To tell the truth, when we come across them while shopping for something else, we're likely to abandon any previously planned menu in their favor. Try them. You'll see.

FEGATO ALLA TOSCANA
Liver, Tuscan Style

Baby beef liver, which is a little meatier than calf's liver, dusted in flour and cooked in herb-flavored olive oil, is another quick dish whose flavor is heightened by lemon juice.

  2 **pounds baby beef liver**
     flour
½ **cup olive oil**
  1 **garlic clove**
  2 **or 3 fresh sage leaves, or 2 or 3 bay leaves**
     salt to taste
     freshly ground pepper to taste
1½ **lemons**

Cut the liver into slices no thicker than ¼ inch. (Slices this thick are sometimes found precut and frozen, in which case, defrost at room temperature before using.) Dredge the slices in flour, patting it on well to make as much as possible firmly adhere. Shake off any loose, excess flour.

Heat the olive oil with the garlic and sage in a big frying pan over medium-high heat. (If you can't get fresh sage, use bay leaves. Dried sage doesn't have the same effect on the liver as does the fresh.) Add the floured liver and sauté it quickly, turning it as soon as the bottom side has browned. Cook the second side only until the juices run. The liver should be almost crisp on the outside, tender and moist inside. Add the salt, pepper, and the juice of ½ lemon to the pan, and heat for a moment. Put the slices on a warm platter and pour on some of the flavored olive oil. Cut 1 lemon into thin wedges, arrange them around the platter, and serve.

FRITTO MISTO ALLA ROMANA
Fried Brains (or Sweetbreads)
Mixed with Vegetables, Roman Style

Fritto misto has many variations, depending on what's available in the regional market. A most frequent combination includes zucchini, artichokes, cauliflower, and either brains (calf's or lamb's) or veal sweetbreads. It can also include potatoes, *ricotta*, liver, and apple slices.

Four main ingredients make a decent choice. Everything is cut into approximately the same bite-sized bits, dipped in an egg batter, deep-fried quickly, and served hot with lemon wedges.

It's the kind of production in which having two cooks in the kitchen makes more than good sense. Both can clean and cut while the *pastella* sits. Then one can dip while the other fries. The bigger the pan, the faster the frying and the better the eating, because this dish should not sit around but be served immediately.

1 double batch *Pastella I*

BRAINS OR SWEETBREADS
   1 pair brains (calf's or lamb's)
   1 tablespoon vinegar
       OR
   1 pair sweetbreads
   1 teaspoon salt

VEGETABLES
   3 zucchini
   3 artichokes
   1 head of cauliflower
   vegetable oil for deep-frying
   4 lemons
   salt

Mix up a double batch of *Pastella I* (page 214) and let it sit for 2 hours.

If using brains: soak them in ice water for about half an hour. Then drain them, remove the skin and membrane, and put them in fresh water to cover. Add the vinegar and simmer for about 15 minutes. Drain and cut in bite-sized pieces, and they're ready for the *pastella.*

If using sweetbreads: soak them in ice-cold salted water for at least 1 hour. Drain them, put them in a quart of fresh water with the teaspoon of salt, and simmer until tender (about 15 minutes). Drain, and then put them into fresh cold water. Drain again and cut away any fat or membrane. Cut them in bite-sized pieces, and they're ready for batter and frying.

Trim off and discard the zucchini tops and bottoms. Cut the trimmed zucchini into long, finger-sized spears. Trim and prepare the artichokes (pages 224 to 226), cutting them finally in wedges no wider than ¼ inch at the base. Soak the artichoke wedges in a quart of water mixed with the juice of 1 lemon until frying time. Break the flowerets off the cauliflower stem, wash them, and they're ready.

Put oil to a depth of at least 2½ inches into a big

pan and heat to 375° (or until hot enough so that batter frizzles and fries immediately on contact). Dip a few morsels of prepared ingredients into the batter, then put them on to fry. (Use your fingers for this, it's messier but easier and quicker.) The pieces will sink to the bottom immediately and slowly rise as they turn golden and cook. They do cook rather quickly, and must be turned over (a slotted spoon is good for this) as soon as they're golden on one side. Remove them when golden crisp all around, replacing them with more batter-covered pieces. Drain thoroughly, first over the hot oil, so that as much oil as possible falls back into the pan, and then on paper towels. Keep the oil at a very high heat during frying, and the process will go quickly. Serve immediately with wedges of lemon.

FEGATO ALLA VENEZIANA
Liver, Venetian Style

Calf's liver, sliced no thicker than ¼ inch, cooked quickly in olive oil on a layer of thinly sliced onions, is unbelievably kind to the palate in taste and texture.

    2 Spanish onions
    ¼ cup olive oil
    3 tablespoons unsalted butter
    ½ teaspoon salt
    2 pounds calf's liver or baby beef liver
    2 tablespoons chopped fresh parsley

Cut the Spanish onions in half, and then slice each half into the thinnest possible slivers to make about 1½ cups. If you don't have Spanish onions, use 1 big Bermuda. If using regular all-purpose kitchen onions, slice them as you would the Spanish onions, but soak them about 10 minutes in ice water and drain them carefully before using.

Heat the oil and butter over medium heat in a big frying pan. Add the slivered onions and sauté them until translucent. Add the salt as they cook.

If the liver is cut in the usual ½-inch-thick slices, put them down on a cutting board and cut horizontally through them to get slices no more than ¼ inch thick.

Add the thinly sliced liver to the onions, and sauté quickly, only 2 minutes per side. If cooked longer, the liver loses both flavor and texture, becomes dried out and dull. It should be just barely pink and moist when you cut into it. Add the parsley, stir, and cook another minute.

Serve with the onions and flavored olive oil on top of the liver.

FEGATO CON VINO BIANCO
Baby Beef Liver in White Wine

This recipe hardly needs an explanation, since it's name tells it all.

    4 tablespoons unsalted butter
    2 bay leaves
    2 pounds baby beef liver
    ½ cup dry white wine
    1 to 2 tablespoons chopped fresh parsley
      salt to taste

Melt the butter in a wide frying pan over medium heat. Add the bay leaves and the liver (which should be sliced no thicker than ¼ inch). Sauté 2 to 3 minutes on each side, and then pour in the wine. Continue cooking until the wine has just about evaporated, or another moment or so. Salt to taste.

Put the slices of liver on a serving platter, sprinkle with the parsley, and pour over them any remaining butter-wine sauce.

FEGATELLI DI MAIALE
Pork Livers

Little bundles of pork liver, cut just bigger than bite size and wrapped in a *rete*. The *rete* is the intestinal membrane, a white, lacy-looking thing you can purchase uncut in Italian meat markets. If you find the liver already cut and wrapped in the *rete,* make sure the butcher wasn't too generous with it, because it is fat, and all you need is just barely enough to wrap and cook the liver in.

    1 to 1½ pounds pork liver
    ½ pound of *rete*
      bay leaves
    2 tablespoons olive oil
      salt to taste
      freshly ground pepper to taste
    3 tablespoons wine vinegar

To prepare the bundles yourself, cut the pork liver into chunks about the size of a small egg. Cut the membrane just big enough to wrap up the chunks. Stick a bay leaf under the last flap of each bundle, and skewer the packet with a toothpick.

Pour the olive oil into a big frying pan, and add the liver chunks as the pan is heating. The membrane will start to melt the minute the pan gets hot. Salt and pepper generously. Sauté quickly, 1 to 2 minutes on a side, until the liver is nicely browned and the juices start to flow. The minute they do, add the wine vinegar, cover, and cook another 2 minutes, or until the vinegar stops sizzling. Serve with just a touch of the pan's sauce and big chunks of hot Italian bread.

ROGNONCINI TRIFOLATI
Veal Kidneys and Mushrooms

The closest we come in translating *trifolati* is "truffle style," which means slicing the kidneys as truffles should be sliced: in paper-thin wedges. But there's more to the dish than the slicing: its distinctive qualities come also from the combination of kidneys and mushrooms in a quick butter-lemon sauce salted by anchovies and garnished with parsley.

1¾ pounds veal kidneys
½ pound fresh mushrooms
2 or 3 anchovy fillets
3 tablespoons olive oil
1 garlic clove
3 tablespoons unsalted butter
  juice of ½ lemon
1 tablespoon chopped fresh parsley
  salt to taste
  freshly ground pepper to taste

Remove any veins and membrane from the kidneys and cut them into thin slices. Clean and cut the mushrooms into thin slices (cut them in half first and then cut each half into as many thin wedges as possible; obviously, big mushrooms are the best for this dish). Mash the anchovies to a paste.

Heat the oil in a medium-sized frying pan. Add the garlic, sauté until golden, and then discard it. Add the kidney and mushroom slices, and sauté over high heat 2 or 3 minutes, adding the butter and the anchovy paste and stirring everything all the while. As soon as the kidneys and mushrooms start to give up their juices, add the lemon juice and chopped parsley. Stir and continue cooking anther moment or two until the sauce has thickened a bit. Taste for salt, adding some if needed. Add pepper to taste and serve immediately.

FAGIOLI E COTICHE
Beans with Pork Rind

This is Italy's contribution to the pork-and-bean recipes of the world, another very hearty, very inexpensive, very nutritious dish for a crowd. The idea of pork (or ham) rind doesn't appeal to a lot of people at first, but they don't have to eat the rind, and invariably they go wild for the beans and the sauce, and eventually end up eating the rind after all.

    ½ **pound pork (or ham) rind**
    3 **tablespoons olive oil**
    2 **cups peeled plum tomatoes, coarsely chopped**
       salt to taste
       freshly ground pepper to taste
    2 **cans white beans** (*cannellini*), **with their packing**
       liquid, or 2 cups dried beans

BATTUTO
    2 **slices lean salt pork**
    1 **garlic clove**
    1 **small onion**
    1 **tablespoon chopped fresh parsley**

Cut the pork (or ham) rind into 1″ × 2″ pieces.
Put them in a pot with at least 2 quarts of water, and
boil, covered, for at least 1 hour, or until tender.

Make a *battuto* (page 24) with the salt pork,
garlic, onion, and parsley, and sauté it until golden in
the olive oil in a large stewpot. Add the plum tomatoes, the liquid in which the beans were canned, salt
and pepper to taste, and the now tender pork (or ham)
rind. Cook for 30 minutes, to reduce the sauce and
blend its flavor. Add the canned beans, heat through,
taste for salt, and adjust the seasonings if necessary.
Serve hot.

If you wish, you can use dried beans. Boil them in
1½ quarts of water for 2 minutes. Remove them from
the heat and let stand 1 hour. Return them to the heat
and simmer until tender. Add 1 cup of the water in
which the beans were cooked to the *battuto* when you
add the tomatoes, and proceed as above.

TRIPPA ALLA ROMANA
Tripe, Roman Style

Fresh tripe, the way Mamma made it, is boiled with
seasoning vegetables, cut in strips when tender, finished
in a sauce of tomatoes and mint, and served with a good
dash of *pecorino* (Romano) cheese.

2 pounds tripe
1 onion
1 carrot
1 celery stalk, with leaves
2 teaspoons salt

BATTUTO
2 slices lean salt pork
1 large onion
½ carrot
½ celery stalk
2 or 3 sprigs parsley

SAUCE
¼ cup olive oil
2 cups peeled plum tomatoes
2 teaspoons salt, or to taste
freshly ground pepper to taste
3 or 4 mint leaves
2 to 3 tablespoons grated Romano cheese

Most of the tripe in American markets has either been pickled or, if fresh, has already been boiled. For this recipe, buy the boiled, fresh tripe, wash it, and put it in a good-sized pot with the seasoning vegetables (onion, carrot, and celery) and the salt, add water to cover, and bring to a boil. Reduce the heat and simmer for at least half an hour, or until tender. Remove the tripe, cool it a bit, and cut it into strips ¼ inch wide, about 3 inches long.

While the tripe is boiling, make a *buttuto* (page 24) of the salt pork, onion, celery, carrot, and parsley. Sauté it until golden in the olive oil in stewpot. When it is golden, and the bits of onion are translucent, add the plum tomatoes, the salt, and several twists of the pepper mill. Bring to a boil, reduce the heat, and simmer about 5 minutes. Then add the strips of tripe, and cook at a slow boil for 1 hour, or until the sauce has thickened and darkened, and the tripe is well flavored and very tender. If the sauce has reduced too much before the tripe is really tender, add ¼ cup warm water.

At the end of the cooking, add the mint leaves and simmer another 5 minutes. Serve with a generous sprinkling of Romano cheese, if you're going Roman all the way. Some prefer half Romano and half Parmesan cheese, as it is less sharp.

SALSE E PASTELLE
Sauces and Batters

Here are 3 familiar sauces to use in cooking and serving meats that don't appear with the sauces in the pasta section.

The batters are for fish, meat, and vegetables.

SALSA DI POMODORO
Basic Tomato Sauce

This smooth, simple sauce is used in the preparation of many dishes and as a condiment as well. If very ripe, fresh plum tomatoes are at hand, use them: the sauce is instantly embellished.

    4 cups peeled plum tomatoes
    4 tablespoons olive oil
    1 carrot
    1 celery stalk
    1 onion
    3 or 4 sprigs fresh parsley
    3 or 4 fresh basil leaves
    2 teaspoons salt, or to taste
      freshly ground pepper to taste

Put the olive oil in a big saucepan and cut the plum tomatoes into bite-sized chunks over the pan so that no drop of juice is wasted. Coarsely chop the other vegetables and herbs, and add everything to the olive oil. Bring to a boil, lower the heat, cover, and simmer ationpt * *

for about half an hour. Uncover, taste for salt, adjust the seasonings if necessary, and simmer another 15 minutes or so, until the liquid has reduced and the tomatoes practically dissolved. Put the whole mixture through a sieve or a food mill, and use it any way you wish. If the sauce seems runny after being sieved, return it to the heat and let it bubble along until it has further condensed.

SALSA DI POMODORO E CIPOLLA
Tomato-and-Onion Sauce

This sauce is used with *Bollito di manzo* (page 115), *Polpette* (pages 129 to 130), and sometimes with fish fillets. It is also the base of certain omelets and vegetable dishes.

    3 medium cooking onions (or 1 huge Bermuda)
    3 tablespoons olive oil
    3 cups whole peeled plum tomatoes (fresh or canned)
    2 teaspoons salt, or to taste
      freshly ground pepper to taste

Cut the onion(s) in half, scoop out the little center core, and slice the halves into the thinnest possible slivers. If using regular all-purpose kitchen onions, you may want to soak them 5 or 10 minutes in cold water to make them milder-tasting. Drain well on paper towels.

Put the olive oil in a large frying pan over medium heat. Add the onions and cook them until they are limp and transparent. Turn off the heat for a few minutes to allow the oil to cool, then add the tomatoes. If using fresh tomatoes: cut them into bite-sized chunks before you add them. If using canned plum tomatoes: mash them a bit as they go in. Add the salt and a few grinds of the pepper mill to the sauce, and turn up the heat until the whole pan boils. Then lower the heat and simmer, stirring occasionally, for 20 to 25 minutes, or until the tomatoes have practically disintegrated and the liquids have reduced almost by half and the color has darkened.

MAIONESE
Mayonnaise

The Italian mayonnaise is the reduction to basics of all the mayonnaises in the world. It contains no spices, just a pinch of finely ground white pepper. The only variation allowed is the substitution of first-quality white wine vinegar for the lemon juice. By law, it should be made by hand: the color and texture are incomparable. Lawbreakers may use a blender, at the expense (minimal) of color and texture and an egg white, countered by the saving of time and nervous energy.

    1 egg at room temperature
    ¼ teaspoon salt
    ¾ cup olive oil
      juice of ½ lemon
      finely ground white pepper to taste

The lawful way to make mayonnaise (by hand): put the egg yolk and the salt in a bowl. Stir well with a wooden spoon. Add a few drops of oil, and stir constantly. As the oil is amalgamated, add a few more drops. This should be done without missing a beat, otherwise the mayonnaise *impazzisce*, literally goes crazy; it curdles. Keep stirring and adding oil by drops until half of the oil has been used. By now the mixture has the look and feel of mayonnaise, but it isn't. Add a few drops of lemon juice, and keep stirring. The mixture gets thinner and lighter with the addition of lemon, so add a few drops of oil to bring back the thickness. If the mixture hasn't gone crazy by this time, you're home safe.

If it has, you need another bowl and another egg yolk. Stir the egg yolk, and add a teaspoon of the crazy mixture. Keep stirring, and when the newly created mixture is well amalgamated, add a bit more of the crazy mixture and so on until you have a sane mixture.

Keep stirring, and watch your pace until all the oil and lemon are gone. Add a pinch of white pepper (don't add black if you have no white), stir well, and you have *maionese,* unforgettable on any poached fish (except for cod) or in *Insalata russa* (pages 238 to 240).

The unlawful way to make mayonnaise (with a blender): break the whole egg into the blender. Add the juice of ½ lemon, the salt, the white pepper, and 2 to 3 tablespoons of the olive oil. Blend until the mixture is homogeneous and thick. Then pour the rest of the oil in a steady trickle into the vortex at the center of the blender. Stop pouring oil only, and if, a small bubble of oil forms in the center. Blend until it disappears, and then add the remaining oil in a steady trickle. Blend a moment more. The final consistency of mayonnaise should be creamy and thick, not runny. When spooned, it should not peak but should slowly search out its own level of rest.

This recipe makes about 1 cup of mayonnaise, enough for 4 *maionese* lovers or 6 discreet admirers, and it doubles easily for more.

SALSA VERDE
Green Sauce

This sauce of parsley, garlic, and capers, held together with oil and vinegar, is a must for *Bollito misto* (pages 116 to 117). When made with lemon, it fancies up any fish in the market. It shouldn't be made in a blender, however, because that homogenizes it and spoils the texture.

      2 **cups parsley leaves**
      2 **tablespoons capers**
      1 **garlic clove**
    ½ **cup olive oil**
    ½ **cup wine vinegar, or the juice of 1½ lemons**
        salt to taste, or 2 chopped anchovy fillets

Chop the parsley, capers, and garlic into fine bits. If using the anchovies instead of salt, add them to the pile, and mince everything some more. Put it all in a mortar and grind to a paste. Add the olive oil, 1 tablespoon at a time, and keep on grinding until a very thick sauce consistency is reached. Then add the vinegar (or lemon, as the case may be) a little at a time in order to dilute the sauce until it is really spoonable. Taste for salt on a bit of bread and adjust the seasonings if necessary.

This sauce can be made ahead of time, and keeps well in the refrigerator with an extra drop or two of olive oil on top. It must, however, be brought to room temperature and stirred vigorously before serving.

PASTELLA PER FRIGGERE I
Batter for Frying I

Here is the basic batter used to fry vegetables like zucchini, artichokes, broccoli, and zucchini flowers, or apples, brains, shrimp, and squid. It's light, tasty, and crisp. This makes enough to fry zucchini for 6 people, for example.

      2 **eggs**
    1½ **tablespoons olive oil**
    ⅔ **cup warm water**
    ½ **teaspoon salt**
    ¾ **cup of flour**

Break the eggs into a bowl, add the oil, water, and salt. Beat until nicely mixed and homogeneous. Slowly sprinkle in the flour, beating constantly, until the mixture has the consistency of a good pancake batter. Let it sit for a couple of hours before using.

When you use this batter to coat cut-up vegetables or anything else, drop in only a few pieces at a time, turn them slowly with a fork to coat all sides, and then take them out and immediately put them into hot frying oil.

PASTELLA (CON LIEVITO) II
Batter (with Yeast) II

This even lighter, crisper batter is traditionally used to fry cod, but it is also delicious with vegetables.

    1 square fresh yeast, or 1 packet dry
 1¼ cups warm water
   ½ teaspoon salt
 1½ cups flour

Dissolve the yeast in the warm water, breaking it up a bit with a spoon and stirring to make sure it all melts. Add the salt and slowly sprinkle in the flour, beating with a whisk or a fork until all the flour is absorbed and the batter is smooth. Let rise in a warm place for at least 1 hour, or until it has doubled in bulk and become light and full of bubbles. Stir and use immediately.

CONTORNI
Vegetables and Salads

Contorni are not just side dishes in the American sense. They are an integral part of second courses, sometimes even bearing the brunt of the course. They are the vegetables and salads whose choice, until recently, depended entirely on the season.

Where garden produce is concerned, the pride and joy of most Italian cooks are the *primizie,* the first of the crop. They are smaller and, because they come from local truck gardens, they are the freshest. Even when crops have traveled a long way to the market, Italians still have a predilection for the smaller vegetables. It's a matter of taste.

Examples of the smaller-the-better philosophy are the 4-inch zucchini, the 6-inch eggplant, tiny peas, and green beans about the size of matchsticks. All of these make exquisite eating. The search for such produce is rewarding and brings to shopping a sort of breathless quality. We hope you'll find yourself exclaiming over new greens at the vegetable stand as we always are.

Our recipes stick with the vegetables usually found in the average American market or those that might show up in the home garden, hence the inclusion of stuffed zucchini flowers. When we recommend fresh plum tomatoes for a sauce, or fresh beans for a salad, we do so because the flavor is not only better but in some cases so different from the canned variety that only if fresh is used will the results be satisfactory. We have found fresh plum tomatoes at harvest time in Italian markets, while shell beans have shown up in the supermarket. For the really devoted cook-gardener, home-grown plum tomatoes aren't any more difficult to raise than salad tomatoes.

When we recommend frozen vegetables, we are simply recognizing the advantages of their enormous convenience: they're clean, cook rapidly, and, if watched and timed properly, are almost as satisfactory in taste and texture in certain dishes as the fresh. They are certainly better than nothing at all out of season.

When it comes to cooking vegetables, the same rigid rule applies as for pasta: they are cooked to the *al dente* stage. Like pasta, many are served with a sauce. The same vegetables also appear dressed with olive oil or deep-fried in basic batter. Some are stuffed, but for those vegetable dishes that have a meat filling, you must turn back to Chapter III.

ASPARAGI ALL'AGRO
Asparagus with Oil and Lemon

The quickest and simplest of dressings for nearly all the green vegetables is olive oil and the juice of a lemon.

    3 pounds asparagus
    2 teaspoons salt (for the water)
    3 tablespoons olive oil
      juice of 1 lemon

Break off the root end of the asparagus, stalk by stalk. It breaks exactly where the edible part begins, and cutting it arbitrarily either leaves a bit of root on or robs you of a bite of tender stalk. Wash carefully, and put in boiling salted water just to cover. (A big frying pan is ideal for this.) Bring the water back to a boil, cover, and reduce the heat a bit. Boil slowly about 5 minutes, or until a fork can easily pierce the broken end of the stalk. Lift the asparagus out with tongs, draining off as much water as possible.

After you've settled them on a serving platter, drain them once more by tilting the platter and spoon-

ing out the last of the water. Pour the olive oil over the
asparagus and baste 2 or 3 times. Add the lemon juice
and baste again, scooping up the dressing with a big
spoon until all the stalks are dressed. (If you haven't
a lemon on hand, use ½ tablespoon of wine vinegar.)
Serve warm or cold, as you wish.

ASPARAGI ALLA PARMIGIANA
Asparagus with Parmesan Cheese

Many, many dishes using Parmesan cheese are called
alla parmigiana. In this instance, bundles of asparagus
are dressed with butter and cheese, topped with a
poached egg, and served with more cheese.

A simpler way of preparing *asparagi alla parmigiana* is just to serve it with melted butter and grated
Parmesan cheese.

    2½ pounds asparagus
     2 teaspoons salt (for the water)
     6 eggs
     8 tablespoons unsalted butter
     6 tablespoons grated Parmesan cheese

Preheat the oven to 400°.

Break off the inedible hard ends of the asparagus
stalk by stalk, and discard them. Wash the asparagus
carefully and plunge it into salted boiling water. Cook
for approximately 5 minutes, or until tender but still
crisp. Drain thoroughly and arrange in 6 piles on an
oven-proof platter.

Poach 6 eggs, removing them from the water when
they are just barely cooked. Put an egg on each pile of
asparagus. Melt the butter and pour a bit over each egg.
Sprinkle with the Parmesan cheese and bake in a hot
(400°) oven for 2 to 3 minutes, or until the cheese has
melted.

ASPARAGI AL PROSCIUTTO
Asparagus with Prosciutto

Here is asparagus in its most elegant guise: fresh stalks are cooked *al dente,* then wrapped in thin slices of *prosciutto* and sprinkled with Parmesan cheese.

    2 pounds asparagus
 1½ teaspoons salt (for the water)
   ¼ pound *prosciutto*
    4 tablespoons grated Parmesan cheese
    8 tablespoons butter

Preheat the oven to 400°.

Break off the root ends of the asparagus stalk by stalk and discard them. Wash thoroughly and put in boiling salted water to cover. Bring to a boil, cover, and cook about 5 minutes, or until a fork goes through the base of the stalk easily. Lift out with tongs and drain on paper towels.

When they are cool enough to handle, divide the stalks into 6 even bundles. Wrap each bundle in a couple of very, very thin slices of *prosciutto,* securing them with a toothpick. Butter a cookie sheet and line the bundles up on it, sprinkle them with the Parmesan cheese, and put in a hot oven (400°) for about 3 minutes, or until the cheese has melted. Melt the butter in a saucepan, and when the bundles come out of the oven, put them on a platter, pour the melted butter over them, and serve.

BIETA ALL'AGRO
Swiss Chard with Oil and Lemon

The only difference between chard and all the other greens served *all'agro* is in the cutting and cooking of the stems, which are as good if not better than the leaves.

2 **pounds Swiss chard**
6 **teaspoons salt (for the water)**
3 **to 4 tablespoons olive oil**
1½ **tablespoons lemon juice**

Wash the chard thoroughly, because the stems are inclined to be packed with fine, black dirt. Cut off the stems and peel the ribs of the sturdiest stalks, which are a bit stringy. Cut all the stems into 2- or 3-inch lengths. Cut the leaves into big pieces.

Bring 6 quarts of water to a boil in a big soup pot. Add the salt and drop in the cut-up stems. When the pot comes back to a boil, add the leaves. When the pot returns to a boil the second time, taste the stems. If they are tender but still crisp, the chard is done.

Drain thoroughly in a colander, squeezing down the whole mass with a plate in order to press as much water out as possible. Put the drained chard into a deep serving platter. Add the oil, turning the chard over and over to distribute the oil evenly. Add the lemon juice, turn again, taste for salt and, if necessary, sprinkle on a bit of salt, and serve.

BROCCOLI ALL'AGRO
Broccoli with Oil and Lemon

Broccoli cooked *al dente* and dressed with olive oil and lemon juice can be served either hot or cold, depending on the day.

3 **good-sized stalks of broccoli**
1½ **teaspoons salt (for the water)**
4 **tablespoons olive oil**
juice of 1 large lemon

Break off all the flowers of the broccoli, and discard most of the stem, using only the top 2 inches, which should be cut into bite-sized pieces. Wash gently and drop into boiling salted water, just enough to cover. Bring back to a boil and cook until the bit of stem on

the flowers is tender but still crisp. Drain thoroughly
and dress with olive oil and lemon juice, turning the
flowers over carefully to coat them well but without
breaking them in the process. Serve warm or cold. If
preparing ahead of time, dress with the olive oil only,
and add the lemon juice at serving time.

BROCCOLI RIPASSATI IN PADELLA
Pan-Cooked Broccoli

Blanched broccoli is cooked in garlic-flavored olive oil.

3 big stalks broccoli
  salt to taste
2 garlic cloves
4 tablespoons olive oil

Break the broccoli heads by cutting off the flowers
one by one. Chop the top third of the stem into bite-
size bits and put both bits and flowers into boiling,
salted water. As soon as the water has returned to a
boil, remove and drain the broccoli. Peel the garlic
cloves, cut them in half, and sauté them until golden
in a frying pan in the olive oil. Discard the garlic, add
the drained broccoli, and cook over medium heat for
about 5 minutes, or until tender but still crisp and bright
green. Sprinkle with salt, and serve.

CARCIOFI FRITTI DORATI
Golden-Fried Artichokes

Thin slices of artichoke, dipped in flour, then in beaten
egg, and deep-fried to a golden crispness: these can be
served alone as a *contorno* or can be part of a *Fritto
misto* (page 194). This, definitely, is one of the dishes
that really merits two cooks: one to dip and one to fry.

6 **medium artichokes**
2 **lemons**
1 **cup flour**
4 **medium eggs**
1 **teaspoon salt**
   vegetable oil for frying

Tear off the tough outer leaves until they snap loudly as they break away. Cut off the bottoms of the stems and peel back with a paring knife over the point where the leaves were broken off to get to the outside of the heart of the artichoke. Turn the artichoke around and cut off about a third of the top of the remaining leaves. Then, as if peeling an apple, pare all the way around the top to cut off any remaining fibrous parts. The artichoke at this point looks like a closed flower bud. Slice the artichoke into quarters, exposing the choke, which looks like a thistle. Cut it out. Then slice the quarters in halves or thirds, so that the base of each piece is no thicker than ¼ inch.

As one by one the artichokes are cut and de-choked, put them in water with the juice of 1 lemon (to keep them from discoloring). When all are prepared, drain them and pat dry with paper towels. Put the flour in one bowl. Beat the eggs in another and add ½ teaspoon of the salt.

Pour frying oil into a big pan to a depth of at least 2 inches and heat it to 375° (or to the point where a drop of beaten egg sizzles and fries instantly). Dredge a few wedges of artichoke at a time in the flour, and then dip them into the beaten eggs and fry. Don't over-crowd the pan. As the artichokes turn golden, turn them to crisp the other side. Take them out when they're a nice toasty color, using a slotted spoon to let as much oil as possible drip back into the pan. Place them on paper towels on a hot platter. Keep on flouring, batter-ing, and frying until all are done. Sprinkle with the remaining ½ teaspoon salt. Serve hot with the other lemon cut into wedges.

In doing a batch this large, you may find the best way to serve everything hot and crisp is to return the fried artichokes to the hot oil for a moment, once they've all been fried. Drain again on paper towels, and serve immediately.

CARCIOFI ALLA PARMIGIANA
Artichokes with Parmesan Cheese

This rich, rich casserole of golden-fried artichokes is layered with tomato sauce and *mozzarella* and topped with Parmesan cheese, and is another really luxurious dish that is easily put together by two cooks in unison.

SAUCE

    1 big Bermuda onion
    4 tablespoons olive oil
    6 cups peeled plum tomatoes
1½ teaspoons salt, or to taste

ARTICHOKES

    6 medium artichokes
    1 lemon
    1 cup flour
    4 eggs
       vegetable oil for frying
    1 pound whole-milk *mozzarella*
 ½ cup grated Parmesan cheese
 ½ cup unseasoned bread crumbs

Preheat the oven to 375°.

To prepare the sauce, slice the onion into the thinnest possible slivers. Put the olive oil in a big skillet, and add the onions and cook over medium heat until they are limp and translucent. Add the plum tomatoes, mashing them as they go in. Add the salt, and simmer 20 minutes, or until the sauce has somewhat condensed, is darker in color, and of sauce consistency.

Prepare and fry the artichokes as in the preceding recipe. When they are drained, they're ready to layer in the casserole.

Slice the *mozzarella* as thin as possible, or grate it as coarsely as you can.

Put a thin layer of sauce in the bottom of an oven-proof casserole, then add a layer of fried artichokes, and add another layer of sauce, and finally a layer of *mozzarella*. Repeat the layering sequence until all the ingredients have been used. Cover with a generous sprinkling of Parmesan cheese mixed with bread crumbs. Bake (at 375°) for 20 minutes, or until the cheese has melted and the crumbs have turned a toasty brown.

If you want to make this dish ahead of time, fry the artichokes, let them cool and drain on paper towels, and make the sauce, but don't assemble the casserole until it is time to bake.

CARCIOFI ALLA ROMANA
Artichokes, Roman Style

Roman artichokes have no choke at all, so it's easy to make a *battuto* of herbs and poke a bit of it in between the leaves before cooking the artichokes gently in olive oil and water. With patience, however, you can de-choke the available kind of these exquisite vegetables.

    6 large artichokes
      juice of 1 lemon
    ½ cup olive oil

BATTUTO
    6 sprigs fresh mint
    ½ garlic clove
    6 sprigs parsley
    1 teaspoon salt
      freshly ground pepper to taste

Prepare the artichokes in the usual fashion (pages 224 to 226), but do not slice them. With your fingers, pry open the cleaned artichoke. Using the sharp point of a paring knife, cut down inside and around the thin center leaves. Then slant the knife to sever the round just cut. Scoop out the center. Next, hold the artichoke under running water and pull out with your fingers any remaining bits of choke. As the artichokes are cleaned, drop them in a bowl of water to which the lemon juice has been added.

Make a *battuto* (page 24) of the mint, garlic, parsley, salt, and pepper (3 or 4 twists of the mill). Drain the artichokes, and put a pinch or two of the *battuto* inside each one.

If you're lucky enough to find fresh, baby artichokes that haven't formed a choke yet, get a dozen of them, clean them, just open a few of the leaves at random, and stuff some of the *battuto* inside.

Put 1 cup of water and the olive oil in a pot (ideally, top-of-the-stove earthenware from Italy) that has a good cover and is just large enough to accommodate the artichokes standing on their heads, stems in the air. Put in the artichokes, cover, bring to a good boil, and then reduce to medium heat.

Cook for about 20 minutes well covered, then uncover, sprinkle with a little salt, and finish cooking, reducing the liquids to practically nothing. (Pierce the heart of the artichoke with a fork, and when it enters easily, the cooking is over.)

Remove the artichokes and place them on a platter, still head-side down. Pour over them any remaining liquid. Serve warm or cold.

CECI ALLA TOSCANA
Chick-Peas, Tuscan Style

Chick-peas, dressed with olive oil and flavored with a hint of rosemary and garlic, are served hot in Tuscany as the main part of a meatless meal. A chunk of tuna fish is a frequent companion, or if meat is served, golden fried cutlets.

2 1-pound cans chick-peas, plus their liquid
2 garlic cloves
1 sprig fresh rosemary, or 1 teaspoon dried
⅓ cup olive oil
   salt to taste
   freshly ground pepper to taste
2 tablespoons wine vinegar (optional)

Put the chick-peas and their packing liquid in a medium-sized saucepan, adding the garlic and rosemary. If you don't have fresh rosemary, which is easily picked out and discarded later, use the dry but wrap it with the garlic in cheesecloth for easy disposal. Add 1 cup of warm water to the pan, bring to a boil, and then simmer gently for 15 minutes. Drain, remove the garlic and rosemary, and dress with the olive oil, salt, and lots of pepper. (If you don't have first-quality olive oil or don't wish to use that amount, add a bit of vinegar, to taste.) Toss and serve.

CIPOLLINE AGRODOLCE
Sweet-and-Sour Pearl Onions

Small white onions can be cooked in a pungent sauce made with brown sugar and vinegar. With their sweet-and-sour flavor, they are a favorite *contorno* with *Bollito di manzo* (page 115), or any of the blander meat dishes.

1½ pounds pearl onions, or 1 24-ounce package
   frozen
8 tablespoons unsalted butter
1 teaspoon salt
3 heaping tablespoons brown sugar
3 tablespoons wine vinegar

If using frozen onions: defrost at room temperature, and spread them out on paper towels to drain off as much water as possible.

If using fresh onions: boil them first in salted water for 5 minutes and drain thoroughly.

Melt the butter over medium heat and add the drained onions. Cook, stirring from time to time, for about 10 minutes, or until tender. Salt, and add the brown sugar, mashing it into the bubbling butter and spreading it evenly around the pan. Cook until the sugar has melted and started to glaze the onions. Add the wine vinegar, bring back to a boil, stir, and cook another 4 or 5 minutes, or until the thickened sauce clings to the onions, and they are cooked through.

CIPOLLINE AL SUGO
Pearl Onions in Tomato Sauce

Onions and tomatoes really go together like salt and pepper, each accenting the other's best flavors. Frozen onions and canned plum tomatoes make it possible to enjoy a summertime dish all year long.

    1 24-ounce bag frozen pearl onions
    4 tablespoons unsalted butter
    1 teaspoon salt
      freshly ground pepper to taste
    1 tablespoon sugar
    1 cup peeled plum tomatoes

Melt the butter over medium heat in a big frying pan, and put in the onions with the salt, pepper (2 or 3 twists of the pepper mill), and the sugar. Stir with a wooden spoon to break up any clumps of onions and bring to a boil. Mash or sieve the plum tomatoes and add them to the onions. Stir, bring back to a boil, lower the heat, and cook about 15 minutes, or until the onions are tender and the tomatoes have been reduced to sauce consistency. Serve hot.

CIPOLLINE E PISELLI
Pearl Onions and Peas

Here is another case in which frozen vegetables can be used successfully in place of fresh. Cooked with a bit of butter, white wine, and sugar, the onions and peas have a sweet-and-sour flavor.

- 1 10-ounce package frozen pearl onions
- 3 tablespoons unsalted butter
  freshly ground pepper to taste
- ½ teaspoon salt
- 2 tablespoons sugar
- ¼ cup dry white wine
- 1 10-ounce package frozen peas
- ½ cup chicken broth (page 55)

Melt the butter in a large skillet, add the onions; freshly ground pepper, salt, sugar, and wine. When the onions have cooked about 5 minutes and are beginning to get soft, add the peas and enough chicken broth barely to cover. (If you don't have broth, dissolve ½ bouillon cube in ½ cup water.) Continue cooking over low heat until the peas are done. Do not overcook. The peas should still be bright green, and the onions shouldn't get soggy.

FAGIOLINI ALL'OLIO
Green Beans with Oil and Lemon

Fagiolini are the smallest of green beans and the most tender, but French-cut frozen beans, just barely cooked, make a year-round everyday substitute.

- 1 24-ounce package French-cut frozen beans
- 1½ teaspoons salt (for the water)
- 3 tablespoons olive oil
  juice of 1 big lemon

Bring about 3 cups of water to a boil, add the salt, and the whole bag of beans. Stir gently to separate bean from bean. Bring back to a boil, and keep a tasting fork handy to check when they are just barely done (about 3 or 4 minutes). They should be cooked, tender but still crisp. Drain immediately, put them in a serving dish, and dress with the olive oil. Toss gently, and then add the lemon juice. Toss again. Serve warm or cold. If preparing ahead of time, don't add the lemon juice until just before you are ready to serve.

FAGIOLI FRESCHI ALL'OLIO
Fresh Shell Beans with Oil

Fresh shell beans, cooked, cooled, and served with olive oil and vinegar, are a summer special, but don't pass this up if you haven't got fresh beans. Canned shell beans, cooked and packed in water and salt only, are a good substitute.

  3 pounds fresh shell beans, or 2 1-pound cans
  3 to 4 teaspoons salt (for the water)
  3 tablespoons olive oil
  freshly ground pepper to taste
  1 tablespoon vinegar (optional)

If using fresh beans: shell, and put them on to boil in abundant water with the salt. When the beans are tender, drain and put them into a serving bowl, cover with the olive oil, a dash of salt, and pepper (2 or 3 twists of the mill). Taste. Add the vinegar if you wish, but an Italian traditionally prefers his beans, especially if fresh, with oil alone. Serve warm or cold, depending on the weather.

If using canned beans: drain them thoroughly. If the liquid they are packed in is obviously thick, put the beans in a sieve to drain, rinse them under cold or warm water, and drain again before putting them in a serving bowl.

FAGIOLI FRESCHI AL POMODORO
Fresh Shell Beans in Tomato Sauce

Those lucky enough to have fresh shell beans and ripe
plum tomatoes owe it to themselves to make this superlative summer dish. While the beans boil the sauce
simmers, and the two finally meet and complete their
cooking together.

> 2 pounds fresh shell beans
> 3 teaspoons salt (approximate)

SAUCE
> 1 onion
> 1 slice lean salt pork
> 1 celery stalk
> 2 tablespoons fresh parsley
> 2 tablespoons olive oil
> 2 pounds fresh plum tomatoes, or 4 cups canned
>   salt to taste
>   freshly ground pepper to taste

Shell the beans, and put them on to boil in about
3 quarts of water and 3 teaspoons salt.

Chop the onion, salt pork, celery, and parsley into
a *battuto* (page 24) and sauté it until golden in the
olive oil in a pan big enough to hold the tomatoes and
eventually the beans.

If using fresh plum tomatoes: drop them in boiling
water for a couple of minutes to loosen their skins,
drain them, peel them, and chop them into chunks.

If using canned plum tomatoes: cut them into
chunks.

When the *battuto* is golden, add the chopped tomatoes and simmer for about 15 minutes, adding salt and
pepper to taste. When the tomato sauce has thickened,
drain the beans, and add them to the simmering sauce
to finish cooking. Serve hot when the beans are tender
to the fork but not so soft they've started to disintegrate.

FAGIOLI E TONNO
Bean-and-Tuna Salad

A traditional summer meal that makes marvelous, simple eating all year round, this salad has a host of variations, depending on how many garden-fresh vegetables are added. If made with fresh beans it has an even better flavor, but takes a bit more time.

BASIC SALAD

- 2 1-pound cans kidney or shell beans, or 3 pounds fresh
- 1 7-ounce can Italian tuna fish
- 4 tablespoons olive oil
- salt to taste
- freshly ground pepper to taste
- 2 tablespoons wine vinegar

POSSIBLE ADDITIONS

- 1 firm (barely ripe) tomato
- 1 medium Spanish onion
- 2 celery stalks
- 1 small cucumber
- ½ green or red sweet pepper
- more olive oil to taste

If using canned kidney or shell beans: drain them, and discard the liquid.

If using fresh beans: shell, and cook them in abundant salted boiling water until just tender. Do not overcook. Drain thoroughly.

Drain the tuna, and put both beans and tuna in a salad bowl. Add the olive oil, salt and pepper, and toss gently. Add the vinegar, and toss again. Serve with hot Italian bread.

If adding the summer vegetables, cut the tomato into quarters, sliver the onion, cut the celery and cucumber into very thin slices, and core the pepper and cut it into long, thin strips. Add to the beans and tuna with 1 or 2 more tablespoons of olive oil, a dash more salt, and 2 or 3 more twists of the pepper mill.

FIOR DI ZUCCHINE FRITTI
Deep-Fried Zucchini Flowers

The delicate lilylike flowers of the zucchini are stuffed with *mozzarella* and anchovies, and then are dipped in batter and fried golden crisp: an unbelievable experience in eating, as well as practical way to use what may have seemed only a decorative element in your vegetable garden. The flowers themselves are seldom seen in the market, as they're too fragile for packaging and shipping, but for those with a garden, a serving of *fior di zucchine* makes up for all the season's weeding.

    18 zucchini flowers
     1 pound whole-milk *mozzarella*
    18 anchovy fillets
     1 batch *Pastella I* (page 214)
       vegetable oil for frying

Remove the pistils inside the flowers and cut off any discolored or wilted part of the petals. Wash carefully in very cold water and set out to dry on paper towels. Dice the *mozzarella,* and cut the anchovies into 3 or 4 pieces each. Open the petals of the flowers, put in 3 or 4 cubes of cheese and 3 or 4 bits of anchovy, or just enough barely to fill but not to overstuff.

Make a batch of *Pastella I,* and gently dip the flowers in it, 1 by 1, coating them well with the batter. Heat the frying oil to 375° (or hot enough so that a drop of batter frizzles on contact), and fry the flowers a few at a time to a golden brown. Drain on paper towels, and serve hot.

FUNGHI TRIFOLATI
Mushrooms, "Truffle Style"

The adjective *trifolati* in this case has been warped with age. Literally, the mushrooms should be sliced like truffles, paper-thin, but the Tuscans have changed all that by slicing them just reasonably thin, so the texture

holds up under cooking. The dish is a delicate blend of
mushrooms, lemon, and parsley, with salt from the anchovies binding all the flavors together.

    1 pound fresh mushrooms
    ½ cup olive oil
    1 medium garlic clove
    2 to 4 anchovy fillets
    3 tablespoons unsalted butter
    ½ lemon
    2 tablespoons chopped fresh parsley

Slice the mushrooms vertically stem to top, first
in half, then in quarters and so on until you have reasonably thin wedges. Put the oil in a medium-sized
frying pan, add the garlic, sauté it until golden (not
fried), and discard it. Add the mushrooms, raise the
heat, and cook quickly while stirring them. Mash the
anchovies (the number depends on how salty they are)
and add them to the mushrooms. Then put in the butter. When the mushrooms are tender but still firm, squirt
them with the lemon juice, stir, and remove from the
heat. Add the parsley, stir again, taste for salt. The anchovies should have provided enough salt but if not,
add more salt. May be served immediately, or cold as
an *antipasto*.

INSALATA DI PATATE
Potato Salad

Potatoes, sliced in thin rounds, dressed in olive oil and
garnished with fresh basil leaves, salt and pepper, really
taste like summer. When prepared ahead of serving
time, their flavor deepens, and they taste even better.
Don't use baking potatoes because they disintegrate too
easily.

12 small all-purpose potatoes
 6 big fresh basil leaves
    salt to taste
    freshly ground pepper to taste
 6 tablespoons olive oil
 3 tablespoons wine vinegar

Scrub the potatoes and put them in boiling, salted water. Cook until tender (about 20 minutes), and then drain and cool them. Peel and slice in thin rounds, about ⅛ inch thick.

Chop the basil leaves coarsely. Put a layer of potato slices in the bottom of a big salad bowl, sprinkle with some chopped basil, some salt and pepper and a bit of olive oil and vinegar. Continue layering until everything is in, including the oil and vinegar. Turn gently until the potatoes are nicely dressed. Serve still lukewarm, or chilled.

INSALATA DI RISO
Rice Salad

Turin's gift of a summer salad is made with rice, tuna fish, eggs, capers, and olives, all tossed with olive oil and abundant lemon juice. Also included are the Italian pickled vegetables (carrots, cauliflower, cucumbers, and others) that are frequently found in the United States labeled "Giardiniera"—they are sour rather than sweet. Traditionally, seasonal fresh vegetables are the perfect substitute, adding the proper color and texture as well as flavor. This recipe serves 6 to 8 generously.

  2 cups long-grain rice
  2 hard-boiled eggs
  2 anchovy fillets
  ½ cup black and green olives
  1 cup Italian pickled vegetables
  2 tablespoons capers
  ½ green sweet pepper
  ½ red sweet pepper
  1 10-ounce package frozen mixed vegetables (2 cups)
  1 7-ounce can dark Italian tuna
  ½ cup olive oil
    juice of 2 lemons
    salt to taste
    freshly ground pepper to taste

Cook the rice in at least 6 cups of salted water, and drain in a colander the minute it's done, rinsing the cooked rice with cold water to wash off any remaining liquid and to separate the grains. Drain thoroughly and put it in a big salad bowl.

Chop up the hard-boiled eggs and anchovies, and add them. Cut the olives in half, and add them, along with the pickles and capers. Slice the peppers into thin, thin strips, and add them.

Cook the frozen mixed vegetables until tender, but be careful not to overcook them. Drain them and add to the rice mixture.

Drain the tuna fish, and break it up with a fork before adding it to the bowl. Pour in the olive oil, enough to dress the salad well. Add the lemon juice, taste for seasonings, and adjust if necessary before tossing again. Chill for at least half an hour, and serve.

INSALATA RUSSA IN GALANTINA
Russian Salad in Aspic

Chilled summer vegetables, seasoned with tart mayonnaise, glazed with gelatin, and decorated with slices of hard-boiled eggs and pickles: this salad comes in two versions, one for a *festa* and one for everyday. It uses either fresh or frozen vegetables, the cook's choice and the season of the year dictating which. Since this is a case of the more the merrier as far as vegetables are concerned, we have included corn, which is not in common use in Italy. This recipe serves 6 to 8 generously.

- 2 medium all-purpose potatoes
- 1 cup corn kernels, or ½ 10-ounce package frozen
- 2 cups peas, or 1 10-ounce package frozen
- 2 cups cubed carrots
- 2 cups French-cut green beans, or 1 10-ounce package frozen
- 2 cups mayonnaise (pages 212 to 213)
- 1 tablespoon wine vinegar or lemon juice (to be added to commercial mayonnaise)
- 1½ envelopes unflavored gelatin
- 2 cups beef (or chicken) stock (pages 53 to 55)
- 2 hard-boiled eggs

Scrub well the all-purpose potatoes (not the baking kind). Then cook them, whole and unpeeled, in boiling salted water until just tender to the fork. Drain, cool thoroughly, peel, and cut into tiny cubes.

Bring a big pot of salted water (1 teaspoon to the quart) to a boil and put in the corn. When it comes back to a boil, add the peas and carrots. When the pot boils again, put in the green beans, and cook the whole thing until the beans are just tender but still crisp and colorful (about 5 minutes). Drain everything in a colander, and let it cool and dry.

Prepare 2 cups of mayonnaise. If you use commercial mayonnaise, add the vinegar or lemon juice and stir well (or mix in a blender).

Put ½ an envelope of unflavored gelatin into 4 tablespoons of cold water in a small saucepan. Stir, and let it sit 3 to 4 minutes. Then put it over low heat, stirring carefully until the gelatin crystals have melted. Cool, and stir it into the mayonnaise.

Make the aspic with 1 envelope of gelatin dissolved in 2 cups cold beef or chicken stock, and heat as above. The stock can be made with 2 bouillon cubes and water, if you don't have the real thing. Cool by placing the pan over a big bowl full of ice cubes, so that you can watch its developing thickness and use it at the right moment.

Mix all the vegetables with the mayonnaise. Chill a big serving bowl or good-sized mold.

When the aspic has cooled to the point at which it is almost syrupy and thick, pour some in the bottom of the chilled mold and swirl it around to coat the bottom and sides. Put the lined mold in the refrigerator a moment or two to set it. Slice the eggs into thin slices and arrange them on the aspic. Pour in more thickened aspic, then half the vegetables. Pour some aspic around the edge of the bowl, filling any cracks. Add the rest of the vegetables, and finish with any aspic that may be left. Cover, and chill in the refrigerator for at least 2 hours.

When it's time to serve, dip the bowl or mold into warm water for a few seconds, cover with a big plate, and turn it over. The *insalata russa* now rests in all its chilled glory on a serving plate.

That's the *festa* way of making Russian salad. If you want to put it together with less ado about something, you can eliminate the aspic. Mix all the vegetables and the thickened mayonnaise. Shape it on a serving platter and decorate with hard-boiled eggs and Italian pickles. Chill, covered with plastic wrap, for 2 hours.

INSALATA
Salad

The normal, everyday salad in Italy is dressed with olive oil, wine vinegar, salt and pepper, and rarely a hint of anything else.

1 **large bunch or head salad greens**
4 **tablespoons olive oil**
  salt to taste
  freshly ground pepper to taste
2 **tablespoons wine vinegar**

No matter which green is used, it should be separated leaf by leaf, washed, drained, wrapped in a fresh kitchen towel, and chilled thoroughly in the refrigerator for half an hour before you cut it, and even then, give the greens a good shake to get out any remaining water.

Head lettuce, whether Boston or iceberg, should be broken in bite-size pieces by hand, as the knife bruises it. Escarole and endive can be either broken by hand or cut with a knife by putting all the stems or bases of the leaves together and slicing through the bunch every ½ to ¾ of an inch. Romaine, *insalata romana*, should also be cut in this fashion, not torn.

Put the broken or cut salad leaves into a big bowl, add the olive oil, and toss gently so that the leaves glisten with oil. Add the salt and pepper to taste, and toss again. Add the vinegar, and taste for seasonings. Adjust if necessary, toss again, and serve.

LENTICCHIE
Lentils

Lentils, cooked with the usual seasoning vegetables, are frequently served with sausage, but they make a good *contorno* for lots of other meats as well.

1 **1-pound bag dried lentils**
1 **garlic clove**
1 **big carrot**
1 **onion**
1 **celery stalk, with leaves**
  freshly ground pepper to taste
4 **peeled plum tomatoes**
3 **to 4 teaspoons salt, or to taste**

Examine the lentils a handful or so at a time in order to sort out and discard any bits of chaff or stone.

Wash them quickly by putting them in a sieve or colander under cold water.

Peel the garlic and the carrot, peel the onion and cut it in half, wash the celery stalk, and put them all, with the tomatoes and salt, in a big pot with the lentils and 9 cups of cold water. Add 3 or 4 twists of the pepper mill. Bring the pot to a boil, skim off any froth that may have formed, and reduce the heat to a simmer. Cook for about 45 minutes to 1 hour, or until the lentils are well cooked, and the liquid has reduced to practically nothing. Check the liquid level toward the end of the cooking time, because a heat that's too high can reduce the liquid before the lentils are tender, in which case a bit of water must be added.

MANTECATO DI PATATE
Whipped Potatoes

This is ordinary mashed potato glorified to golden yellow by beating in eggs and butter and flavoring it with a hint of nutmeg.

    6 to 8 baking potatoes
    ¼ to ½ cup milk
    1 teaspoon nutmeg
    4 tablespoons unsalted butter
    2 eggs

Peel the potatoes and cut them into quarters. Put them in cold, salted water, and cook them over a high flame. When the water boils, reduce the heat and cook about 20 minutes, or until soft to the fork.

Drain the potatoes thoroughly and put them back into the pan over very low heat. Using either an electric beater or a hand potato masher, beat the potatoes smooth, adding the milk a bit at a time, and the nutmeg and butter as you go along. The exact amount of milk depends on the size and quality of the potatoes: some take a little more, some take a little less. Aim for a finished product that's a little less stiff than regular mashed potatoes but not runny. When the potato is completely beaten and smooth, add the eggs, beat again, and continue cooking and beating another 2 minutes over low heat. Serve with almost any meat cooked in a sauce. If you want to be fancy about the dish, make peaks on the top with a fork or spoon, and put it under the broiler for a couple of minutes to toast before serving.

MELANZANE A FUNGHETTO
Eggplant, "Mushroom Style"

This is the best possible introduction to eggplant. Use it at its smallest size when it has the nicest texture and flavor: no more than 5 inches in length and 2½ inches in diameter. This size has a tender skin, fewer seeds, less bitterness. If you can't find eggplant of this description in your market or garden, turn to another recipe. In making *melanzane a funghetto,* eggplant is cooked to the color and texture of a small mushroom or *funghetto.*

>   6 small eggplants
>   5 tablespoons olive oil
>   2 garlic cloves
>   1 teaspoon salt
>   1 tablespoon minced fresh parsley
>   2 or 3 peeled plum tomatoes, coarsely chopped

Most small eggplants aren't bitter as are the big ones, but just to be on the safe side, cut them in half lengthwise, salt them liberally, and let stand for 15 minutes. Then scrape away the moist salt, cut again lengthwise into three spears and then into 1-inch wedges.

Heat the olive oil in a large frying pan, add the garlic, and sauté over medium heat until golden. Discard the garlic, add the eggplants, and stir as they cook for a few minutes. When the eggplants have absorbed the oil, salt them, and they'll release their own juices. Add the minced parsley, cook and stir for a moment, then add the coarsely chopped tomatoes. They'll add not only a bit of color but also some moisture to the sauce. Stir gently, lower the heat, and simmer for about 10 minutes, or until the eggplants can be easily pierced with a fork. (The length of time depends on the actual size and age of the eggplants.) The pulp of the eggplants should be tender but firm, the color and consistency about like a properly cooked little mushroom.

MELANZANE ALLA PARMIGIANA
Eggplant Parmigiana

Thin slices of eggplant, dipped in flour, deep-fried, and then layered in a casserole with tomato sauce and topped with Parmesan cheese, is what this recipe is all about. When two cooks are sharing the honors, one can make the sauce while the other does the frying. In any case, the eggplant must be sliced open and salted for the first step in this rather special casserole.

FRIED EGGPLANT
> 4 **small or 2 medium eggplants**
> **salt**
> 4 **tablespoons flour**
> **vegetable oil for frying**

SAUCE
> 1 **garlic clove**
> 1 **small onion**
> ⅓ **cup olive oil**
> 3 **cups peeled plum tomatoes**
> 3 **or 4 fresh basil leaves**
> **pinch of salt**
> **freshly ground pepper to taste**
> ½ **cup grated whole-milk** *mozzarella*
> 1 **cup grated Parmesan cheese**
> ½ **cup unseasoned bread crumbs**

Preheat the oven to 350°.

Slice the eggplants in half, salt liberally, and let stand about 20 minutes to get the bitterness out of them.

While the salted eggplant is waiting, prepare the sauce. Slice the garlic in half and mince the onion, and sauté both until golden in the olive oil in a medium-sized frying pan over medium heat. When the onion is transparent and the garlic golden, discard the garlic and add the tomatoes, basil, salt, and a few grinds of pepper. Let simmer about 15 minutes.

Scrape the now-moistened salt off the eggplant and cut the halves into lengthwise slices no thicker than ½ inch. Dredge the slices in flour, coating them well, and fry in hot oil until golden brown on both sides. Drain on paper towels.

In an oven-proof baking dish or shallow casserole, spread a layer of tomato sauce, then a layer of fried eggplant, sprinkle with some of the grated *mozzarella* and some of the Parmesan cheese. Repeat until everything is used up, finishing with tomato sauce. Sprinkle with bread crumbs and bake (at 350°) for about 15 minutes, or until the bread crumbs are toasted and the *mozzarella* melted.

MELANZANE RIPIENE
Stuffed Eggplant

Anchovies, olives, parsley, and capers, all chopped together, are the main flavorings in the stuffing, which is rounded out with unseasoned bread crumbs and a couple of plum tomatoes.

- 6 small or 3 medium eggplants
- 4 anchovy fillets
- ½ cup pitted black olives
- 1 tablespoon chopped fresh parsley
- 1 tablespoon capers
- 2 peeled plum tomatoes
- 2 tablespoons grated Parmesan cheese
- ½ cup unseasoned bread crumbs
- ½ cup olive oil

Preheat the oven to 350°.
Cut the eggplants in half lengthwise. Salt liberally,

let stand 30 minutes, and then scrape away the moist salt. Scoop out and reserve most of the pulpy center, leaving a ½-inch-thick shell. Put the pulp aside in a bowl. Blanch the shells in boiling water, drain, and let dry on paper towels.

Mince the anchovies, olives, parsley, and capers and add them to the eggplant pulp. Cut the tomatoes into chunks and add them along with the Parmesan cheese. Mix well, and add enough bread crumbs to firm up the filling and fill the eggplant shells. Sprinkle the remaining bread crumbs over the filled shells.

Oil a baking dish just large enough to hold the shells, and line them up in it. Dribble olive oil over the pan, making sure that each half-eggplant gets some. Bake (at 350°) for about 20 minutes, or until easily pierced with a fork. (The larger the eggplants, the longer the baking time.) Put them on a serving platter and pour over any juices left in the pan. These are served hot from the oven as a *contorno*, or cold as an *antipasto*.

PEPERONATA
Peppers with Onions and Tomatoes

Traditionally this dish was prepared ahead of time, and served cold as an accompaniment to any meat. The peppers and tomatoes had to be in season, which limited serving it to summertime. In the United States, however, green peppers are available almost year round, so the dish can be served hot in midwinter, when it is just as appetizing.

Romans, blessed with the light, dry *castelli* wines, have always made *peperonata* with wine. Southerners substitute water and wine vinegar, or just vinegar.

3 tablespoons olive oil
1 garlic clove
4 or 5 sweet peppers (red, green, and yellow)
3 medium onions
2 cups peeled plum tomatoes
1 teaspoon salt, or to taste
   freshly ground pepper to taste
⅓ cup dry white wine, or 3 tablespoons wine vinegar
   and 3 tablespoons water

Put the olive oil in a good-sized pot (with a cover) over medium heat. Cut the garlic in half, add it to the oil, sauté it to a golden brown, and then discard it. Cut the peppers open, discard their cores and stems, and slice them into long, thin strips. Cut the onions into quarters and cut off the bit of core at the bottom of each quarter. Add the peppers and onions to the flavored olive oil, and cook briskly, stirring constantly. As soon as they start to wilt, add the tomatoes, salt, and a few grinds of pepper. Stir well, and when the mixture is back to a boil, reduce the heat, and cover the pot. Simmer for 15 to 20 minutes, stirring occasionally. Then raise the heat, add the wine (or wine vinegar and water), stir, and boil uncovered 5 minutes, or until the sauce has condensed a bit and the vegetables have cooked. Serve hot or cold.

PEPERONATA E MELANZANE
Peppers, Onions, and Tomatoes, with Eggplant

There are French, Spanish, and Greek versions of this moist Mediterranean dish, a bouquet of peppers, onions, and chunked eggplant cooked with plum tomatoes. The Italian difference is that the vegetables are cooked to the *al dente* stage, retaining shape and texture, yet exchanging flavor.

3 small eggplants
4 sweet peppers
3 medium onions
1 garlic clove
1 red pepper pod, seeded, or a dash of Tabasco
3 tablespoons olive oil
2 cups peeled plum tomatoes, coarsely chopped
1 teaspoon salt, or to taste
  freshly ground pepper to taste
⅓ cup dry white wine, or 3 tablespoons wine vinegar

Half an hour before cooking time, wash the eggplant and cut it in half lengthwise. Sprinkle liberally with salt and set aside. When the salt has drawn out the bitterness of the eggplant (about 20 minutes), scrape it away with the blade of a knife. Cut into quarters and then into 1-inch chunks. Cut the peppers open, remove the core and seeds, slice into ½-inch strips. Cut the onions into quarters or thick wedges.

Put the garlic, pepper pod, and oil in the bottom of a big pot over medium heat. When the garlic is golden and the pepper dark brown, discard them, raise the heat, and add the peppers and onions. Cook quickly, stirring, until they begin to wilt. Then add the eggplant, and after 5 minutes add the chopped tomatoes (without their juice), the salt, and a few grinds of pepper, and stir well. Cover, lower the heat, and simmer for 15 minutes, stirring occasionally. When the vegetables are cooked, tender but still somewhat firm to the bite—and yet easily pierced with a fork—raise the heat, add the wine, stir, and boil for 3 minutes to blend the flavors and wine in the sauce and to reduce slightly the quantity of the sauce itself. Serve hot or cold.

PISELLI ALLA ROMANA
Peas, Roman Style

This is another dish claimed by the Romans for their proud use of *primizie*, the first tiny vegetables of the season, in this case, tiny new peas. Those lucky people with gardens can harvest their own new peas and make this recipe with them—that's real Italian cookery. If, however, you use the frozen tiny peas available at the ordinary American market and cook them with a hint of onion and *prosciutto* (or lean salt pork), you can achieve almost the same delicacy all year round.

- 2 10-ounce packages tiny frozen peas
- 4 tablespoons unsalted butter
- 1 small onion
- 4 slices lean salt pork, or 6 medium-thick slices *prosciutto*
- ½ cup dry white wine
- 1 tablespoon sugar

Defrost the peas at room temperature for an hour or so before cooking.

Melt the butter in a deep, wide (11-inch) frying pan. Mince the onion, cut the salt pork into ½-inch strips, and sauté both slowly in the butter until they are translucent. Add the peas, wine, and sugar, and cook over medium heat about 5 minutes, or until the peas are tender. Check for moisture in the pan during cooking, and if the peas don't provide enough to keep things juicy, add a little warm water (almost but don't quite cover the peas). When the peas are tender but still firm, some of the liquid will have evaporated, and the sauce, an integral part of this dish, will have thickened slightly.

If you wish to make this recipe fancier, substitute *prosciutto* for the lean salt pork. If you can't get tiny frozen peas, use the larger frozen ones, but watch out that they don't add too much moisture to the sauce. If they do, remove the peas to a hot serving dish when they're cooked, and reduce the sauce by cooking it over medium heat another 4 to 5 minutes. Pour the sauce over the peas, and serve.

POMODORI CON BASILICO
Tomato Salad with Basil

A salad of almost ripe, thinly sliced tomatoes, coarsely
chopped fresh basil, olive oil, and vinegar: it's simple
if you have the proper elements. The final flavor depends on having fresh basil and summer tomatoes, just
picked and not quite fully ripened. They must be still
slightly green, only pale pink on the bottom, firm
to touch, but red on the inside. Tomato fragrance and
flavor is at its height at this stage, which explains why
a lot of us grow tomatoes, now that we're so far from
the Italian markets, where they arrive on the very day
they're picked.

It is frequently served with a slice of fresh Italian
mozzarella, as well as with a piece of fresh Italian bread
so you can get up all the juices at the end.

    6 medium-sized, underripe tomatoes
    4 or 5 fresh basil leaves
      salt to taste
      freshly ground pepper to taste
    2 tablespoons olive oil
    1 tablespoon vinegar

Cut the tomatoes in half, then quarters and eighths
and so on, until you end up with ¼-inch wedges. Spread
them out on a deep platter or wide shallow bowl. Break
the basil leaves into bits and sprinkle them over the
tomatoes. Sprinkle with salt and 2 or 3 grinds of the
pepper mill, and add the oil and vinegar. To avoid
turning the tomatoes over and over, tilt the dish up on
one side, and with a big spoon scoop up the dressing
and baste the tomatoes over and over to get the essence
of basil thoroughly mixed with the oil, vinegar, and
tomato juices. Let stand about 15 minutes before
serving.

POMODORI GRATINATI
Stuffed Tomatoes

These tomatoes, stuffed with anchovies, capers, and bread crumbs, and baked in an oven, can be served hot as a *contorno* or cold as *antipasto*.

    6 big ripe but firm tomatoes
    6 anchovy fillets
    2 tablespoons capers
    ½ to ¾ cup unseasoned bread crumbs
    ½ cup olive oil
    ½ teaspoon salt
      freshly ground pepper to taste

Preheat the oven to 350°.

Mince the anchovies and capers together, add half the bread crumbs, the oil, salt, and pepper, and mix well until a good, solid paste has formed. If the mixture is too moist, add a bit more bread crumbs.

Cut the tomatoes in half and scoop out the seeds and center pulp, which you then put through a sieve, saving the nice juice that passes through. Fill the tomatoes, and add a bit of tomato juice to each one. Sprinkle with the remaining bread crumbs, and put a drop or two of oil on top of each tomato half.

Oil the bottom of a baking dish and line up the halves in it. Bake (at 350°) for half an hour, or until the tomatoes are cooked through.

SPINACI ALL'AGRO
Spinach with Oil and Lemon

Like all the other *all'agro* recipes, this is a simple matter of briefly cooking the greens in salted water, draining them well, and dressing them with olive oil and lemon juice. The amount of spinach really must be determined by the appetite of the group.

    2½ pounds fresh spinach
     1 teaspoon salt
     3 tablespoons olive oil
    1½ tablespoons lemon juice

Wash the spinach thoroughly and break or cut off any thick stems, saving only the tender, thin ones. Put about ½ inch of water in the bottom of a big pot. When it boils, put in the spinach, salt it, and stir carefully with a wooden spoon until the heat has wilted the spinach and the water has come back to a boil. Cook over medium heat for 3 or 4 minutes, stirring a couple of times. Drain when the spinach is just tender but still a lovely green. Press against the sides of the colander to get as much water out as possible. Spread the spinach out on a platter, sprinkle with the oil and lemon juice, and turn over gently, as you would a salad. Serve warm or cold.

ZUCCHINE ALL'OLIO
Zucchini with Oil and Lemon

Zucchini, the smaller the better, just barely cooked in boiling salted water, are served with a breath of garlic and parsley, olive oil, and lemon juice. This is not a dish for big zucchini, as they are too pulpy on the inside, too sturdy on the outside. It can be eaten warm or cold, depending on the mood.

    12 very small or 6 medium zucchini
        salt
     1 tablespoon fresh parsley
    ½ garlic clove
     2 tablespoons olive oil
        juice of 1 lemon (no more than 1 tablespoon)

Wash and clean the zucchini, cutting off the tops and bottoms and any bruised spots. Bring to a boil enough water to cover, add salt, and boil the zucchini whole, 3 or 4 minutes for the small ones, 8 to 10 minutes for the medium.

As soon as the zucchini are cooked and tender but still firm, drain them and cut them lengthwise, first in half and then in quarters. Put them on a serving platter. Mince the parsley and garlic together into fine, fine bits, and sprinkle them over the zucchini. Add the olive oil and lemon juice. Tilt the dish, scoop up the dressing, and baste over and over so that the oil and lemon pick up the garlic and parsley aromas and penetrate the zucchini without everything having to be tossed around. If you prepare the dish ahead of time, don't add the lemon juice until the last minute before serving.

ZUCCHINE AL SUGO
Zucchini in Tomato Sauce

If two cooks are on hand, one can make a tomato sauce while the other slices up the zucchini. Then everybody tastes to make sure the zucchini aren't overcooked and the sauce is the right thickness and flavor. (If the ingredients are garden-fresh, there is the real danger the dish will never get to the table, having been eaten away at tasting time.)

 1 big Bermuda onion, or 3 ordinary kitchen onions
 2 tablespoons olive oil
 ½ red pepper pod, seeded
 3 cups peeled plum tomatoes
 1 teaspoon salt, or to taste
 6 medium zucchini

Cut the onion into thin slivers and sauté them until golden in the olive oil over medium heat, stirring them to make sure they become translucent without browning. If using kitchen onions, soak the slivers 10 minutes in cold water, drain, and pat dry before you sauté them. While the onions are cooking, add the half pepper pod to them, discarding it when it turns dark brown. Cut the plum tomatoes into chunks and add them to the now translucent onions with the salt. Bring the mixture to a boil, reduce the heat, and simmer about 15 minutes (probably 20 if you are using fresh, ripe plum tomatoes), or until the liquid has reduced and the sauce has thickened and darkened in color.

Clean the zucchini, and slice into thin rounds. When the sauce is ready, add the zucchini and continue to simmer about 5 minutes, or until *al dente,* tender but not mushy. Taste for salt and correct the seasoning if necessary. Serve hot.

DOLCI
Desserts

Any native Italian or anyone who has ever been to Italy knows that Italian sweets, all of them, rank right up at the top in any international list of lovely desserts. Probably most world travelers have tasted *crostata, monte bianco, zuppa inglese,* and have enjoyed that mixed offering of taste and texture that only pastry can provide.

Many, many pastries are made daily in thousands of pastry shops up and down the peninsula, and are sold at a modest price. Preparing them is not necessarily complicated, but it is time-consuming. Hence, in most families, when it seems to be time to set aside the omnipresent fruit and to crown a meal with an especially festive dessert, someone is sent to the pastry shop.

Yet the tradition of homemade desserts is long, and most families have one, two, or three favorite recipes for cakes and cookies that go back generations. Some of them call for ingredients not always found around the proverbial corner. Some do take a lot of time, and that's not easily found either. We've chosen recipes that can be made at home, and don't always take a lot of time to prepare, such as fruits elaborated into *dolci.* Some have stood the test, not only of generations but also of various rather makeshift kitchens where practical limitations were overcome by the wish to make a proper dessert to culminate a proper feast. In fact, most family sweets do go with feast days, whether it be the celebration of a saint, a child, a republic, or a labor day. Some just represent the need to get together, family or friends, and enjoy a special morsel. With this group of recipes we invite you to treat yourself to some of the most delicious of Italian traditions.

ARANCI ALLA SICILIANA
Oranges, Sicilian Style

Peeled seedless oranges are sliced thin, dressed with lemon juice and olive oil, and sprinkled with black Sicilian olives. A dash of salt brings out all the flavors.

   6 seedless oranges
   6 tablespoons olive oil
   ½ teaspoon salt, or to taste
   24 black olives (Sicilian or Greek)
      juice of ½ lemon

   Peel the oranges, taking off as much of the white inner peel as possible. Slice in thin rounds and spread out on a large serving plate. Sprinkle with olive oil and salt (to your taste, but ½ teaspoon is the average amount).

   Marinate the olives in the lemon juice, 10 to 15 minutes. Distribute the olives over the orange slices. Tilt the plate, and with a large spoon scoop up the olive oil and juices and baste the oranges. Press down gently on some of the slices, so that more juice mingles with the oil. Baste a bit more and serve.

CILIEGE SOTTO SPIRITO
Preserved Cherries

Some of the best cherries of the season should be saved for winter: spices and vodka do the job. In Italy, grain alcohol is used, but that's not easily available in the United States. Serve 2 or 3 cherries to a person, with a teaspoon or so of the aromatic liquor, as an after-dinner treat.

   1½ **pounds Bing cherries**
   ½   **cup sugar**
   6   **cloves**
   1   **3-inch stick of cinnamon**
   2   **cups vodka, or enough to cover the cherries**

When you buy cherries for this kind of preserving, be sure they are not dead ripe. Choose very firm, red Bing cherries, fresh enough so that their stems are still bright green and well attached to the fruit. Wash the cherries and spread them out on a clean towel to dry. When they are dry, cut off the top of each stem, leaving just ¼ inch. (Don't use cherries without stems, because they tend to fall apart in the jar.)

Put the sugar in the bottom of a 1-quart sterilized jar with a good seal. Add the cloves, cinnamon, and cherries. Give the jar a shake or two to settle the fruit, and pour on enough vodka to cover completely the cherries. Seal tightly and let stand at least 4 weeks before serving.

FRAGOLE AL LIMONE
Strawberries with Lemon

Originally this was the one and only treatment given to wild strawberries in season. The fruit was washed in white wine, once as available in Italy as drinking water, drained, and then marinated. Domestic strawberries react nicely to almost the same routine.

   1½ **quarts fresh strawberries**
   ½   **to 1 cup confectioners' sugar, depending on the fruit's sweetness**
   juice of 2 lemons, strained

Wash the berries thoroughly and remove the stems. Crush a handful of them and leave the rest whole. Put them all in a bowl, pour on the sugar, and mix gently. Add the lemon juice and mix again. Chill in the refrigerator for at least half an hour before serving.

MACEDONIA
Italian Fruit Cup

A seasonal mixture of fruits, fresh and dried, cut into small pieces and flavored with white wine and Maraschino liqueur. In the summer, one can add melons, strawberries, cherries, raspberries, nectarines, and peaches. Just be sure not to crush any of the more delicate fruits in cutting and stirring.

> ½ cup seedless raisins
> ½ cup white wine
> 1 apple
> 1 pear
> 1 orange
> 1 small bunch red grapes
> 1 small bunch green seedless grapes
> 4 dates
> 4 dried figs
>   juice of ½ lemon
> 3 tablespoons sugar, or to taste
> 1 jigger (3 ounces) Maraschino liqueur
> 1 banana

Put the raisins to soak in the wine. Chop the apple and pear into bits (about ¼-inch pieces, so that you can get 3 or 4 morsels per spoonful) and put them into a serving bowl. Peel the orange, and cut it likewise. Slice the grapes open, seeding the red ones, and add them to the other fruits. Cut up the dates and figs, and add them. Pour in the raisins with their wine. Add the lemon juice, sugar, and Maraschino liqueur. Stir gently with a big spoon, and chill for at least half an hour. Just before serving, add the banana, sliced or diced. Stir once more.

MELE COTTE
Baked Apples

Baked apples with raisin and marmalade filling, cooked with a bit of white wine.

6 baking apples
½ cup raisins
½ cup white wine
6 tablespoons marmalade (orange, cherry, or apricot)
¼ to ½ cup sugar

Preheat the oven to 350°.

Put the raisins to plump and soak in the white wine. Wash and core the apples, making sure all the seeds are removed. Butter a baking dish that is just large enough to hold the apples and put them in. Put some raisins in the bottom of the well in each apple, add a tablespoon of marmalade (more if you desire), and then put in the rest of the raisins, filling each well. Sprinkle with the sugar, and pour the wine in which the raisins soaked into the bottom of the baking dish.

Bake for half an hour (at 350°), or until the apples are soft and puffy and the wine has mingled with the apple juices to make a splendid semi-thick sauce in the bottom of the dish. Baste with the sauce and serve hot or cold.

PESCHE RIPIENE
Stuffed Baked Peaches

Big, ripe peaches, whose stones are replaced by crushed almonds or almond cookies, are basted and baked in wine.

6 large Freestone peaches
1 large egg
½ cup confectioners' sugar
4 Italian macaroons, or 2 ounces slivered almonds plus ½ teaspoon almond extract
½ cup dry white wine

Preheat the oven to 375°.

Wash the peaches, dry them, and cut them in half. Remove the stones. With a spoon scrape out the red pulp around the hollow, and save it. Beat the egg and sugar until pale yellow and fluffy.

If using macaroons (*amaretti*), crush them, and add to the egg and sugar along with the peach pulp. Mix well. If using slivered almonds, toast them in the oven (as it is heating) 10 minutes, and then crush or mince them on a chopping board. Add to the egg and sugar along with the peach pulp and the almond extract.

Fill the centers of the peach halves with the prepared mixture. Butter a baking dish just large enough to accommodate the peaches and put the halves in. Sprinkle with the wine and bake (at 375°) for half an hour. Baste the peaches with the syrup in the bottom of the pan and return them to the oven for another 10 minutes. Serve warm.

GRANITA DI CAFFÈ
Coffee Ice

Strong black coffee with sugar, frozen in crystals, topped with whipped cream, is a favorite refresher all during the summer. It tastes like the best after-dinner coffee and makes any meal the better for its addition.

ICE

    3 cups very strong Italian coffee
  15 teaspoons sugar

WHIPPED CREAM

    1 cup all-purpose cream
    3 teaspoons sugar, or to taste

To get the right flavor, use an *espresso* coffeepot and Italian-roasted coffee.

While the coffee is still hot, pour it into a large Pyrex pitcher, stir in the sugar, and keep stirring until it has dissolved. Let the coffee cool a bit, then put it into ice trays in the freezer section of the refrigerator. After about an hour (depending on how cold the freezer really is), stir the contents of the trays with a fork, breaking up the crystals of frozen coffee that will have formed around the edges. Freeze another hour, stir again with a fork. By now the coffee is nearly completely frozen. Freeze for another hour, stirring at the halfway point and at the end. The *granita* is ready for serving when it's all frozen into crystals and is neither solid ice nor runny. If left in the freezer beyond this stage, it loses its characteristic texture of tiny particles of coffee ice, and should be broken up with a fork in a bowl before serving.

To serve, whip the cream, adding the sugar. Take 6 small glasses, put a tablespoon of whipped cream in the bottom of each glass, add to it ⅙ of the *granita,* and top each serving with 2 tablespoons or so of whipped cream.

MONTE BIANCO
Riced Chestnuts with Whipped Cream

Boiled chestnuts, flavored with vanilla and rum, whipped and sent through a potato ricer make the *monte* (mountain), which is capped with whipped cream for the *bianco* (white) of this rich and elegant dessert.

CHESTNUT PUREE

> 2 pounds chestnuts
> 1½ teaspoons salt
> 1 cup warm milk (approximate)
> 5 tablespoons confectioners' sugar
> 1 jigger brandy or rum, or 1½ teaspoons vanilla

WHIPPED CREAM

> 1 cup all-purpose cream
> 1 teaspoon vanilla
> 5 tablespoons confectioners' sugar

Score the chestnuts with a sharp knife and put them to boil in water to cover. Add the salt and cook them at least 25 minutes, or until soft. Drain, shell, and peel off the inner skin as quickly as possible (because they peel more easily while still warm).

Put the chestnuts back into a saucepan over very

low heat. Add some warm milk and mash them with an ordinary potato masher. At first they tend to break up into pea-sized pieces, but gradually they turn into a puree. Add more milk, a little at a time, and keep on mashing until all the lumps are gone.

When the chestnuts are a smooth, thick puree, add the confectioners' sugar and the rum or brandy (or the vanilla, if you wish to substitute it for the liquor). Mash a bit more and then pack the puree into either a cookie press with a ricer disk or into a potato ricer. Press all the puree through, letting it fall either into individual dessert dishes in little mounds or 1 big mound on a serving plate. Chill thoroughly.

Whip the cream, adding the vanilla and the sugar. Using a pastry bag, decorate the mounds (or mound) of chestnut puree with whipped cream as snow would cover a mountain peak.

ZABAGLIONE

One of Italy's most famous and favorite sweets is from the Piedmont. Made with beaten eggs and Marsala, it is served either warm or chilled in small glasses. It's also considered a great restorative, so much so that it's part of the language: a losing soccer player is greeted with jeers of "Go get yourself a *zabaglione!*"

  6 egg yolks
  6 tablespoons sugar
12 tablespoons Marsala wine

A round-bottom copper bowl is ideal for making *zabaglione*. Use the bowl as the upper part of a double boiler. If you don't have one, simply use an ordinary double boiler. Put the egg yolks into whichever container you are using, add the sugar, and beat until very pale and fluffy. Then put the container in hot but not boiling water, keep on beating, using a whisk or the blending speed of an electric beater. Add the Marsala

a little at a time, and keep on beating until the mixture
thickens to the consistency of a light batter.

Remove from the heat, beat a few moments longer,
and pour into 6 dessert glasses. It can be served lukewarm or, and we think it's much better, cold.

ZABAGLIONE BISCUÌ
Neapolitan Zabaglione

A Neapolitan variation of *zabaglione* uses egg whites
and whipped cream to make a richer but lighter dessert.

    1 recipe Zabaglione (page 264)
    3 egg whites at room temperature
    ½ cup all-purpose cream

Make the *zabaglione* as described in the preceding
recipe. When it is the consistency of light batter, beat
the egg whites until they are stiff and fold them gently
into the *zabaglione*. Whip the cream and fold that in,
too. Spoon the mixture into 6 dessert glasses or custard
cups and place them in the freezer for half an hour.

AMARETTI
Macaroons

The Italian macaroon is made with hand-crushed sweet
and bitter (*amare*) almonds, but finding the bitter ones
sometimes poses a problem for the American cook. This
adaptation of the traditional recipe uses almond extract
and canned almond paste to approximate the authentic
amaretti flavor and texture.

    1 8-ounce can almond paste
    1 cup granulated sugar
    4 egg whites (approximate) at room temperature
        pinch of salt
    2 teaspoons almond extract
    1 tablespoon confectioners' sugar

Mash up the almond paste in a bowl with a fork,
adding the granulated sugar as you mash. Add 1 egg

white and, using an electric mixer, beat until smooth (about 3 minutes).

In a separate bowl, beat ⅓ cup of egg whites (approximately 3 egg whites, but it depends on the size of the egg) until stiff but not dry. Add a pinch of salt midway in the beating.

Add the egg whites to the sugar and almond paste mixture and continue beating about 3 minutes, or until the batter is nice and light. Mix in the almond extract.

Butter and flour 3 cookie sheets and drop the batter by the half teaspoonful (demitasse spoons are good for this), leaving approximately 1½ inches between the cookies. Put the confectioners' sugar in a sieve and sprinkle each cookie with a bit of it. Let stand 1½ hours.

Preheat the oven to 350°. Then bake the *amaretti* for about 20 minutes, or until golden brown in color. Cool before removing from the cookie sheets with a spatula. Makes about 60 to 70 cookies.

BISCOTTI AI PIGNOLI
Pine Nut Cookies

These almond-flavored cookies, decorated with pine nuts, resemble Italian macaroons.

    1½ cups sugar
     1 tablespoon almond paste
    ½ teaspoon salt
     4 large eggs
     2 cups flour
    ½ teaspoon baking powder
     2 teaspoons almond extract
     2 tablespoons pine nuts
     2 tablespoons confectioners' sugar

Preheat the oven to 350°.

Place a mixing bowl over hot but not boiling water, or use a big double boiler. Put the sugar, almond paste, salt, and eggs into the bowl, and beat for 5 minutes, or until the mixture is lukewarm and looks like pancake batter. Make sure that the almond paste is well beaten also.

Take the bowl off the hot water and continue beating for another 5 minutes, or until the batter is cool and looks almost like frosting. Sift the flour with the baking powder and fold it gently into the batter. Add the almond extract and fold again.

Using a teaspoon, drop cookies 1½ inches apart on buttered and floured cookies sheets, decorate with pine nuts, and sprinkle with confectioners' sugar. Let stand about 5 minutes, and then bake for 15 minutes (at 350°), or until toasty and crisp on the outside. Makes about 60 cookies.

PASTA FROLLA
Sweet Pastry Dough

This is a rich, soft, sweet pastry dough, which is the basis of many cakes and tarts, most notably *Crostata* (below).

    2 cups unbleached flour
    ½ cup plus 1 tablespoon sugar
    7 tablespoons unsalted soft butter
    3 tablespoons vegetable shortening
    3 egg yolks
    1 whole egg
    1 tablespoon grated lemon or orange rind

Sift the flour and make it into a mound on your counter or pastry board. Add the sugar and turn the mound into a crater as for *pasta all'uovo*. Add the soft butter and the shortening in small dabs. Lightly beat the egg yolks with the whole egg and add them to the center of the crater. Start beating the egg more thoroughly with a fork, around and around the center, picking up flour, butter, and shortening as you beat. Continue until the flour, shortening, butter, and egg are all well mixed. Add the grated rind, put aside the fork, and work with your hands until everything begins to stick together and form a buttery, soft dough. It is very like cookie dough and should not be handled excessively. Shape it into a ball, wrap it in plastic wrap, and chill it for at least half an hour in the refrigerator. When it's chilled, sprinkle the counter with flour and roll it as needed.

CROSTATA
Sweet Pastry Tart

This looks like any other big tart but its crust is sweeter while its jam filling is sharper than that of similar pastries. The jams most frequently used in Italy are the pungent cherry or plum. American Damson plum comes close to the Italian, but American cherry is much sweeter. *Crostata* can be made in a pie pan, a rectangular cookie sheet, or a springform pan.

> 1 recipe *Pasta frolla* (page 267), chilled
> 1 jar plum or cherry jam (10 ounces approximately)
> 1 egg white, lightly beaten

Preheat the oven to 375°.
Butter the pan to be used.
Divide the chilled ball of *pasta frolla* into 1 large and 1 small ball. Roll the larger ball into a round or rectangle about ¼ inch thick and just big enough to fit your pan and come up no more than ¾ of an inch on the sides. If the dough does develop a crack or two because of its richness, it can be manipulated easily and pushed together again. Fill the crust with the jam.

Put the second smaller ball of dough on a floured surface and press it into a disk about ¼ inch thick. Cut it into strips ½ inch wide and place them lattice fashion on the jam. Brush with some of the lightly beaten egg white. Make a final long strip of dough and put it around the edges of the *crostata,* covering all the ends of the lattice. Crimp all the way around. Brush with the remaining egg white.

Bake for 10 minutes (at 375°), then reduce the

heat to 350° and bake for 20 minutes, or until the crust is toasty, puffed up a bit, and baked through. Chill before serving.

PASTIERA NAPOLETANA
Neapolitan Easter Cake

In Naples, it wouldn't be Easter without this cake made with sweet pastry crust, filled with whipped *ricotta*, eggs, and chocolate, flavored with zest of lemon and rum, and baked in an oven. The original uses whole-wheat kernels (softened for 8 days and cooked in milk) and rosewater as ingredients. This modern version using rice is just as acceptable and certainly more feasible.

    1 recipe *Pasta frolla* (page 267), chilled
    ½ cup long-grain rice
    2 squares baking chocolate
    1 pound *ricotta*
    1½ cups sugar
    3 medium egg yolks at room temperature
    1 tablespoon candied citron
    ¼ teaspoon cinnamon
        grated rind of 1 lemon
    ¼ cup rum, or 1 teaspoon vanilla
    2 egg whites at room temperature

Make the *pasta frolla* and chill it.

Cook the rice, rinse it with cold water in a colander, and set it aside to cool.

Melt the chocolate in a small double boiler and cool.

Preheat the oven to 350°.

Put the *ricotta* in a large bowl and beat it with an eggbeater until smooth. Add 1 cup of the sugar and stir in the egg yolks, 1 by 1, mixing after each addition until well blended. Add the citron, cinnamon, lemon rind, chocolate, and rum (or vanilla). In a separate bowl, whip the 2 egg whites with the last of the sugar until stiff and fold them into the egg-*ricotta* mixture. Lastly, fold in the cooked rice.

Break off about ⅔ of the *pasta frolla*, roll it into a round, and place it in the bottom of a buttered 10- or 12-inch cake or springform pan. Spread it out carefully along the bottom of the pan, pushing with your fingers, and up the sides about 1½ inches. Pour in the beaten *ricotta* mixture. Flour the counter, roll out the remaining piece of *pasta frolla* until it is about ½ inch thick, cut into ½-inch strips with a pastry cutter or knife, and place them lattice fashion on top of the *pastiera*. Brush with a bit of slightly beaten egg white (use one of the whites left over from the *pasta frolla*).

Bake for 1 hour, or until the lattice of the *pasta frolla* is nicely toasted and cooked through. Cool before serving.

BIGNÈ DI SAN GIUSEPPE
St. Joseph's Day Pastries

These light, puffy pastries can be baked and then filled with pastry cream, or deep-fried and then dusted with confectioners' sugar. *Bignè* are a must for St. Joseph's Day (March 19), but are so delicious the saint gets celebrated far more often than just on his feast day.

PASTRY
- 1¼ cups water
- 5 tablespoons unsalted butter
- ¾ cup flour, sifted
- 4 eggs
- 1½ tablespoons sugar
- ½ teaspoon grated lemon rind
- 1½ tablespoons cognac, or 1 tablespoon vanilla

BAKED BIGNÈ
- 1 recipe *Crema pasticcera* (pages 278 to 279)

FRIED BIGNÈ
- 1 quart vegetable oil
- confectioners' sugar

Bring the water and butter to a boil in a saucepan over high heat, and the minute the mixture boils, take the pan off and add the flour all at once. Stir immediately and vigorously with a wooden spoon, putting the pan back over the heat. The mixture turns into a paste right away and must be stirred continuously until it forms a ball and no longer clings to the sides or bottom of the pan. Keep on stirring a little more, until the paste sounds as if it were frying. Remove it from the heat, and cool.

Add the eggs, 1 at a time, stirring each in completely before adding the next. Keep on stirring until the soft dough is perfectly amalgamated, smooth, and rather like drop-cookie batter. Then stir in the sugar, the lemon rind, and the cognac (or vanilla). Cover and let stand 15 minutes in a cool place.

To bake: drop by the tablespoonful on a buttered cookie sheet, leaving at least 2 inches between them. Bake in a preheated 400° oven for 25 minutes, or until golden brown in color, crisp on the outside, and nearly doubled in size. Remove from the oven, break open gently, and cool. When cooled, fill with vanilla or chocolate *crema pasticcera,* or with sweetened whipped cream.

To fry: heat 1 quart of vegetable oil to 300° in a deep pan, and drop the dough in by the tablespoonful. It helps to work with 2 spoons, 1 for dipping up the dough and the other for scraping it off the first spoon (both should be dipped in the oil). Don't drop in more than 4 or 5 *bignè* at a time, and leave plenty of space for them to swell up. As they fry, they will keep turning themselves over, once the first side is done to a toasty brown. The temperature of the oil will go up as the *bignè* cook, and since they must start at a lower than frying heat, turn the heat down after each group has cooked, so that the second and third installments start, like the first, at about 300° and finish cooking at 350°. Starting with oil that is too hot will overcook the *bignè* outside and leave the inside undercooked.

When nicely browned and puffed-up, remove with

a slotted spoon, drain on paper towels, and finally sprinkle with a bit of confectioners' sugar.

BABÀ

A sweet bread baked as a big cake or more commonly as individual cupcakes soaked in a rum-flavored syrup. So perfect a sweet is this that to describe someone or something terribly good, a Neapolitan would say, "È nù babà!"

SWEET BREAD

    ½ cup golden seedless raisins
    ½ cup unsalted butter
    ½ cup warm (110°) water
  1½ packages dry yeast
    3 cups flour
    2 eggs plus 1 egg yolk
    ⅓ cup confectioners' sugar
    ½ teaspoon salt
    1 teaspoon vanilla

RUM SYRUP

    1 cup sugar
    1 cup water
    ¾ cup dark rum

Soak the raisins in a bowl of hot water in order to plump them up.

Melt the butter over a low flame, and let it cool. Heat the water until it is hot to the touch (110°) and dissolve the yeast in it. Mix with 1 cup of the flour until you have a soft, sticky dough. Cover and let rise in a warm place for about half an hour, or until doubled in bulk.

In another bowl, beat the eggs and sugar until very pale and fluffy. Slowly sift a cup of flour into the egg mixture. Add the melted, cooled butter, mix well, and add the raised dough, the salt, and the vanilla. Keep on mixing until the egg mixture and raised dough are well amalgamated. Slowly add enough of the last cup of flour to turn the dough into a soft bread dough. Knead it well (using the last of the flour) on the counter, until it is smooth, elastic, and soft. Punch it down on the counter, sprinkle with the plumped-up raisins, and knead them in.

The dough may be cooked in a tubular pan (8 inches in diameter and 3 inches tall is a good size) or in cupcake pans. In either case, butter the pan well, sprinkle with a bit of granulated sugar, and shake out any extra. Put only enough dough in the pan to fill ⅓ of it. Let rise 1½ hours, or until well over the edge of the pan, in a closed, unheated oven. When the dough has risen, leave the pan in the oven and turn on the heat, setting the thermostat at 400°. Bake for 35 to 45 minutes if using the tubular pan, 25 minutes for the cupcake pans. The top should be a toasted brown. Test with a toothpick or a long, slim skewer; if the *babà* is well done, the skewer comes out clean.

Cool the *babà* slightly, and put it on a platter.

To make the rum syrup, boil the sugar and water over a high heat for 10 minutes, add the rum, boil another minute, and the syrup is ready to use. Pour it over the cooling *babà,* and baste from time to time until all the syrup has been absorbed.

CANNOLI ALLA SICILIANA
Sicilian Filled Pastries

This is a double treat from Sicily: crisp fried pastry and creamy *ricotta.* Either one could definitely stand on its own, but combined they become *cannoli.* The pastry was once fried wrapped around pieces of *canna* (bamboo cane), hence the name. Today we substitute for the cane 1-inch aluminum piping available in Italian or European cookware shops. As for the filling, this recipe calls for the addition of whipped cream to achieve the light texture of the traditional one made with delicate, fresh, Sicilian *ricotta.*

PASTRY
- **1 cup flour**
- **¼ teaspoon salt**
- **1 scant tablespoon sugar**
- **1 tablespoon soft unsalted butter**
- **¼ cup white wine**
  vegetable oil for frying

FILLING
- **2 cups *ricotta***
- **1 cup whipped heavy cream**
- **3 tablespoons sugar (or more if you wish)**
- **2 tablespoons candied fruits, or 3 tablespoons cocoa and 2 tablespoons chocolate bits (jimmies)**
- **1½ teaspoons vanilla**

PASTRY: place the flour in a mound on a pastry board or counter. Make a well in the center, and put in the salt, sugar, and dabs of the soft butter. Add the wine, and with a fork start stirring in the center. Keep on until most of the flour has been absorbed, and you have a paste you can work with your hands.

Knead the paste until it is smooth and has picked up almost all the remaining flour. Roll it out no thicker than a noodle, and cut it into 3½″ × 3½″ squares, if you are using 5-inch-long, 1-inch-diameter *cannoli forms*. The diagonal of the squares should not be longer than the forms, so adjust the size of the squares to the length of the forms.

Place the *cannoli* forms diagonally on the squares. Wrap the pastry around the form, 1 corner over the other, and press the corners to hold them together. If the corners don't stick with pressure, moisten a finger with water, apply it to the contact point, and press again.

Cover the bottom of a frying pan with about ¾ inch of vegetable oil and heat it to 375°. If you don't have a thermometer, drop a bit of dough in. If it immediately starts to blister and turn a toast color, the temperature is right. Because *cannoli* cook very fast and swell in size during the process, you may find 3 is a

good number to cook at a time. Put them in the hot oil,
turning them carefully when one side is done. Remove
them as soon as they have become crisp, a uniform
toast color, and rather blistered all around. The forms,
naturally, get terribly hot: a pointed pliers is the easiest
tool with which to lift them out of the pan. Hold the
form with the pliers and give a gentle push with a fork
to slip the fried *cannolo* off the form. Drain the *cannoli*
on paper towels. Put the forms aside to cool. When
cooled, rewrap, and continue frying until all are done.
If you want to work very quickly, have about 18 forms
on hand (which is approximately what this recipe
makes) all wrapped and ready before you begin frying.

Cannoli, when cooked and left unfilled, will keep
crisp a day or so in a tin or a dry place.

If you want to make more than 18 *cannoli,* the
recipe doubles easily using 2 cups of flour, ½ teaspoon
salt, 1½ tablespoons sugar, 2 tablespoons soft unsalted
butter, and ⅔ cup of wine. If you are kneading and
rolling on a pasta machine, which is ideal for this particular dough, start at the highest number and bring it
down to #3.

FILLING: put the *ricotta* in a bowl and fold in the
whipped cream, adding the sugar as you fold. Chop the
candied fruits to tiny slivers no bigger than grains of
rice and fold in all but about a teaspoonful. Add the
vanilla.

Using a spatula or a broad knife, fill the *cannoli*
first from one end and then from the other. Press the
filling in gently to make sure the center is full. Scrape
each end to smooth out the cream and decorate the
ends by dipping them in the remaining candied fruit
slivers.

If you want to make the filling chocolate, substitute cocoa for the candied fruits in the cream-*ricotta*
mixture, and decorate with grated chocolate or the
chocolate jimmies.

The *cannoli* should not be filled too long before
serving, as that softens the pastry. The filling, however,

can be chilled, and both parts of this elegant dessert can be made ahead of time and assembled shortly before the meal.

FRAPPE
Sweet Fried Pastry

The traditional sweet for Carnevale, *frappe* are made with the same dough as *cannoli,* cut into strips, tied in a single knot, deep-fried, and dusted with powdered sugar.

> **1 batch pastry for *Cannoli* (pages 273 to 276)
> confectioners' sugar**

When you reach the point of cutting the pastry dough, cut it into strips 1½ inch wide and about 6 inches long. Take each strip and make a single knot in the center.

Heat the frying oil to 375° or to the point at which a piece of dough frizzles and blisters immediately on contact. Fry a few knotted strips at a time (they fry very quickly), turning them the minute they are a golden toast color on one side. When golden on all sides, remove immediately with a slotted spoon, let them drain a minute over the pan, and then on paper towels. Sprinkle with confectioners' sugar, and serve warm or cold.

TORTA MADDALENA
Maddalena Cake

Similar to a sponge cake, *torta Maddalena* is very light, very delicate, but its top crust is almost like a meringue or frosting. The main secret in the making is the beating: lots of it, most simply done with a hand-held electric beater.

8 tablespoons unsalted butter
3 large eggs at room temperature
2 egg yolks
1½ cups sugar
1¼ cups pastry flour
¼ teaspoon salt
1 lemon peel, grated

Melt the butter over a low flame, and cool.

Preheat the oven to 375°.

Heat water in a big pan almost but not quite to boiling. Combine the eggs, egg yolks, and sugar in a heat-proof bowl big enough to fit comfortably in the hot water. You can use a big double boiler, but a bowl makes beating and scraping much easier. A copper bowl, the kind used for beating egg whites high and stiff, is ideal. Beat the mixture with an electric beater over the hot water until it becomes very, very pale yellow and thick and nicely warm to the touch. This should take about 2 minutes. Remove the bowl from the water and continue beating until the mixture is completely cool and very thick (about 3 minutes). Sift the flour 3 times, adding the salt. Put aside the beater, and very slowly fold the flour into the eggs. Fold in the cooled, melted butter, and when completely blended, fold in the grated lemon rind.

Butter and flour a 12-inch round cake pan. Pour in the batter and bake (at 375°) for about 30 minutes. Cool completely before removing from the pan; otherwise, the crusty top will crack. A springform pan is even better than an ordinary pan.

PAN DI SPAGNA
Sponge Cake

Literally, the name means "Bread of Spain," but in the very beginning it was probably called *pan di spugna,* or sponge bread. A light, bright yellow versatile cake, it is delightful by itself as well as part of other desserts.

     5 large eggs at room temperature
1½ cups sugar
1½ cups unbleached flour
    1 teaspoon vanilla
    ½ teaspoon grated lemon peel

Preheat the oven to 350°.

Separate the eggs, putting the yolks in a large bowl and the whites in a smaller but still adequate one. Add the sugar to the yolks, and beat until pale yellow and the consistency of a good frosting. Beat the whites until they stand stiff in peaks. Gently fold the whites into the yellows, using a flat spoon or spatula, putting in a bit at a time and slowly turning the batter over and over until the egg-sugar mixture is all absorbed. When folding, be sure to go all the way to the bottom of the bowl and around the edges.

Sift the flour 3 times and fold it in slowly a bit at a time. By now the batter has doubled in bulk. Fold in the flavorings.

Butter and flour 2 9-inch layer-cake pans or 1 8-inch square pan. Pour in the batter and bake (at 350°); layers take approximately 20 minutes and the square pan takes 30. When done, the cake should be toasty and crisp on top, and a toothpick comes out clean when stuck into it.

Layers usually don't rise above the pans' edges, and can be turned upside down to cool. The square cake rises above the edge and unless you have a special rack, must be cooled face up. Either way, *pan di spagna* must be cool before you work with or cut it.

CREMA PASTICCERA
Pastry Cream

This is a basic pastry cream; it can be either vanilla with a hint of lemon flavor or all chocolate. This recipe provides enough for filling and topping a *Zuppa inglese* (pages 280 to 281) or filling a batch of *Bignè* (pages 270 to 272).

4 tablespoons sugar
4 egg yolks
4 tablespoons flour
2⅔ cups milk
1 teaspoon vanilla
2 ounces unsweetened baking chocolate, grated, or
1 teaspoon grated lemon peel

Put the sugar, egg yolks, and flour in a saucepan, and stir hard and fast with a wooden spoon until the mixture is smooth and light yellow and all the sugar has dissolved (which has happened when you can't hear it grating on the sides of the pan).

In another saucepan heat the milk to scalding (it will form a skin on top just before it boils). Slowly pour the hot milk into the egg mixture, stirring constantly over medium heat. Keep stirring (always in the same direction to prevent curdling) and cooking over medium heat until the mixture starts to boil and thicken and coat the spoon. Add the vanilla. Lower the heat at this point, add either the chocolate or the lemon peel, and continue cooking for another 4 minutes or so until the *crema* is really thick, the consistency of pudding. Remove from the heat and put a piece of plastic wrap right down on the surface of the *crema,* to prevent a skin from forming as it cools.

The *crema* is ready to spread when it has cooled to room temperature. It may also be made hours ahead of use and stored in the refrigerator, but if you do that, bring it to room temperature before spreading.

To make a batch that is half chocolate and half vanilla to use in *zuppa inglese:* divide the cream into 2 saucepans just as it starts to thicken. Add 1 ounce of grated unsweetened chocolate to one of the pans and ½ teaspoon grated lemon peel to the other. Reduce the heat, and continue cooking and stirring both pans for about 4 minutes, or until the *crema* is of pudding consistency. Cover and cool as above.

ZUPPA INGLESE
Layered Sponge Cake with Pastry Cream

Zuppa means "soup" and *inglese* means "English." This dessert vaguely resembles a glorified English trifle, and many people consider this the reason for its name. We prefer to believe the source is the vernacular distortion of *inzuppare* (to soak, to drench) and of *intriso* (medley), which in some Italian dialects sounds like *inglese*. There are many regional versions of *zuppa inglese*, but the ingredients remain basically the same. The two most common versions are the layered *zuppa* and the *zuppa* in a mold. The latter sometimes uses *savoiardi* (ladyfingers) instead of *pan di Spagna* (sponge cake). Rosolio, a red Italian liqueur made of rose essence and spices, is commonly used for color and flavor. As for the other liqueurs, the choice is dictated by preference or by what is available in the family pantry. Here is our way of assembling the layered and the molded versions.

1 recipe *Pan di Spagna* (pages 278 to 279)
1 recipe *Crema pasticcera,* half vanilla and half chocolate (pages 277 to 278)
½ cup Rosolio
¼ cup rum
¼ cup brandy
½ ounce unsweetened baking chocolate, grated (for layered *zuppa* only)

LAYERED ZUPPA: Bake 2 layers of *pan di Spagna* in 9-inch round pans; prepare the vanilla and chocolate *crema pasticcera.*

The first step in assembling the *zuppa inglese* is to cut in half horizontally each round of cake, making a total of 4 layers. Work slowly and use a serrated knife. (1) Put the first layer crust-side down on a serving platter. Sprinkle with ¼ cup of the Rosolio. Spread this layer with half the chocolate *crema,* smoothing it to the edge with a wide knife. (2) Put the second layer on, crust-side down, sprinkle with the rum, and spread with half the vanilla *crema.* (3) Put the third layer on, crust-side down, sprinkle with the brandy, and spread with the remaining chocolate *crema*. (4) Sprinkle the cut side of the fourth and final layer with the remaining ¼ cup of Rosolio, and then put this layer on, crust-side *up*. Spread with the rest of the vanilla *crema,* and sprinkle with the grated chocolate. Chill at least half an hour before cutting.

MOLDED ZUPPA: Bake 1 *pan di Spagna* in an 8-inch square pan; prepare the vanilla and chocolate *crema pasticcera*.

Cut the cake in thin (less than ½ inch) slices, and then cut all of them in half vertically. Take a deep bowl (4 inches deep and 9 inches in diameter is a good size) and line the sides with half-slices of cake, sponge-side against the bowl. Cover the bottom with 2 or 3 slices, sponge-side down. If necessary to trim the pieces to size for this first layer, reserve the scraps to fill in gaps. (2) Dribble ¼ cup of the Rosolio on the slices in the sides and bottom. Spread the bottom with chocolate *crema*. (3) Cover with more slices of cake, sprinkle with the rum, and spread with vanilla *crema,* using some to fill the cracks in the side walls. (4) Add another layer of slices, sprinkle with the brandy, and spread with chocolate *crema*. Use any remaining *crema,* chocolate or vanilla, to finish crack-filling. (5) Place a final layer of slices over the entire top, using any reserved scraps of cake to fill in gaps in what will be, when the bowl is inverted for serving, the base of the *zuppa inglese*. Sprinkle with the remaining ¼ cup of Rosolio.

Chill for at least half an hour. Unmold by turning the bowl upside down onto a serving plate. To serve, slice in wedges as you would a layer cake.

SVOGLIATURE
Snacks

The Italian *svogliature,* in terms of food, can be translated as snacks. They do stay the appetite while you are waiting for a more structured meal, but even more than that, they are designed to satisfy a socio-gastronomic whim of the moment. "Let's have a pizza" is a clarion call among friends to get together and have a good time, sharing a pizza and a few glasses of wine. Formalities, ponderous thoughts, or the worries of the day are not allowed around the table: they would definitely spoil a pizza, *calzone, crostino,* or any other *svogliature.*

PIZZA

Pizza, like pasta, has been internationally elected to represent Italian cookery. "Pizza pie" is an accepted term, even if in translation it means only "pie-pie." For a pizza *is* a pie, and therefore covers a multitude of variations whose common attribute is a bottom crust of bread dough baked in an oven. If the real pizza could stand up, it would surely be *pizza napoletana:* a thin, crisp crust of bread dough, a bit of olive oil, *mozzarella* cheese, fresh, ripe plum tomatoes, a pinch of oregano, a few anchovies, and that's all.

It is fair to assume that the pizza's origins are as old as bread-making. When all the loaves had been shoved in the oven, the baker would take a small ball of leftover dough, flatten it into a disk, flavor it with whatever was handy, and cook it in the hot oven. Time and imagination have produced many kinds of *pizze*. Purists tend not to recognize them and stay with the classic *napoletana*. Yet all *pizze* should be appetizingly light and tasty, with the flavors well balanced and not overpowering.

The secrets (if they can be called that) of a good pizza are the right bread dough, the freshness of the ingredients, and, most of all, the oven. Ideally, this should be a wood-fired brick oven, but this is practically impossible to find today. Even in Italy, brick ovens are dying of old age, and are being replaced by gas or electric ones. *Sic transit gloria pizzae.*

This fact alone, however, should not deter anybody from trying a homemade version. With a minimum of care, and a bit of love and enthusiasm, a very acceptable pizza can be produced. The following are a few guidelines:

THE DOUGH:

(1) Flour should be the unbleached, all-purpose kind.

(2) Cake yeast is preferable, dissolved in lukewarm water, but dry yeast is easier to find and will work well if you use quite warm water to dissolve it (110°). Water that is too hot will let all the zip out of the yeast before it has a chance to work in the dough.

(3) Go easy on the salt. Sprinkle it on after the yeast and water have amalgamated with the flour.

(4) Knead until you have a smooth, elastic ball of dough.

(5) Roll out the dough no more than ⅛ inch thick.

(6) Pizza may be made in rounds in individual pizza tins or in pie pans, but most home pizza-makers use cookie sheets to bake large rectangular pies that will serve a crowd.

THE TOPPING:

(1) The topping or filling should not be runny,

not overloaded with spices, and not too complicated a combination of flavors.

(2) Use whole-milk *mozzarella* cheese, as it melts more like Italian *mozzarella* and retains more of its softness on cooling.

(3) Use fresh mushrooms, not canned.

(4) Use fresh (if possible), very ripe, peeled plum tomatoes, cut into chunks. If they're not available, use canned, but do not use the liquid; sometimes tomatoes are put up in a very watery juice that will make a soggy mess of a pizza.

(5) Preheat the oven to 450° to 475°, and keep an eye on the baking pizza the first few times you make it, to correct the timing if necessary.

Each recipe for the various *pizze* that follows is enough for a full batch of dough, but if you want to make different kinds of *pizze* at one time, as we do, adjust the quantities in the toppings accordingly. We find that this system is more fun and satisfies and varying tastes of 6 to 8 people.

PASTA PER PIZZA
Pizza Dough

No two pizza-makers seem to produce the same dough, and no ordinary kitchen stove has an oven that bakes like the old-fashioned brick oven. This recipe, adapted for the American oven, produces 4 12-inch rounds or 4 10″ × 15″ rectangles (the size of cookie sheets).

> 5 cups unbleached flour
> 2 packets active dry yeast
> 2 cups warm water
> 1 teaspoon salt
>   olive oil

Put the flour in a mound on your counter or pastry board and make a well in the middle. Pour the powdered yeast in that well. Add just a bit of warm water to the yeast and start stirring it with a fork. As it gathers flour and a paste starts to form, add more water. Keep on stirring and adding water to the paste until all the water is used.

Then start working with your hands. At first the dough seems hopeless and very raggedy. But in about 2 minutes it takes on the tough shape and consistency of play dough, and will continue to pick up the remaining flour as you knead back and forth. Add the salt. Keep on kneading until the dough is soft, smooth, and warm. At the end of about 15 minutes you should have a very smooth ball, so light in texture you can see your handprint briefly before the dough bounces back. If, after all the original flour has been used, the dough begins to stick to the counter, sprinkle with some extra flour.

Put a teaspoon or so of olive oil in a bowl at least twice as big as the finished ball of dough. Roll the dough around in the oil until it is well coated. Cover the bowl with plastic wrap, sealing it well. Put in a warm place and let it rise until doubled in size.

Preheat the oven to 450°.

Punch the dough down, cut in fourths, and flatten each piece out on a floured surface. Roll the pieces into rectangles to fit a cookie sheet (10″ × 15″) with a border ½ inch high, or into circles to fit pizza or pie pans. Flour the pans very lightly, and put the dough on them. Push the dough with your fingers up and into the corners and around the edges to make a slight border to hold any kind of topping. Now you are ready to add your topping.

Bake (at 450°), the time depending on the type of pizza. Usually it takes about 20 minutes total timing to get a well-baked pizza, one that's toasty and crisp on the bottom and edges.

PIZZA NAPOLETANA
Neapolitan Pizza

Possibly the pizza most familiar to all of us is made with a layer of slightly crushed ripe plum tomatoes and grated *mozzarella* cheese, salted with anchovy fillets and flavored with just a hint of oregano.

    1 recipe Pizza Dough (pages 287 to 288)
    olive oil
    3 to 4 cups peeled plum tomatoes
    1 pound whole-milk *mozzarella*
    1 2-ounce can anchovy fillets
    ½ teaspoon oregano
    salt to taste

Preheat the oven to 450°.

Prepare and roll the pizza dough, and brush it lightly with a pastry brush dipped in olive oil.

Cut the plum tomatoes into chunks, discarding as many seeds and liquid as possible, and spread them over the dough more or less to cover it. Grate the *mozzarella* as coarsely as you can, or chop it into tiny bits. Sprinkle generously over the tomatoes. Cut the anchovies into inch-long pieces and spread them around. Sprinkle with oregano and dribble a bit of olive oil over the entire surface. Salt lightly.

Bake in a hot oven (450°) 20 to 25 minutes, or until the crust is crisp and golden, the cheese melted and blended with the tomatoes. Serve hot.

PIZZA COI FUNGHI
Pizza with Mushrooms

A favorite variation on a theme, this pizza takes advantage of fresh mushrooms.

1 **recipe Pizza Dough (pages 287 to 288)**
1 **pound fresh mushrooms**
   olive oil
2 **to 3 cups peeled plum tomatoes**
1 **pound whole-milk** *mozzarella*
   salt to taste
   freshly ground pepper to taste

Preheat the oven to 450°.
Prepare the pizza dough.
Slice the mushrooms as finely as possible.

Brush the pizza dough with oil, using either a pastry brush or your fingers. Cut the tomatoes into chunks and spread them out on the dough. Grate the *mozzarella,* or chop it finely, and sprinkle it over the tomatoes. Add sliced mushrooms to cover the entire pizza. Salt lightly and add a bit of freshly ground pepper. Sprinkle with drops of olive oil and bake about 20 minutes (at 450°), or until it is crisp and toasty around the edges, the cheese melted, and the mushrooms cooked.

PIZZA AI FUNGHI
Mushroom Pizza

This is a pizza without tomatoes and cheese. The mushrooms do the whole job.

1 **recipe Pizza Dough (pages 287 to 288)**
1½ **pounds fresh mushrooms**
   olive oil
1 **garlic clove, minced**
¼ **teaspoon salt**
2 **tablespoons fresh parsley, minced**

Prepare the pizza dough.
Preheat the oven to 450°.
Slice the mushrooms as finely as possible, and then sauté them briefly in a big frying pan with 6 tablespoons of olive oil and the minced garlic. As soon as the mushrooms have absorbed most of the oil, add the salt and the parsley, stir, and cook 1 minute longer.

Spread the mushrooms over the pizza dough, salt

snacksy(at

lightly, and dribble olive oil over the surface. Bake (at 450°) 15 to 20 minutes.

PIZZA CON MOZZARELLA E PROSCIUTTO
Pizza with Mozzarella and Prosciutto

This is a relatively nondrippy pizza which, if cut into bite-sized squares, is a marvelous snack to go with before-dinner drinks.

    1 recipe Pizza Dough (pages 287 to 288)
      olive oil
    ½ pound thinly sliced *prosciutto*
    1 pound whole-milk *mozzarella*

Preheat the oven to 450°.
Prepare the pizza dough and brush it with olive oil.
Cut the *prosciutto* into pieces about 1-inch square and spread them on the dough.
Grate the *mozzarella* or chop it into tiny bits and sprinkle all over the pizza.
Bake (at 450°) about 20 minutes, or until the dough is nicely toasted and the cheese has melted. Cool 5 minutes or so before cutting.

PIZZA CON CIPOLLE
Onion Pizza

This is an old family favorite: pizza flavored with slivered onions and rosemary.

    1 recipe Pizza Dough (pages 287 to 288)
    1 big Bermuda or Spanish onion
    1 teaspoon coarse salt
      freshly ground pepper to taste
    3 teaspoons dried rosemary
      olive oil

Preheat the oven to 450°.
Prepare the dough, spreading it out on the tins and brushing it with olive oil.

Slice the onion into thin slivers and sprinkle them over the dough. Pat lightly in order to press them into the dough. Sprinkle with coarse salt, a generous amount of freshly ground pepper, and finally add the rosemary. Dribble olive oil over everything.

Bake for about 20 minutes (at 450°), or until the dough is crisp and toasted, as will be some of the onions.

PIZZA MARGHERITA

This is a pizza for those who love the semisharp flavor of Parmesan cheese which, blended with tomatoes, is a pleasant contrast to the *mozzarella*.

> 1 recipe Pizza Dough (pages 287 to 288)
>   olive oil
> 3 to 4 cups peeled plum tomatoes
> 1 pound whole-milk *mozzarella*
> ¾ cup grated Parmesan cheese
>   salt to taste
>   freshly ground pepper to taste (optional)

Preheat the oven to 450° and prepare the dough, brushing it lightly with olive oil.

Cut the tomatoes into chunks and spread them around on top of the dough. Top the tomatoes with grated *mozzarella*. Sprinkle the pizza with grated Parmesan cheese as evenly as possible. Salt (and pepper, if you wish) very lightly, and sprinkle with olive oil.

Bake 20 to 25 minutes (at 450°), or until golden, the cheeses having melted completely and blended with the tomatoes.

CALZONE
Pizza Turnovers

This is a pizza in disguise: the dough is the same but the topping becomes a filling. The translation of *calzone* is "breeches," but don't ask why. Perhaps because the filling should never be bigger than its breeches; if it is, you have a catastrophe in the oven.

> 1 recipe Pizza Dough (pages 287 to 288)
> 2 eggs
> 1½ cups *ricotta*
> ½ cup grated Parmesan cheese
> ¼ teaspoon salt
> ½ pound whole-milk *mozzarella*
> ⅓ pound *prosciutto*

Preheat the oven to 450°.

When the pizza dough has risen, roll it out on a floured surface and cut it into circles about 8 inches in diameter.

Put the eggs in a bowl and add the *ricotta*, Parmesan cheese, and salt. Mix well.

Cut the *mozzarella* into tiny cubes and the *prosciutto* into ½-inch strips.

Put some of the cheese-egg mixture on the center of each round of dough. Add some *mozzarella* and *prosciutto*. Fold the round in half to enclose the filling and press down all around the edge to seal the dough shut.

Lightly oil 2 (perhaps 3, depending on their size) cookie sheets, and put the *calzone* on them. Brush the top side of the *calzone* with oil.

Bake for 25 minutes, or until the edges are toasty and the tops golden. Serve hot (with knife and fork).

CRESCENTI
Pastry Pillows

The name *crescenti* means "something that rises or swells up." Made of a simple flour-and-water dough rolled very thin, *crescenti* are first cut into strips and then diagonally into pieces about 1½ inches long. Our children nicknamed them *gonfiati* (blowups) and ate them with confectioners' sugar or honey as a snack with hot chocolate or *caffe latte*. In the Emilia-Romagna region, *crescenti* are served plain with *salame* or *prosciutto* and a good dry wine.

    4 cups flour
    2 tablespoons olive oil or shortening
    ½ teaspoon salt
    ½ teaspoon baking soda
    ½ cup water
      oil for frying

Put the flour in a heap on your counter, table, or pastry board. Make a well in the middle, add the oil, salt, and baking soda. Add the water to the center and mix the liquids around and around with a fork, picking up flour as you go. Keep mixing (if necessary, add a bit more water) until a thick dough forms. Put aside the fork and knead the dough thoroughly until it is soft, elastic, and uniform, like pasta dough. Form into a ball. Tidy up the working surface, removing any stuck-on pieces of dough.

Sprinkle the working surface with flour and roll the dough out like a piecrust until it is as thin as a coin, as they say in Italy. Cut into 2-inch-wide strips, and then on the diagonal into pieces about 2½ inches long. Use either an ordinary table knife for this or a pastry cutter.

Heat the frying oil to 375°, or until a piece of dough dropped in frizzles and start to swell on impact. Put as many pieces of cut dough into the hot oil as will fit comfortably. Turn them over the minute they've swelled on the top side and turned toasty brown on the under side. When both sides are crisp and golden, remove with a slotted spoon and drain on paper towels.

Serve hot or cold, with or without powdered sugar.

SUPPLÌ
Rice Croquettes

Another solution for a snack or even an *antipasto* is a batch of rice croquettes. They're held together with a bit of *ragù,* flavored with nutmeg and Parmesan cheese, rolled into shapes the size of an egg, and have a morsel of *mozzarella* hidden in the center. No one we know makes the *ragù* especially for *supplì* so this recipe simply happens when you have an extra cup of sauce.

> 3 cups long-grain rice
> 3 teaspoons salt
> 3 tablespoons unsalted butter
> 1 cup *Ragú I* (pages 50 to 51)
> 2 large eggs
> ¼ teaspoon nutmeg
> 2 tablespoons grated Parmesan cheese
> ½ pound whole-milk *mozzarella*
> 1 cup unseasoned bread crumbs
>   oil for frying

Combine the rice, salt, butter, and 6 cups of cold water in a big saucepan, and bring to a boil. Stir, cover, reduce the heat, and simmer for 12 minutes, or until the rice is just cooked, *al dente.* Stir a couple of times while cooking. Let the rice cool to lukewarm.

Mix the *ragù,* eggs, nutmeg, and Parmesan cheese into the lukewarm rice. Cool completely.

Cut the *mozzarella* into ½-inch cubes.

Take a heaping tablespoon of rice, about the size of a jumbo egg, place it in the palm of your hand. Put 1 or 2 cubes of *mozzarella* more or less in the center of the rice in hand. Compact the rice ball as you would a snowball, and then pat it into an oblong shape. Roll it in bread crumbs, patting gently to get as many crumbs as possible to stick to the outside. Continue scooping, stuffing, rolling until all the rice balls are made. Let them rest about 10 minutes before frying.

Put about ¾ inch of frying oil in the bottom of a heavy skillet. Bring to a high heat, lower the *supplì* one by one into the hot oil, and brown thoroughly on all sides, turning gently. Drain on paper towels, and serve warm.

SUPPLÌ IN BIANCO
Rice Croquettes II

Any dish served *in bianco* means it's served without sauce. These croquettes, not necessarily white, can be made without waiting for that extra cup of *ragù* to come around.

>   3 cups long-grain rice
>   3 teaspoons salt
>   3 tablespoons unsalted butter
>   ¼ teaspoon powdered saffron (optional)
>   3 tablespoons grated Parmesan cheese
>   2 large eggs
>   ¼ teaspoon nutmeg
>   ½ pound whole-milk *mozzarella*
>   1 cup unseasoned bread crumbs
>   oil for frying

Cook the rice as in the preceding recipe, adding the saffron during the last 3 minutes of cooking. Stir in the Parmesan cheese, cool the rice to lukewarm, and then mix the eggs and nutmeg into it.

Shape and fry the *supplì* as in the preceding recipe.

CROSTINI
Oven-Toasted Sandwiches

An extra 15 minutes is all you need to make *crostini* for 2 that taste and look like a party. The bread is layered with *mozzarella, prosciutto,* and a touch of anchovies. You have to eat them with a fork.

>   8 slices Italian bread
>   6 thin slices *mozzarella*
>   3 slices *prosciutto*
>   2 to 3 tablespoons olive oil
>   2 tablespoons unsalted butter
>   3 anchovy fillets

Preheat the oven to 450°.
Cut the crusts off the bread and put 4 slices in

each of 2 individual small casseroles that are just large enough to hold the slices standing upright. Put the slices of *mozzarella* between all the bread slices in both casseroles. Put *prosciutto* next to the *mozzarella* in 1 of the casseroles. Sprinkle the 2 sets of slices with olive oil and bake until toasted (at 450°) for 15 minutes.

Meanwhile, melt the butter. Mash the anchovies and add them to the butter, heating just long enough to blend the two.

When the *crostini* come out of the oven, pour the anchovied butter over the bread slices that have no ham between them. Divide each of the *crostini* in half, and serve with a glass of cold dry white wine.

BRUSCHETTA
Grilled Bread

Slices of Italian bread, brushed with olive oil and even more lightly with garlic, toasted over hot coals; this may be the ancestor of America's garlic bread. Those who wish to forego the garlic may substitute a few drops of vinegar. Both versions are usually served together when an outdoor grill is going or there's a picnic.

1 round loaf Italian bread
1 or 2 cloves garlic (depending on the number of slices of bread used)
  wine vinegar (optional)
  olive oil
  salt to taste

Cut the bread into slices about ¾ inch thick. Cut the garlic in half and rub 1 side of each slice of bread lightly with it (or sprinkle on a few drops of vinegar instead). Brush the same side with olive oil. Place the slices with the oiled sides up on an open grill. When they are toasted, turn and grill the second sides. Add a few drops of olive oil and salt. Serve with country dishes, or use as antipasto with a glass of wine while waiting for the rest of the meal.

Menu Suggestions

One day in Bologna, while checking old recipes against the new, we came across a turn-of-the-century cookbook, perhaps the first to be used widely as such in a country of mother-to-daughter recipes. The book, addressed to "Dear Housewife," lists sample menus for everyday consumption. One of these, taken at random, reads like this:

Open with various antipasti
Broth
Boiled veal and chicken with spinach
Cold rabbit
Intermezzo: mussels in white sauce
Suckling veal cutlets with truffles in red sauce
Roast venison (quail)
Sweets: French cream; angel cake
Close with fruit and assorted cheeses

There were twenty-three other such samples, all reading more like an opera libretto than a family menu, especially for that time. If anything, they represent, in that day of the emerging middle class, either something to dream about or something to strive for in case the king came to dinner. There aren't many kings these days, and so we suggest in a spirit of realism the following combinations of dishes likely to be found any day or Sunday on a family table. Then and now.

Recipes for all the specific dishes suggested in the following seasonal menus appear in this book. Consult the index for page references; consult your local market for fresh fruits and salad greens.

PRIMAVERA
Spring

Antipasto misto	Mixed Appetizers
Riso e scampi alla veneziana	Rice with Shrimp, Venetian Style
Carciofi alla parmigiana	Artichoke with Parmesan Cheese
Insalata	Mixed Green Salad
Crostata	Sweet Pastry Tart
Fettuccine alla panna	*Fettuccine* with Cream
Saltimbocca	Veal Slices with *Prosciutto*
Cipolline agrodolce	Sweet-and-Sour Pearl Onions
Frutta di stagione	Fresh Fruit
Pastina in brodo	Pasta Bits in Broth
Costolette d'abbacchio panate	Breaded Lamb Chops
Broccoli all'agro	Broccoli with Oil and Lemon
Fragole al limone	Strawberries with Lemon
Vermicelli alle vongole	Thin Spaghetti with Clam Sauce
Seppie coi piselli alla romana	Squid with Peas, Roman Style
Macedonia	Italian Fruit Cup
Risotto alla milanese	Rice, Milanese Style
Ossobuco	Veal Shanks
Frutta di stagione	Fresh Fruit
Tonnarelli alla burina	Thin Noodles, Peasant Style
Fegato alla Veneziana	Liver, Venetian Style
Insalata di patate	Potato Salad
Frutta di stagione	Fresh Fruit
Stracciatella	Broth with Beaten Egg
Petto di tacchino dorato	Golden-fried Turkey Breast

| Asparagi all'agro | Asparagus with Oil and Lemon |
| Amaretti | Macaroons |

ESTATE
Summer

Prosciutto e melone	Prosciutto and Melon
Fettuccine al pomodoro e basilico	Fettuccine with Tomato and Basil Sauce
Pollo arrosto con patate	Roast Chicken with Potatoes
Melanzane a funghetti	Eggplant, Mushroom Style
Pesche Ripiene	Stuffed Baked Peaches
Insalata di riso	Rice Salad
Costolette alla milanese	Veal Chops, Milanese Style
Pomodori con basilico	Tomato Salad with Basil
Frutta di stagione	Fresh Fruit
Pomodori al riso	Tomatoes Stuffed with Rice
Fritto misto di pesce	Mixed Fried Fish
Zucchine all'olio	Zucchini with Oil
Frutta di stagione	Fresh Fruit
Spaghetti alla pescatora	Spaghetti, Fishermen's Style
Piccata di vitello	Veal in Lemon-and-Wine Sauce
Peperoni arrosto	Roast Peppers
Biscotti ai pignoli	Pine Nut Cookies
Spaghetti all'ortica	Spaghetti, "Nettle Style"
Zucchine ripiene	Stuffed Zucchini
Insalata d'indivia	Endive Salad
Frutta di stagione	Fresh Fruit
Antipasto di mare	Seafood Cocktail
Trance di pesce alla griglia	Grilled Fish Steaks
Insalata russa in galantina	Russian Salad in Aspic
Granita di caffè	Coffee Ice

Linguine al pesto	Linguine with *Pesto*
Pollo alla diavola	Chicken, Devil's Style
Fagiolini all'olio	Green Beans with Oil and Lemon
Bruschetta	Garlic Bread
Frutta di stagione	Fresh Fruit

AUTUNNO
Fall

Lasagne, paglia e fieno	Yellow and Green *Lasagne*
Piccata di petto di tacchino	Turkey Breast in a Piquant Sauce
Bieta all'agro	Swiss Chard with Oil and Lemon
Torta Maddalena	Maddalena Cake
Riso e indivia	Rice-and-Endive Soup
Stufatino in umido	Shinbone Stew
Cipolline e piselli	Pearl Onions and Peas
Frutta di stagione	Fresh Fruit
Penne all'arrabbiata	Macaroni in Hot Tomato Sauce
Rollato di vitello	Rolled Breast of Veal
Mantecato di patate	Whipped Potatoes
Zabaglione biscuì	Neapolitan *zabaglione*
Gnocchi verdi	Green Dumplings
Fettine alla pizzaiolo	Beef Slices in Pizza Sauce
Insalata Mista	Mixed Green Salad
Frutta di stagione	Fresh Fruit
Quadrucci e piselli	Pasta Squares and Peas in Broth
Fegatelli di maiale	Pork Livers
Broccoli ripassati in padella	Pan-cooked Broccoli
Frutta di stagione	Fresh Fruit
Zuppa di pesce alla siciliana	Sicilian Fish Soup
Cannoli alla siciliana	Sicilian Filled Pastries

Cannelloni ripieni alla
 toscana

Cannelloni, Tuscan Style

Scaloppine al marsala

Veal Cutlets with Marsala
 Wine Sauce

Piselli alla romana

Peas, Roman Style

Frutta

Fresh Fruit

INVERNO
 Winter

Carciofini all' olio

Articoke Hearts in Olive
 Oil

Cappelletti in Brodo

Cappelletti in Broth

Bollito misto con salsa verde

Mixed Boiled Meats with
 Green Sauce

Spinaci all'agro

Spinach with Oil and Lemon

Zuppa inglese

Layered Sponge Cake with
 Pastry Cream

Minestrone alla milanese

Vegetable Soup, Milanese
 Style

Frittatine al sugo

Little Omelets with Tomato
 Sauce

Frutta e formaggio

Fruit and Cheese

Spaghetti alla carbonara

Spaghetti, Charcoal Makers'
 Style

Fettine in padella

Pan-cooked Beef Slices

Funghi trifolati

Mushrooms, "Truffle Style"

Mele cotte

Baked Apples

Spuntature (e salsicce) al
 sugo

Spareribs (and Sausages)
 in Sauce (with or without
 polenta)

Insalata mista

Mixed Green Salad

Frutta di stagione

Fresh Fruit

Riso al burro e parmigiano	Rice with Butter and Parmesan Cheese
Pollo alla cacciatora	Hunters' Chicken
Peperonata	Peppers with Onions and Tomatoes
Frappe	Sweet Fried Pastry
Pasta e ceci	Chick-pea Soup
Baccalà al sugo alla romana	Cod in a Roman Sauce
Finocchio all'olio	Fennel with Olive Oil
Frutta di stagione	Fresh Fruit
Brodetto d'Ancona	Fish Soup in the Style of Ancona
Aranci alla siciliana	Oranges, Sicilian Style

Index

ABOUT THE AUTHORS

MARGARET ROMAGNOLI, an American who has taken Italian citizenship, and FRANCO ROMAGNOLI, an Italian who is now an American citizen, met in Rome. Franco was a radio engineer who answered Margaret's call for technical help when she worked for the Marshall Plan Radio Information Service. Because she married "a foreigner," Margaret was fired from government service; Franco came to America to pursue his interest in cinematography. He says, "Even though I grew up in Italy, where men are rarely in the kitchen, in my home in Rome, the kitchen was the heart of the house." The Romagnolis, who have lived alternately in America and Italy, now live in Watertown, Massachusetts, with their four children; and their kitchen, as it was in Rome, is still the heart of their home.

KITCHEN POWER!

Bantam Book Catalog

Here's your up-to-the-minute listing of over 1,400 titles by your favorite authors.

This illustrated, large format catalog gives a description of each title. For your convenience, it is divided into categories in fiction and non-fiction—gothics, science fiction, westerns, mysteries, cookbooks, mysticism and occult, biographies, history, family living, health, psychology, art.

So don't delay—take advantage of this special opportunity to increase your reading pleasure.

Just send us your name and address and 50¢ (to help defray postage and handling costs).

The Romagnolis' Table

Margaret and Franco Romagnoli prove that two cooks in the kitchen *do not* spoil the broth. They have been chopping, slicing and sizzling together for 22 years. In addition, they have captivated audiences coast to coast with their lively, expert, TV cooking show.

Create authentic, yet refreshingly simple, everyday Italian dishes in no time. Whip up a wondrously wicked zabaglione. Make a zesty Italian-style pizza. Prepare your own pasta from scratch. Try a luscious zuppa inglese or "English soup." In THE ROMAGNOLIS' TABLE you'll find a superb collection of recipes—from appetizers to desserts—arranged in the order they appear on your family table. All real old-fashioned Italian eating at its very best.

14926

0

76783 00275

ISBN 0-553-14926-1

THR

Fine Fo